Dreaming and Memory

DREAMING AND MEMORY

A New Information-Processing Model

STANLEY R. PALOMBO, M.D.

Basic Books, Inc., Publishers   New York

The author gratefully acknowledges permission to reprint excerpts from the following sources:

The Interpretation of Dreams, by Sigmund Freud. Translated from the German by James Strachey. Published in the United States by Basic Books, Inc., New York, by arrangement with George Allen & Unwin, Ltd. and the Hogarth Press, Ltd, London.

"Remarks on the Theory and Practice of Dream-Interpretation," by Sigmund Freud. In the *Standard Edition of the Complete Works of Sigmund Freud,* Vol. 19. Acknowledgment is made to Sigmund Freud Copyrights, Ltd., The Institute of Psychoanalysis, and The Hogarth Press for permission to quote from this material. Published in the United States by Basic Books, Inc., New York.

Portions of chapters 2, 3, and 6 appeared in "Dreams, Memory, and the Origin of Thought," by Stanley R. Palombo, in Vol. 2, *Thought, Consciousness, and Reality* of the *Psychiatry and the Humanities* series (Yale University Press, 1977). Copyright © 1977 by the Forum on Psychiatry and the Humanities of the Washington School of Psychiatry.

A portion of chapter 2 has been revised and extended from "The Dream and the Memory Cycle," by Stanley R. Palombo, originally published in *International Review of Psychoanalysis* 3(1976):64–84.

Library of Congress Cataloging in Publication Data

Palombo, Stanley R
    Dreaming and memory.

    Bibliographical references: p. 223
    Includes index.
        1. Memory—Physiological aspects.   2.   Dreams—
Physiological aspects.   3.   Human information
processing.   I.   Title.   [DNLM: 1.   Dreams.
2.   Memory.   3.   Psychoanalytic theory.   4.   Models,
Psychological.   WM460.5.D8 P181d]
    QP406.P34   153.6'3   78–53812
    ISBN: 0–465–01708–8

To my children

Marielle, Adria, Jessica

CONTENTS

CONTENTS

CONTENTS

PREFACE

There is a character in Congreve who is said to "rely on his memory for his wit, and on his wit for his memory." The symmetrical phrasing reveals a psychological abyss. The man who repeats an old joke is nothing but a bore. But the one who improvises the record of his past life calls into question the continuity and integrity of his identity as a person.

The decision to incorporate a new experience into the permanent record of the self and the way in which this new experience is related to the accumulated experience of the past, have a determinative influence on the basic structures of personality and their capacity for meaningful action in new life situations. The idea that dreaming plays a significant role in these critical processes has been in the scientific literature for more than ten years. *Dreaming and Memory* proposes a specific theoretical model for these processes and demonstrates how they operate during an extended episode of psychoanalytic treatment.

The data for this demonstration were derived from transcribed analytic sessions and from dream reports recorded when the subject was awakened in the sleep laboratory after periods of dreaming sleep. My aim is to show that a particular sequence of psychological processes which I call *the memory cycle*, exists in nature and that this sequence operates through a predictable (and predicted) series of observable events. I do not attempt to establish the conditions under which the memory cycle functions optimally, although in the case under study, the progress of the treatment clearly had an effect on success or failure of the cycle in evading the influence of the dream censorship discovered and described by Freud.

Further research is needed to elucidate these important questions. Replication of the experimental procedure described here should be especially useful. However, I am willing to risk the claim that the data presented herein are sufficient to demonstrate that the memory cycle is not simply a theoretical construct but a functioning reality in the day-to-day activity of the human mind.

The memory cycle model suggests that every dream must incorporate the representation of an event in the (often remote) past of the dreamer.

Since very few of these memories appear spontaneously in the associations of analytic patients, it had been my impression that they could be retrieved only through the data obtained in the sleep laboratory, where the dreams least altered by the censorship are most likely to be found. Without expecting any evidence to the contrary, however, I began to ask patients first and then friends whether a reported dream or any of its more graphic details reminded them of an actual experience early in life.

To my surprise I found that they were quite often able to recall a memory that was unmistakably a source of the dream imagery, even though these recollections had not occurred to them before my questioning. If this observation can be confirmed, it may provide the opportunity for collecting data through a relatively simple procedure which lends itself to research problems that rely on statistical methods for their solution. It may conceivably add something useful to the clinical practice of dream analysis, though I have as yet no basis for making a claim of any kind in this area.

Finally, beyond the ultimate fate of any of the specific proposals offered in *Dreaming and Memory*, I hope that this book provides its readers with a new and stimulating way of looking at the complexities and multiple relationships underlying the ordinarily observable surface of mental activity.

I feel personally grateful to so many people in my family and among my friends and teachers for helping me to see for myself that any attempt I make to acknowledge my indebtedness is necessarily both incomplete and inadequate. I therefore offer my thanks and my apologies both to those who are not mentioned and to those who are.

To my grandparents, who grew up on the Eastern margins of western civilization, I owe the benefit of their difficult crossing. My parents, who made the voyage with them, had to discover the modern world for themselves. They passed on to me a restless curiosity about the human mind and an unrelenting love for its marvelous creations.

At Harvard College I was taught by Archibald MacLeish and William Matchett how to interrogate a poem. During my psychiatric training I learned from Hilde Bruch and Elvin Semrad, among many others, how to read the disclosures of a suffering patient, rather than the signs of an illness. I hope this rather meager text retains some indication of their influence on me.

I became aware of information theory as a conceptual tool when I heard Herbert Simon's William James Lectures at Harvard in 1962. My attempt to apply Simon's work to fine structure of the psychoanalytic interaction became the seed from which much of my current thinking grew. My interest in the information-processing function of dreaming led me to the work of Ramon Greenberg and Chester Pearlman, who had reached a similar position through a different route. Greenberg and Pearlman offered me their own ideas and their continued encouragement. Although we are in disagreement about some important issues, their personal generosity has been unfailing. Without their support I would never have written *Dreaming and Memory*.

Among the many friends and colleagues who contributed to the development of this book through their encouragement and challenging conversation over many years, and through their critical reading of portions of this manuscript, I wish to pay special tribute to Joseph and Marilyn Caston, Stanley Cavell, Aaron Glassman, Albert Grokoest, Allen Grossman, Carol Horn, Jacob Katzow, Wolfgang Lederer, John Merrifield, Werner Nathan, Douglas Noble, Richard Onorato, Richard Reinitz, Arlene and Arnold Richards, Earle Silber, Bennett Simon, Nancy Veret, Edith Weigert, Stephen Weissman, and David Wolfe. None of them, of course, have any responsibility for the deficiencies of the author's style or thought.

The anonymous contributors to *Dreaming and Memory* are perhaps the most important of all. I refer to the analyst and the patient and the research scientists whose combined efforts led to the collection of the data examined in this study. The confidentiality of the therapeutic relationship prevents me from identifying them. I wish them to know, however, that I consider their willingness to share this material with me to be quite extraordinary. I can only hope that the result of our unusual collaboration will compensate them in some way for their gift.

My list of references is not intended to be a review of the relevant literature. Many important related works were not included only because I was not aware of them while I was in the process of writing this book. However that may reflect on me, no omission should be considered a judgment on my part of the value of a colleague's contribution to our collective enterprise.

Last but not least, I wish to express my regret to all the important people in my life who were inconvenienced or neglected because of my absorption in the writing of *Dreaming and Memory*. Perhaps someday it will seem to all of us to have been worth it.

Dreaming and Memory

CHAPTER 1

Introduction

The Psychology of Dreams

Since ancient times, people have believed that dreaming constitutes a meaningful expression of the inner psychological state of the dreamer. Only in our narrowly materialist modern civilization has the dream been considered the random by-product of a primarily physiological state—a state which may be as ordinary as indigestion or as esoteric as the repeated self-stimulation of the reticular activating system of the pontine brain-stem. Freud entered the controversey as a defender of the popular view, which is still disputed today in some scientific circles.

The question facing the dream psychologist remains what it has always been: why, if dreams are meaningful, are the formal properties of dreams so unlike those of waking thought? The traditional answer is that dreams express themselves in what amounts to a secret code or an unknown language, and that the task of the interpreter is to decode or translate the imagery of the dream into an equivalent text in everyday narrative prose.

But why the strangeness of the dream language? Here the explanations are more varied, but they have usually pointed to a source of the dream which is alien to ordinary human consciousness, a source for which the language of dreams is in some way a more natural language. The earliest assumption, of course, was that dreams originate in a supernatural world. To the ancients the logical and contextual constraints of human language and thought were considered to be representative of the more general limitations of human life, limitations which could be transcended with impunity by the gods or demons responsible for the dream message. The identification of the divine or demonic agent, however, was a continuing problem to the dream interpreter of antiquity.

Nevertheless, as the belief in an external, supernatural source of dreams receded, so also did the belief that dreams are meaningful. If they originate within the dreamer, but outside his consciousness, the argument went, then they must be the product of physiological rather than mental activity. Freud took the decisive step of locating the dream world within an unconscious portion of the dreamer's own mind, with his demonstration of the associative linkages between the dreamer's waking thoughts and the obscure imagery of the dream. This discovery, in turn, led to a host of new questions about the nature of the unconscious mind.

In the analysis of his hysterical patients, Freud recognized that the defensive repression of forbidden wishes was responsible for the inaccessibility to consciousness of much of the patient's experience associated with those wishes. This observation immediately suggested an explanation for the strangeness of the dream world. Like the neurotic symptom, the dream might result from the transformation of a forbidden wish into an expression which was unintelligible to ordinary consciousness. The manifest content of the dream would then be a deliberately distorted and disguised representation of "latent dream thoughts" associated with the forbidden wish.

For Freud the peculiar imagery of the dream was not simply an alternative system of representation, a different "language," but the product of a deliberate effort to conceal the meaningfulness of underlying "thoughts." Dreaming thus became a kind of pathological mental activity, analogous to neurotic symptom formation. The question of divine or demonic influence at work in the origin of dreams had been resolved, at least from the point of view of the distorting mechanisms of the dreamwork, in favor of the demonic.

Freud's position in the history of dream psychology is therefore somewhat paradoxical. Although he did far more than anyone either before or since to elucidate the meaningful aspect of dream content, his model of dream construction shifted the emphasis of dream interpretation from the *deciphering* of an unusual message communicated by the dream to the *unmasking* of a commonplace (though disavowed) meaning hidden by the dream censorship.

For the psychoanalytic practitioner, Freud's new emphasis was and remains a most powerful clinical tool. The analyst's aim in his daily work is to overcome the manifold varieties of self-deception responsible for the sufferings of his patients. Freud's discovery that dreaming, like other mental activities, is influenced by the defensive intrusion of the ego, made the dream an appropriate object for analysis. The fact that in dreaming, the defensive operations of the patient tend to be less familiar to him, and less idiosyncratic than those of his waking state, eases a bit the burden of self-discovery which ordinarily follows analytic interpretation. If the analyst believes that the ego defenses not only influence the content of the dream but actually play the primary role in dream construction, then he is in a position to avoid other aspects of dreaming which might distract him from his essential therapeutic goal.

For the dream psychologist, however, Freud's model for the process of dream construction is incomplete in some important ways. It is not very precise about what it is that the dream censorship is censoring, as we shall discuss later at some length in chapter 5. Moreover, it attributes the unusual form of the dream not to the *original* content of the dream, the "message," as it were, from the interior dream world, but to the defensive process through which this meaning is distorted and disguised.

Here Freud seemed to be breaking with the tradition that sees the dream as a special kind of internal communication; no longer a prophetic message from a divinity, perhaps, but at least a glimpse into an internal source of creative and integrative mental activity. Nevertheless, the apparent relationship between the "symbolic language" of dreams and the expressive achievements of literature and the arts has continued to be a major concern both within and without the clinical arena of psychoanalytic practice.

I will try to show here that the manifest content of the dream as it is remembered by the dreamer is actually the result of a dynamic interplay between primitive *adaptive* and *defensive* mechanisms. One can do justice to Freud's clinical discoveries without slighting the adaptive significance of the process of dreaming. This adaptive process can be shown to do its work on the materials of the dream prior to and independent of the conflict observed by Freud between the emergence of repressed childhood wishes and the countervailing action of the dream censorship.

Although he did not emphasize the adaptive aspect of dreaming in his major writings on the subject, Freud was clearly aware that an adaptive process might, in fact, play an important role in the process of dream construction. In *Beyond the Pleasure Principle* (1920), he offered some tentative suggestions about the nature of such a function:

It is impossible to classify as wish-fulfillments the dreams we have been discussing which occur in traumatic neuroses, or the dreams during psychoanalyses which bring to memory the psychical traumas of childhood. They arise, rather, in obedience to the compulsion to repeat, though it is true that in analysis that compulsion is supported by the wish (which is encouraged by "suggestion") to conjure up what has been forgotten and repressed. Thus it would seem that the function of dreams, which consists in setting aside any motives that might interrupt sleep, by fulfilling the wishes of the disturbing impulses, is not their *original* function. It would not be possible for them to perform that function until the whole of mental life has accepted the dominance of the pleasure principle. If there is a "beyond the pleasure principle," it is only consistent to grant that there was also a time *before* the purpose of dreams was the fulfillment of wishes. This would imply no denial of their later function. (Pp. 32–33)

Of the many investigators who have tried to elucidate the adaptive purpose of dreaming, I will confine my attention here to the important group of analysts, psychotherapists, and psychologists who have felt that the dream itself—and not merely the interpretation of the dream— plays a positive, integrating role both in normal emotional development and in the intensified self-examination of the therapeutic process.

Carl Jung (1933) was among the first to reemphasize this aspect of dream psychology. He speaks of the unconscious mind, as exemplified in the dreaming state, as performing a complementary or compensatory role in relation to waking consciousness. What is neglected in the daytime world of urgent activity is taken up again by the nocturnal unconscious in a way that allows a wider set of relationships to the dreamer's overall life experience to be established. Jung's problem, like that of many psychologists who have been influenced by his work, was to show how this integrating function expresses itself in the actual construction of the dream. Again, why the strange and irrational quality of the integrated product?

Lacking a solution for this problem which could be based on a scientific understanding of the individual human mind in its day-to-day functioning, Jung retreated to a new version of the ancient idea that the dream has its source outside the dreamer. His *collective unconscious* is, in effect, a suprahuman world. Messages from this external world, expressing themselves in the universal language of archetypal symbols, are generated in the mind of the individual dreamer as he sleeps, where they provide an extended context for his individual experience. Their effect is benign, or meant to be, and Jung's psychology drifts regressively into a kind of religious anthropology.

Perhaps the most original contributor to post-Freudian dream psychology was Samuel Lowy (1942), who anticipated many of the findings of the sleep laboratory in his view of dreaming as a purposeful psycho-

6

logical process which nevertheless serves an essentially different function from that of waking thought. According to Lowy, this function is accomplished during sleep, does not require that the process itself be remembered, and is not *conscious* in the normal, waking sense of that term.

The remembering of a dream, which Lowy recognized to be an exceptional event, provides the opportunity for the information contained in the dream to be utilized in the more familiar problem-solving activity of waking consciousness, such as, for example, dream interpretation. For Lowy, the interpretation is not simply an undoing of the disguising function of the dream censorship, nor is it a reading of the messages sent by a knowing unconscious to the waking mind. It is an activity which deliberately links the content of the dream to other aspects of the dreamer's experience; an activity which is separate and distinct from the unconscious adaptive purpose normally performed by the unremembered dream. The benefits of interpretation represent a "secondary gain" additional to that produced by the dreaming process itself.

Lowy's conception of the adaptive purpose intrinsic to the process of dreaming itself is not fully developed. In general, it follows Jung's notion of a compensatory or complementary reorganization of waking experience. But Lowy adds an emphasis lacking in Jung. He sees the dream as a series of connections between present and past experience:

By means of the dream-formation, details of the past are continually reintroduced into consciousness, are thus prevented from sinking into such depths that they cannot be recovered. Those of our experiences which are not at the moment accessible to consciousness are thus kept in touch with consciousness, so that in case of necessity association with them may become easier.

This connecting function of the dream-formation is reinforced considerably by formation of symbols. When this function takes a hand and condenses masses of experiences, perhaps a whole period of the dreamer's life, into one single image, then all the material which is contained in this synthesis is reconnected with consciousness. Dream-formation thus causes not only a connection of single details, but also of whole "conglomerations" of past experience. But this is not all. Through the constancy and continuity existing in the process of dreaming, there is created a connection with this dream-continuity. Which fact greatly contributes to the preservation of the cohesion and unity of mental life as a whole. (Pp. 201–02, quoted in Jones, 1970)

As we shall see, Lowy's idea of the motive for the connecting of present and past experience in the dream is different from the one to be suggested here, but his description of the resulting process approaches it very closely. I believe that, like most of the investigators concerned with the adaptive function of dreams, Lowy attributes too much complexity to this function. As a result, he fails to recognize the specific mechanism responsible for the manner in which the links between present and past experience are actually constructed in the process of dreaming.

Calvin Hall (1953, 1966) and Thomas French (French and Fromm, 1964) have provided an empirical basis for the study of dream sequences. This important topic was neglected by Freud because, I believe, his model of dream construction did not suggest a rationale for the existence of thematically related sequences (see chapter 5). Hall, working in the psychology laboratory, and French, based on his clinical work as a psychoanalyst, have each documented the thematic relationship between dreams occurring on a single night and dreams reported over a period of weeks and months in the clinical situation.

Both Hall and French postulate that this relationship is the result of an unconscious process akin to the "working through" which takes place in psychoanalytic therapy. Each dream in the sequence sheds some new light on what French and Fromm call "the focal conflict" which currently preoccupies the dreamer. Hall emphasizes the "spotlight dream," which illuminates a series of related dreams and perhaps indicates a resolution of the conflict which has been represented in various forms throughout the series.

French and Fromm demonstrate that the dreams in a given sequence call attention to situations and conflicts in the dreamer's past which have formal and emotional connections with his current preoccupation. These past situations are scrutinized in the hope that they will suggest a resolution for the still-unsolved problem of the present. I believe that this idea comes close to the mark. However, it does not take into account Lowy's distinction between the primary function of the unremembered dream and the secondary gain which results from waking elaboration and interpretation.

As I will try to show, the dream sequence is actually a sequence of dreams *and* waking revisions of remembered dreams. The "working-through" aspect of the sequence is the result of daytime activity (both conscious and preconscious) which is then incorporated into the later dreams in the sequence. Without this distinction, French and Fromm once again attribute too much problem-solving sophistication to the primary nocturnal function of dreaming. They fail to explain how a mechanism with this degree of sophistication might produce as the result of its efforts an object as cognitively crude as the manifest dream content.

Many others (e.g. Ullman, 1959) have contributed to our perception of the dream as an adaptive or expressive element in the mental life of the dreamer. Jones (1970) provides an extremely valuable summary and synthesis of their ideas, as well as important insights of his own. In none of this work, however, does the missing ingredient appear: the repetitive mechanism which produces an adaptive result by distorting and degrading the representations of experience which enter into the construction of the dream.

Freud's successors—both his followers and his critics—seem to have been beguiled by the intimate association in Freud's thinking between the concept of *defense* and the concept of *mechanism*. In order to suggest an alternative to defensive activity as the primary source of various integrative and adaptive psychic functions, one is drawn somehow to suggest that an alternative to the notion of a mechanism is also required.

The alternative usually chosen is a kind of humanistic holism, characterized by the effort to relate even the smallest units of psychic activity to the overall aims and interests of the "whole person." This achievement is of course the ultimate goal both of therapeutic practice and theoretical understanding. In pursuing this goal prematurely and indiscriminately at all levels of the hierarchic organization of the psychic apparatus, however, we are put in the false position of having to understand the whole person before being able to explain any of the details of his thought and behavior.

The investigator who adopts this strategy tends to lose interest in the observation of lower-level adaptive functions. He may even come to deny that they exist, on the grounds that adaptation is a function of the whole organism, and that "mechanisms" are by definition rigid and inflexibile. To follow this course is to lose touch with the means by which adaptation is achieved. The organism, human or otherwise, survives through the incorporation of simple mechanical performance into increasingly complex patterns of contingent organization. (Miller et al, 1960; Simon, 1969; Pattee, 1973).

The result of the holistic approach has been that much has been learned about the associative networks which connect the elements of the dream to the overall personality of the dreamer (e.g., Erikson, 1954) but little about the process of dream construction itself. Freud's model remains the only one detailed enough to generate precise hypotheses about the process through which the particular elements of the dream are incorporated into the final structure of the manifest content. It must serve as the point of departure for anyone who wishes to understand how dreams are made, or what stuff they are made of.

In the concluding pages of *The New Psychology of Dreaming*, Jones (1970) suggests that further progress in dream research may lie in the direction indicated by Breger (1967) and Dewan (1967), who, along

9

with Greenberg and Leiderman (1966) and Hawkins (1966), proposed that dreaming represents a stage in the transfer of newly acquired experiential information into the permanent memory structure. This hypothesis gives us for the first time the clear statement of an adaptive function which must be carried out in a routine and repetitive fashion, that is, which requires a "mechanism" operating on a much lower level of information processing than the problem-solving activity of waking consciousness.

This mechanism can be identified. In fact, it was clearly observed by Freud himself, although its significance could not be fully grasped within the framework of Freud's theory of dream construction. The acitvity of this adaptive mechanism is *computation*, not *communication*.

It is my hope that the new theory which I propose and try to demonstrate here will be of interest to all who are concerned with dream psychology. For a practicing psychoanalyst like myself, it is especially important that a new theory be concordant with the therapeutic effects of dream interpretation as they appear in the everyday work I share with other analysts. The nonpsychoanalytic reader may feel at times that I am digressing into areas of controversy which may have meaning only within the psychoanalytic community itself.

Nevertheless, psychoanalysts talk and write about dreams in a language based on the traditional theory. A theory of dreams which could not be represented in that language would be an anomaly. At the same time, I have found it necessary to redefine some traditional terms which I find misleading, including the central concept of the "latent content" of the dream. To modify a theory so closely intertwined with the therapeutic enterprise of psychoanalysis requires justification. I have tried to supply it, for my colleagues as well as for myself.

My point of departure, then, will be the traditional psychoanalytic theory of dreams as formulated by Freud in the *Traumdeutung* and later works. My aim, however, is not to confine the theory of dreams within this tradition, but rather to enlarge the theoretical framework provided by Freud in a way that will allow the research findings of dream physiology and the recent contributions of information theory and cognitive psychology to fit comfortably within it, not to mention the work of the dream psychologists who have labored all along outside the theoretical boundaries set by Freud and his direct successors in the psychoanalytic world.

Psychoanalytic Ego Psychology

Psychoanalytic ego psychology came into its own with the publication in 1936 of Anna Freud's *The Ego and the Mechanisms of Defense*. This important work demonstrated that the discoveries of psychoanalysis extended beyond the hidden world of unconscious wishes to the relatively neglected defensive functions of the ego. The establishment of the principle that major aspects of ego functioning may themselves be unconscious opened the way for the study of unconscious adaptive mechanisms which might be identified for the first time from the perspective of psychoanalysis.

The contributions of Heinz Hartmann and his coworkers, beginning in 1939 with Hartmann's *Ego Psychology and the Problem of Adaptation*, developed a broad theoretical foundation for further progress in the psychoanalytic study of the ego. Hartmann's work brought much of what was already known about the ego, from psychoanalytic sources and from the behavioral sciences generally, into relationship with the earlier psychoanalytic explorations of unconscious impulses and their conflicts with the mechanisms of defense. The stage was set for new discoveries about the as yet poorly understood integrative mechanisms of the ego.

Important advances came through the psychoanalytic study of ego development in early childhood. The work of Anna Freud (1946), Erik Erikson (1950), René Spitz (1959, 1965) and others demonstrated that adaptive ego functioning is present from the very beginning of life. This finding was confirmed by the developmental psychology of Jean Piaget, introduced to American psychoanalysts by Peter Wolff (1960). Later contributors, including Jacobson (1964), White (1964), Bowlby (1969), and Mahler (1968), have diverged in their detailed views of the process of ego development. But all have agreed that it takes place in accordance with an autonomous maturational ground plan which begins to unfold as soon as the baby is born.

As a result of this important work, we now have a clear idea that the primitive cognitive and affective structures we observe in children are the direct precursors of the more familiar conscious and rational problem-solving mechanisms we associate with the adult ego (Holt, 1967). It is well understood that these primitive structures never disappear and that they may reassume control of the psychic apparatus under unusual circumstances, as in the various forms of psychopathology. It is not generally understood, however, how much and to what extent the more primitive structures of the adaptive ego may play a continuing part in the *nonconscious* (as distinct from *preconscious*) adaptive functioning of the mature adult ego.

The area in which our current state of knowledge is most deficient is that which pertains to the synthetic or integrative functions of the ego. These are the functions which evaluate the vast quantity of new information continually impinging on us, select from it what is important enough to retain, and then connect this new information wherever appropriate with preexisting psychic structures. This integrative work is carried on as a prelude to conscious problem-solving, outside our normal awareness.

Much of our successful responsiveness to the ordinary demands of everyday life is due to the nonconscious integrative functions of the ego. These functions have a special importance for psychoanalysis, in addition, since the therapeutic benefits of analytic treatment cannot be fully accounted for by the patient's conscious insight into his neurotic difficulties. We speak of "regression in the service of the ego," but this useful formulation of Kris's (1932) suggests an occasional excursion from the conscious norm, rather than the massive infrastructure which supports the specialized capabilities of conscious verbalization.

Rapaport (1960) calls attention to some of the unsolved problems which lie in this area of investigation:

> We suggested above that a prerequisite of the theory of the therapeutic technique may be a theory of communication. Data for building such a theory are needed. The data and concepts of the existing attempts at a communication theory do not seem to be relevant. The focus of such a theory must be the laws which govern the tendency of communication to engender or to prevent reciprocal communication. Moreover, it should be a theory in which the communicants' becoming conscious of something is equivalent to [latent] verbal or non-verbal communication. The methods by which data relevant to such a theory can be obtained have yet to be worked out. (P. 136)

Since the time of Rapaport's writing, important developments have occurred in the biological sciences. Success in adaptation is now closely linked with the capacity of an organism to extract information from its environment and store it internally in meaningful configurations. This principle, dramatically established by the breaking of the genetic code, is currently being elaborated at the higher levels of psychological integration (Lindsay and Norman, 1972).

A major step for psychoanalytic ego psychology was taken by Peterfreund in his *Information, Systems and Psychoanalysis* (1971). Peterfreund demonstrated the feasibility of translating the language of psychoanalysis into terms compatible with the developing information sciences. Rosenblatt and Thickstun (1977, 1978) have been carrying this effort forward. The reader unfamiliar with information theory will be substantially assisted by these works which cannot be adequately summarized here.

The advent of the information sciences has supplied us with many of the conceptual tools specified by Rapaport as necessary for the carrying out of the project mentioned in the quotation above. *Dreaming and Memory* will describe and illustrate one of the principle intrapsychic processes which make possible the restructuring of the analytic patient's personality through the medium of his communications with the analyst.

Dreaming and Memory

An earlier paper (Palombo, 1976)* described an autonomous mechanism of nonconscious adaptive ego functioning called "the memory cycle." The memory cycle is a sequence of processes through which new experiential information is introduced into adaptively suitable locations in the permanent memory structure. The most striking hypothesis of the memory-cycle model is that the critical step in the sequence—the step which matches representations of new experiences with the representations of closely related experiences of the past—takes place during dreaming. (How this happens will be explained in the next section.)

The study reported here applies the theoretical model of the memory cycle to new data from an ongoing psychoanalysis. These new data confirm the picture of the memory cycle generated by the earlier model, as well as clarifying many details only roughly sketched out in the original theory. In particular, they demonstrate for the first time the precise relationship between the adaptive function of dreaming in the memory cycle, that is, the matching of representations of current and past experience, and the defensive operations of the dream censorship, which act to prevent the matching from taking place.

These new findings have significant implications for the psychoanalytic theory of dreams, which will be discussed at length later on. Equally important, however, is the new understanding they provide of the process

* Most of this paper is included in chapter 2.

through which the therapeutic effect of psychoanalysis is achieved. Two major points may be mentioned:

1. Dream interpretation appears to have a special efficacy in the building of those intrapsychic structures which restore and renew the incomplete self and object representations acquired during the patient's childhood. This effect results from a synergistic collaboration between the analyst's interpretive activity and the adaptive functioning of dreaming in the memory cycle. It is distinct from, but complementary to, the role played by dreams in providing new data from that part of the patient's memory structure which is ordinarily inaccessible to consciousness.

2. The intrapsychic counterpart of the analyst's dream interpretation is a new dream which incorporates the originally reported dream together with the new information supplied by the interpretation. This new dream, which I have called "the correction dream," results in the introduction of the information contained in the interpretation into the precise location in the permanent memory structure which contributed its contents to the originally reported dream. (The nature of the correction dream will be described in detail in the next section.)

Eissler (1969) suggests that there may be issues in psychoanalytic theory which cannot be resolved through the exclusive use of data gathered in the clinical practice of psychoanalysis. As his chief example, he cites the theoretical problems created by the regular quantitative and periodic aspects of dreaming, as revealed by studies in the sleep laboratory, findings not easily reconciled with the traditional psychoanalytic explanation for the genesis of dreams.

He raises the question whether new theoretical formulations derived from data other than free association will prove to be compatible with the psychoanalytic paradigm developed by Freud from clinical practice. The study reported here should help to answer this question. Although the data comes primarily from the clinical process of psychoanalysis as recorded during two consecutive analytic hours, it also includes the patient's descriptions of his dreams after being awakened in the sleep laboratory on the night following the first recorded hour.

These nocturnal dream reports play an essential role in filling what might otherwise have been a fatal gap in the data of free association. The memory-cycle model predicts that correction dreams will in general be accompanied by little anxiety, will therefore be unlikely to awaken the dreamer, and will in most cases be neither remembered nor reported. For this reason, the data from the sleep laboratory were brought into the study.

It should be emphasized that the gap in the associative data with which we are concerned is caused not simply by defensive inhibition of adaptive functioning, but, as Eissler suggests, by normal operating characteristics of the psychic apparatus which have escaped our attention in the past.

In brief, then, this investigation provides an empirical demonstration of the memory cycle at work. While the memory-cycle model offers a new vantage point for the understanding of individual dreams, its most novel contribution to our knowledge of intrapsychic events is concerned with the new light it casts on the continuous and cumulative relationships between sequences of dreams and the waking experiences (including the experience of psychoanalytic treatment) incorporated into them over a series of successive days and nights.

The Memory Cycle

The memory cycle is the process through which new information which has entered the state of waking consciousness is transferred to the memory structure for permanent storage. The new information may arise from external perception, the recall of an earlier memory, fantasy, or problem-solving activity.

This new information is stored during the day in a short-term memory of large but limited capacity. Only a small portion of its contents can be transferred to the permanent memory structure in each twenty-four-hour period. The contents of the short-term memory must therefore be reduced in volume by a process which selects only the most important of them for permanent storage. The selection may take place in waking consciousness, or, more reasonably, during nondreaming sleep, when the short-term memory is temporarily freed from its usual function of accepting new information.

The representations of new experience which survive the selection process are what Freud called the "day residues." They are not the insignificant odds and ends that Freud thought them to be, however, but precisely those experiences whose novelty of meaning and associated affect make them worth preserving for future reference. Why the day residues of reported dreams so often appear to be "innocuous" is a question that will be answered in this study.

The critical problem to be solved in the transfer of the day residues to the permanent memory is the determination of suitable locations for them. The permanent memory is organized associatively: it is not indexed by subject matter or by any logical system (Palombo, 1973). The day residues must be matched with items already in the memory structure which they closely resemble. To make this determination, a number of related items already contained in the permanent memory must be compared with each new day residue. The procedure which can accomplish this task most quickly and efficiently is *comparison by superimposition.*

The two items to be compared are projected simultaneously in the sensory projection mechanisms. If the superimposition which results is a coherent composite image, the match is considered to be successful and the new item is stored in a location adjacent to that of the memory item with which it was matched. Freud compared this process, which he called "condensation," to Galton's technique of superimposing photographic images of individual family members in order to find the common features of the family as a whole.

Dreaming is the stage of comparison by superimposition in the operation of the memory cycle. The coherence of the dream determines the success of the match and the desirability of introducing the day residue into a location directly accessible to the older memory item. This means that every dream has two distinct experiential sources "hidden behind" the composite image of the manifest content: one consisting of the day residues it incorporates, and the other of the memory items from the past with which they are being matched.

An exceptionally clear example of the matching process at work is given in Freud's essay, "On Dreams" (1901):

From every element in a dream's content associative threads branch out in two or more directions; every situation in a dream seems to be put together out of two or more impressions or experiences. For instance, I once had a dream of a sort of swimming-pool, in which the bathers were scattering in all directions; at one point on the edge of the pool someone was standing and bending towards one of the people bathing, as though to help her out of the water. The situation was put together from a memory of an experience I had had at puberty and from two paintings, one of which I had seen shortly before the dream. On was a picture from Schwind's series illustrating the legend of Mélusine, which showed the water-nymphs surprised in their pool (see the scattering bathers in the dream); the other was a picture of the deluge by an Italian Master; while the little experience remembered from my puberty was of having seen the instructor at a swimming school helping a lady out of the water who had stopped in until after the time set aside for male bathers. (Pp. 648–49)

Freud went on to say (P. 650): "The dream-work then proceeds just as Francis Galton did in constructing his family photographs. It superimposes, as it were, the different components upon one another. The common element in them then stands out clearly in the composite picture, while contradictory details more or less wipe one another out."

Galton's purpose in constructing his family photographs was not aesthetic, of course. He was trying to discover what the family resemblance actually consisted of, what features were common to its members, and what, if any, relationship existed between these common features and other aspects of the family identity. In this sense his method was an investigative and evaluative procedure. As I have suggested, Galton's method is employed in dreams for a strictly analogous purpose.

The Correction Dream

An anxiety dream which awakens the dreamer brings to consciousness an unusual or disproportionately large gap between the cognitive and affective elements of a day residue and the past memories with which a match has been attempted. Awareness of the anxiety dream in his waking state gives the dreamer an opportunity to bridge the gap with a new mediating experience which enlarges the connection between the experiences of present and past. The data of this study will indicate that the most likely source for a mismatch is the direct interference of the dream censor in the matching process.

When the anxiety dream is brought into contact with other thoughts, affects, and memories during waking consciousness, this new information is attached to the representation of the anxiety dream in the formation of the day residues for the next night's dreaming.

The process through which the remembered dream and the new experience make contact may be exclusively preconscious in a given instance. Simply having the dream "in mind" during the day is often sufficient to alert the integrative mechanisms of the ego to incoming information which may be relevant to the problem posed by the dream. Either in unconscious processing during the day, or in predreaming sleep, the connections can be made explicit as the day residues are sifted and assembled into dream-sized units for the matching process.

More can be accomplished if a deliberate effort is made to relate the remembered dream to current experience and to the actual memories of the past which are evoked by the dream. This can be done by the dreamer on his own, but the effort is certainly enhanced by the collaboration of a psychoanalyst who is trained to make the required connections.*

The part of the new day residue formed by the remembered dream already contains a component derived from a memory of the past which is located in the permanent memory structure. During the matching process, this component of the day residue will be successfully matched with the other representations of the same memory in the permanent structure. As a result of the successful matching, the entire day residue connected with the past component will be introduced into the permanent memory at those locations which contributed their contents to the original dream. If the day residue contained a dream interpretation, this would be included, too.

The new dream during which this successful matching takes place is the correction dream. It has three identifiable components:

1. The material of the original anxiety dream, including the derivatives of both the day residue and the past memories matched with it.
2. The new material added during the waking experience, stimulated by the original dream and incorporated into the new day residue together with it.
3. New historical material from the immediate vicinity in the permanent memory structure of those precise locations which contributed the mnemonic component of the original anxiety dream. This material forms the past component of the new dream, which is matched with the new day residue compounded from items (1) and (2).

Thus, in the case of a dream reported and interpreted during an analytic hour, the reported dream would act as a kind of tracer which carries the interpretation back to the specific locations in the memory store whose contents had been incompletely or unsuccessfully matched in the original dream.

The introduction of the interpretation at these locations in the permanent memory would then have the effect of bringing the memory structure into closer accord with current reality, or, put another way, of repairing an informational defect in the memory structure which had been exposed by the reported dream.

---

* Children seem to have a natural tendency to review their recent dreams before going to sleep. For a long time, Jessica, age 2½, appeared to be malingering when she claimed that she could not fall asleep because she was having bad dreams. This misunderstanding was cleared up a few months later when Marielle, age 7½, following an explanation of the correction dream by her father, reported that she routinely reviews her remembered dreams of the previous night after going to bed.

INTRODUCTION

Once the characteristics of the correction dream are known, it is not difficult to find examples among the dreams ordinarily related to us by analytic patients, even though correction dreams are relatively low in anxiety level and therefore less likely to awaken the dreamer and be reported. The dreams referred to by Freud as "confirmation dreams" or "corroboration dreams" were most probably correction dreams, as were the "spotlight dreams" reported by Hall (1969).

With so many theoretical issues at stake, however, we cannot be satisfied with dreams which only *appear* to be correction dreams. We will have to demonstrate the existence of a dream which cannot possibly be anything but a correction dream, with all of the components and complex relationships predicted for it by the memory-cycle model unmistakably in evidence.

To do this, we cannot rely on anecdotal reports from analytic hours. We must have clinical records which can tell us each of the following:

1. The experiences of the first dream day which contributed to the day residues incorporated into the original dream.
2. A sufficiently detailed report of this dream.
3. The extra-analytic experiences of the second dream day, the day on which the original dream was reported to the analyst.
4. The contents of the analytic hour in which the dream was reported.
5. A sufficiently detailed report of the correction dream that follows the first analytic hour.
6. The contents of the second analytic hour in which the correction dream was reported. (This will allow us to check, through the patient's associations, that the correction dream is related in depth as well as by manifest content to the original dream.)

With good fortune, this material could be provided through the recording and transcription of two successive analytic hours, since items (1), (2), (3), and (5) might very well be included in the contents of the hours in sufficient detail to give us the information we need. Item (5) presents a special problem, however, since a successful correction dream is less likely to come to the dreamer's attention and be reported in analysis than the original dream which awakened him.

In order to be certain that we have a full report of the correction dreams in this study, we shall take advantage of a research technique developed by other investigators who were studying the effect of dreaming on emotional conflicts aroused during a psychoanalytic hour which occurred on the dream day.

The Present Study

The analysand in this case, M. A., was an unmarried man in his early thirties who came for treatment shortly after his father died. His complaints included anxiety connected with his father's business, which he was now managing, and difficulties in forming close emotional ties with any of the woman he was dating.

M. A.'s illness had the mixed features of an obsessive-compulsive psychoneurosis and a narcissistic character structure. In the sample we shall be considering, the neurotic elements appear to predominate. The Oedipal conflict is conspicuously present and colors the material which emerges in both hours and in the correction dreams. Pre-Oedipal issues are also clearly in evidence, and the level of M. A.'s object relations appears to fluctuate between those typical of the anal and phallic stages of libidinal development.

Because M. A. lived at a distance from the analyst, it was arranged that he make two trips to Washington each week, where he had an evening analytic hour, stayed overnight, and saw the analyst again early the following morning. For the research on dreams, M. A. was willing to spend some of his nights between analytic hours in the sleep laboratory, where he was awakened at the end of each REM (rapid eye movement) period and his dreams recorded. He was paid for this participation, although the money was not an important motivating factor for him.

During the first year of the analysis, there were twelve dream-recording nights separated by intervals of one to several weeks. The extended clinical example to be presented here was recorded on one of these nights and during the analytic hours immediately preceding and succeeding it. I am extremely grateful to the original investigators, and to the patient and analyst who participated in their study, for their unstinting generosity in making this material available to me.

The importance of the sleep laboratory for our purposes here was not simply that it provided a record of M. A.'s dreams with a minimum of secondary elaboration, but more importantly that the nocturnal recording session gave M. A. the opportunity to report the dreams in full during the morning analytic hour and to associate to them in all their rich detail.

Besides making this study possible, the use of original transcripts provides us with a number of checks on the objectivity of the interpretations which follow. The data were collected several years before the memory-cycle model was conceived, so that the process of collection could not have been influenced by the theoretical approach under study here.

At the time the theoretical description of the memory-cycle model had been formulated, I was not personally acquainted with the original investigators, had not discussed with them the possibility of my using their data, and had not seen any of it. The theoretical model was therefore not influenced in any way by the nature of the data.

Finally, I was not personally acquainted with M. A.'s analyst at the time this study was written and had not read any of his writings which may have contained references to the case. The analyst's influence on my view of M. A. is therefore restricted to whatever is reflected by his interpretive statements in the transcript themselves.

We shall be concerned with the events taking place during a Thursday-evening analytic hour, with the dream descriptions recorded that night, and with the analytic hour early the following morning. During the Thursday-evening hour, the patient reported two dreams he had had at home on Tuesday night, after his analytic hour on Tuesday morning. This report was followed by an interpretation by the analyst which was directed not to the content of the dreams but to their obscurity and lack of associated affect. The patient then associated to affect-laden memories of his father which were directly relevant to the current transference situation. During the hour, the analyst pointed out to the patient the anxiety-producing elements contained in these memories which ordinarily led the patient to avoid them.

Three dreams were recorded on Thursday night and then reported by the patient with some minor changes in the analytic hour the next morning. Two of these dreams were closely related thematically to the Tuesday-night dreams. All contained references to the patient's father which appeared in a variety of affective contexts related to the transference.

The Thursday-night dreams, two of which were correction dreams, illustrate the operation of the memory cycle in several ways. First of all, they show a return to the content of the Tuesday-night dreams, but with the addition of the missing figure of the patient's father recovered by the analytic work of the Thursday hour.

Second, the Thursday residues, which included the reported Tuesday dreams enriched by the Thursday interpretations, were matched in the second series of dreams with new historical material from precisely the same areas in the memory structure which had supplied the imagery of the earlier dreams.

Third, the construction built up from the interconnected interpretations of the Thursday hour evoked and was matched with many more memory nodes in these areas than were the unenriched Tuesday residues. (This is shown not so much by the increased detail of the Thursday dreams, which cannot be fairly compared with the Tuesday dreams because of their different conditions of collection, but by the richness of associations to the content of the Thursday dreams in the Friday hour.)

Fourth, instinctual material is represented in the Thursday dreams in a relatively undisguised form, in contrast with the obscurity of the earlier dreams.

Fifth, the principal day residue of the Tuesday dreams, together with the past memory with which it was originally matched, emerge not in the Thursday analytic hour in which the Tuesday dreams were reported, but as associations to the Thursday-night correction dreams after they had been reported during the Friday-morning hour.

The concept of an ongoing interchange between the problem-solving activity of waking consciousness and the information-storing function of the permanent memory structure, mediated by the matching process in dreams and facilitated by the information-monitoring and structure-building activities of the psychoanalyst, is, of course, a complex and unfamiliar one. In order to see the reality behind the concept, we will have to examine our data with a thoroughness impossible in the actual practice of psychoanalysis and unusual in the psychoanalytic literature on dreams. This effort will enable us to see the dream not as an isolated and fortuitous event in the mental life of the dreamer, but as the essential bridge which links his childhood experience with his contemporary psychological world across the span of intervening years.

Organization

Chapter 2 is an exposition of the theory of the memory cycle. It appears (with minor changes) as it was written before the study which forms the major part of this monograph was undertaken. The reader will thus have an opportunity to judge the extent to which the empirical findings of the study confirm the model proposed earlier on theoretical grounds. (I should add that the model was stimulated by and in full accordance with my clinical experience as a psychoanalyst, although no systematic collection of data was involved in the original statement of the model.)

My aim in writing this exposition was to describe the adaptive function of dreaming without attempting to account for the modifications introduced into the process of dream construction by the censorship mechanisms. In fact, my understanding of the interaction between adaptive and defensive operations in the formation of dreams was not clarified until I had the opportunity to review the new (to me) data. The changes brought about by this clarification will become apparent when the data is presented later on.

Chapter 3 presents the new data as they emerged from the associative flow of the recorded analytic hours and sleep-laboratory reports. My intention here was to demonstrate the complementarity between the interpretive activity of the analyst and the adaptive functions of the memory cycle and the correction dream.

In chapter 4 the dream material is extracted from the analytic process and is used to directly illustrate the mechanism of dream construction. Here I have stressed the action of the memory cycle as a general mechanism which, although it is most clearly observed in the context of an ongoing analysis, has a life of its own quite apart from the therapeutic interaction.

Chapter 5 discusses the results of the study as they apply to the traditional psychoanalytic theory of dreams. Freud's writings on dreams throughout his career are reviewed, and a number of puzzling inconsistencies between his observations and his theoretical formulations are shown to be resolvable through the memory-cycle model. One of Freud's basic assumptions comes into question here; that mental activity is initiated when a single item of content with a high charge of "psychic energy" imposes itself in a self-aggrandizing way on another item with a lower charge. Freud's usual explanation for the genesis of dreams follows this assumption. The memory-cycle model and the confirming data presented here indicate that the dream is formed when two items of content, each one of importance to the adaptive functioning of the dreamer, are brought together by a higher-order information-processing structure for the purpose of comparison and evaluation.

In chapter 6 the new model for the mechanism of dream construction is generalized to other aspects of primary-process activity. This procedure leads to the conclusion that the Id, when it is viewed in terms of primitive organization of its contents, must be considered an archaic portion of the adaptive ego. It is therefore suggested that a distinction be made between the *adaptive ego,* with a small *e,* and the *Ego* as defined by the criterion of accessibility to consciousness. Under this arrangement, all structured activity of the psychic apparatus, including the primary process, is classified according to its place in the hierarchical structure of the adaptive ego.

The Ego, the Id, and the Superego, which I prefer to call psychic *superstructures,* may contain or cover any of the structures, at any level of complexity, which belong to the adaptive ego. The apportionment of these structures to the various superstructures, and the boundaries between the superstructures, are determined for each individual by the activity of his defense mechanisms. While the more primitive structures of the adaptive ego tend to remain inaccessible to consciousness, and therefore to appear clinically as Id contents, the tendency is not by any means absolute. Moreover, the inaccessibility of these primitive structures is not a given built into the psychic apparatus biologically, but a secondary development very much influenced by individual experience. If this were not so, psychoanalysis, as a therapeutic method, would be impossible.

Chapter 7 discusses the restraints placed on the development of psychoanalytic theory as a general psychology by the therapeutic success of psychoanalysis in its clinical application. Freud always chose the formulation which most dramatically underlined the therapeutic aims of the analyst. The resulting theory places great emphasis on the subjective feeling states of the patient, and assumes that these feeling states provide the principal motivation for behavior and symptom formation. The memory-cycle model and the findings of this study indicate that these subjective states are the outcome of evaluative procedures carried out unconsciously by the adaptive structures of the archaic ego.

Many analysts are concerned that any alteration in the framework of psychoanalytic theory would require them to abandon some of the technical procedures which have proven useful to them. But this is not the case here. If the patient's concealed affective states are not the ultimate source of his motivations, they are nevertheless of critical importance to the understanding of his inner life. The clinical usefulness of Freud's theoretical language depends in only a limited way on its ability to identify the psychological processes underlying the patient's subjective state. To the extent that this language is clinically useful at the present time, it will remain useful no matter what additional understanding of the underlying processes we acquire.

The history of science is full of examples of incomplete theoretical systems which persisted for long periods of time because of their association with practical techniques of proven value. In all such cases, theoretical advances were retarded by this association, and in every case the theoretical advance, when it finally came, helped to refine and improve existing techniques.

CHAPTER 2

The Dream
and the
Memory Cycle

Introduction

My purpose here is to present a new theoretical model of the process by which the structure and contents of the human memory store are modified and extended through new experience. This chapter will continue the psychoanalytic study of memory begun earlier in "The Associative Memory Tree," (Palombo, 1973) in which I attempted to define the structure of the memory storage system as it is revealed through the pattern of free association which unfolds during the psychoanalytic hour.

As my title indicates, the pathway leading to the permanent memory passes through a territory already familiar to psychoanalysts, the world of dreams. In fact, the dreaming state constitutes the crucial step in the introduction of new experiential material into the existing structure of the memory. In what follows I shall refer to the sequence of events through which a newly recorded sensory impression is processed and stored as *the memory cycle*.

The earliest suggestions that dreaming performs an information-processing function involved in the transfer of perceptual information from the short-term memory to the permanent memory were made independently by Greenberg and Leiderman (1966), Dewan (1967), and Breger (1967). Hawkins (1966) also pointed to the adaptive function of dreaming by relating it to the memory system through Freud's metaphor of the "Mystic Writing Pad" (1925).*

A terminological note is necessary here. To most experimental psychologists, the "short-term memory" is a structure that can hold up to seven items of memory in full consciousness for about twenty seconds after immediate sensory registration. Information retained for longer than this period is considered to have been transferred to the "long-term memory."

What we are concerned with here is a short-term memory structure that accumulates the meaningful experience of a normal waking day, only a small portion of which will actually be transferred to the permanent memory. For example, a patient whose medial temporal lobes were removed in an effort to treat his intractable epilepsy was prevented from transferring new information into permanent storage, as described by Milner et al. (1968):

During three of the nights at the Clinical Research Center, the patient rang for the night nurse, asking her, with many apologies, if she would tell him where he was and how he came to be there. He clearly realized that he was in a hospital but seemed unable to reconstruct any of the events of the previous day. On another occasion he remarked, "Every day is alone in itself, whatever enjoyment I've had, and whatever sorrow I've had." Our own impression is that many events fade for him long before the day is over. He often volunteers stereotyped descriptions of his own state, by saying that it is "like waking from a dream." His experience seems to be that of a person who is just becoming aware of his surroundings without fully comprehending the situation, because he does not remember what went before. (P. 217)

In addition to a deficiency in his short-term memory, this patient was unable to transfer the accumulated day residues into his permanent memory structure. The short-term memory referred to in this paper is the memory structure that stores the day's events. In the case example above, this structure represented the outer limit of the patient's powers of retention. The long-term memory contains the items normally retained beyond this limit, items that can be recalled decades later without reinforcement during the interim.

---

* This chapter was complete in all essentials before I became acquainted with the very valuable work of these writers. I take this as an indication that the information-processing model of memory is a paradigm whose time has come. Although many of my own thoughts were anticipated in the works cited, and in Breger, Hunter, and Lane (1971), there are also many differences. Since I have decided not to interrupt the continuity of my presentation in order to compare it in detail with these earlier works, I wish to make clear my acknowledgment of their priority wherever applicable.

One of the advantages of the approach developed here is that it reconciles two views of dreaming often thought to be in opposition. The dreaming state functions as an adaptive process necessary to the integration of new experience and at the same time as a conduit through which unconscious infantile wishes gain access to the realm of contemporary waking consciousness. These two aims will be seen to be mutually complementary.

The Memory System

At the input terminus of the memory system we can imagine a gigantic funnel which takes a flood of sensory impressions recorded in many sensory modalities, converging and directing them to a more central area for processing and evaluation (see Figure 1). At the storage terminus is a vast container, capable of holding all the significant memories gathered during a span of time which is enormous when compared with the brief moment necessary to record an individual im-

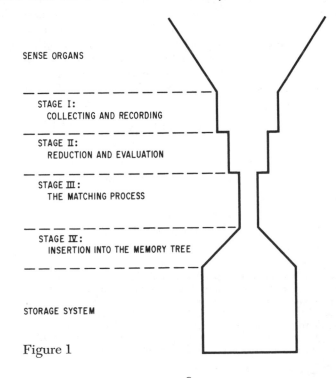

SENSE ORGANS

STAGE I:
COLLECTING AND RECORDING

STAGE II:
REDUCTION AND EVALUATION

STAGE III:
THE MATCHING PROCESS

STAGE IV:
INSERTION INTO THE MEMORY TREE

STORAGE SYSTEM

Figure 1

pression. Between these terminal components is an evaluating and processing system which must perform a great many discrete operations on each chunk of information passing through it. We will have to find a way to bring the requirement for precision and complexity in the processing system into accord with the requirements imposed by the great volume of information waiting to be processed.

The memory cycle consists of four distinct stages:

I.   At the input terminus the sensory impression is recorded, arranged in a simple ordering with other impressions, and transmitted to the central processing mechanism.

II.   In the central processing mechanism, a sequence of sorting and selection operations establishes that the sensory impression in question is of sufficient interest to warrant its introduction into the permanent memory store.

III. Also in the central processing mechanism, the specific locations in the permanent memory structure into which the new sensory impression will be introduced are determined.

IV.   The new sensory impression is transferred into the permanent memory store at the locations determined in Stage III.

Our attention will be directed primarily to Stages II and III, where the decisions are made that determine which new sensory impressions are to be introduced into the permanent memory and where they are to be located. Stage III is of special interest to the psychoanalyst, for it is during this stage of the memory cycle that dreaming occurs.

Stage III is of interest for other reasons as well. From the information-processing point of view, the determination of the most suitable locations for storing the new sensory impression is extraordinarily difficult. A brief explanation is in order here, because we will find later on that dreaming provides the specific solution to this difficulty.

In order for a new sensory impression to be introduced into a suitable location, such a location must first be discovered. As we will see, a suitable location is one that is adjacent to a closely related past memory already incorporated into the memory structure. *This means that for each new sensory impression to be introduced into the permanent memory, a closely related past memory must be recovered from it.*

It is a relatively simple matter to recall a memory which has been deliberately stored in a clearly marked location from which it will be accessible for repeated use, like a telephone number. But finding a past memory to meet the requirements of an entirely new problem situation is quite different. (The storing of *each* new and unanticipated sensory impression constitutes a new problem situation for the memory cycle.) A trial-and-error search of the permanent memory is ruled out by its

29

huge size. Nor is it possible simply to look for a particular kind of memory on a correspondingly numbered shelf, as it might be if the permanent memory were arranged according to a predetermined index like the Dewey decimal system.

The structure of the memory is more in the nature of a labyrinth. If an isolated memory is to be recovered from it on demand, an associative pathway leading to it must already have been marked out clearly, like Ariadne's thread. In "The Associative Memory Tree," I indicated how the psychoanalyst helps the patient piece together the segments of this thread as they emerge from his apparently disconnected associations.

In psychoanalytic work, as in other creative mental activities, a recurring requirement is the location of a significant memory for which no previously-marked-out associative pathway exists. Heuristic strategies for searching the permanent memory can be developed; yet, when all of the cognitive techniques of waking consciousness are brought into play, including the highly sophisticated techniques of free association and psychoanalytic interpretation, the time consumed in the search for even a single significant memory may stretch from minutes to hours or years.

We recognize that the ability to "summon up remembrance of things past" is an attribute of the greatest art. But we are generally ignorant of the fact that in order to make our way through the everyday world, we are required to summon up our own memories of the past on a mass-production schedule. It is this remarkable feat which is accomplished routinely during Stage III of the memory cycle, through the use of the technology of the dream. Without it there would be no way for us to transfer the enormous volume of our daily experience into the vast container of our memory, and to do it meaningfully.

Stage III therefore occupies a narrow bottleneck in the progress of a new sensory impression from input to permanent storage; a bottleneck which poses a serious threat to the adaptive functions of the psychic apparatus. The permanent memory is in constant danger of being out of touch with current reality, for although the memory store is floating in an ocean of sense data, it is nevertheless continually athirst for the new information which can enter it only through the slender opening of the dream.

It is in order to minimize this danger that Stage III is given a very high priority among the activities of the psychic apparatus, both in the distribution of operating time and in the consumption of energy (metabolic *and* psychic). In the dreaming state, we see the most powerful of cognitive tools—the sensory-projection systems—withdrawn from contact with the outside world for a considerable period every day so that they may serve the requirements of the memory cycle. Without their use, the determination of suitable locations in the permanent memory for new sensory impressions could not take place within any reasonable length of time,

As it is, the use of the sensory-projection mechanisms limits the amount of new information to be processed to roughly the quantity that can be held in conscious awareness at any given time. This amount is infinitesimal when compared with either the quantity taken in by the sense organs during a single day or the quantity already stored in the permanent memory at any time after earliest infancy. For all these reasons, Stage III must operate with extreme rapidity and efficiency.

Seen from this perspective, the peremptory qualities of dreaming brought to our attention by the physiological investigations of Aserinsky and Kleitman (1953), Dement (1960), Fisher (1965), Hartmann (1973), and others are not at all surprising. These investigations indicate that all mammals are required to spend a relatively fixed amount of time in the dreaming state, from 5 to 10 percent of their total life span, in fact.

Dreams occur in human subjects with strict regularity during the final ten to twenty minutes of successive ninety-minute sleep and dream periods. Deprivation of dreaming sleep causes noteworthy mental and emotional stress (Greenberg and Pearlman, 1974). During the nights immediately following several nights of experimental dream deprivation, subjects invariably increase the proportion of dreaming sleep until 80 to 90 percent of the lost dreaming time has been recovered.

The well-known rapid eye movements and an extreme activation of the brain as well as the neuroendocrine systems occur in the dreaming state (Hartmann, 1967). Cerebral blood flow, maintained at a constant level during even the most strenuous waking activity, is markedly increased during dreaming (Reivich et al., 1968). Clearly, dreaming is not an occasional mental operation called into action only to deal with unpredictably dangerous stimuli. Dreaming is directly involved in our ability to survive as organisms through its role in the construction of a framework of past experience within which the psychic apparatus can perform its daily duties.

The Associative Memory Tree

The memory tree is a structure discovered by Newell, Shaw, and Simon (1957) in their now-historic work on the programming of the digital computer to simulate complex human psychological processes. The tree structure may be realized in any information-processing system, whether this system is an animal brain, a digital computer or something else not yet anticipated.

In the memory tree, an item of memory content is stored in a given location, to be called here a *nodal point* or *node*. Along with this item is stored the address of another location or locations, which are to become nodal points *subordinate* to the original node. New items of memory content related to the original content are introduced into the locations whose addresses are stored together with the original item of content. The subordinate nodal points, in turn, contain the addresses of still other locations which become the next rank of subordinate nodes. The result is a branching structure which can grow to any size (see Figure 2).

When the item of memory content stored in the original location (now the superordinate nodal point) is recovered, the addresses of the

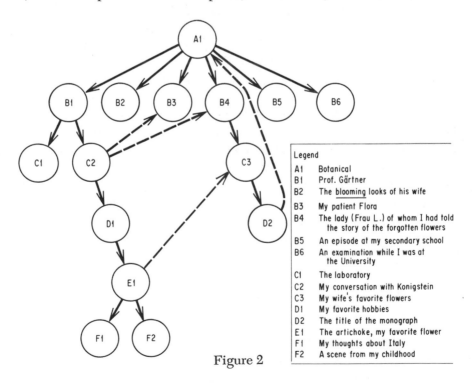

Figure 2

Legend

A1	Botanical
B1	Prof. Gärtner
B2	The blooming looks of his wife
B3	My patient Flora
B4	The lady (Frau L.) of whom I had told the story of the forgotten flowers
B5	An episode at my secondary school
B6	An examination while I was at the University
C1	The laboratory
C2	My conversation with Konigstein
C3	My wife's favorite flowers
D1	My favorite hobbies
D2	The title of the monograph
E1	The artichoke, my favorite flower
F1	My thoughts about Italy
F2	A scene from my childhood

first rank of subordinate nodes are recovered as well, and the contents of these nodes become accessible. Which, if any, of these new contents will actually be explored depends on the affective values (positive or negative, strong or weak) assigned to them. In this way, a dynamically determined associative pathway may be traced out through a portion of the tree. (It should be noted that the *physical* locations of the various nodal points may be scattered randomly through the computer memory or brain. The connections in the memory tree are made through the addresses of subordinate nodes and a routine procedure for finding the physical locations when these addresses are known.)

Like the programmed associative-memory structures that it resembles, the structure of the human permanent memory appears to have a number of features that present obstacles to any systematic procedure for searching out and locating a particular item of information. These obstacles exist prior to and independent of whatever additional difficulties may be created by the mechanisms of repression discovered by Freud. They must be dealt with by adaptive mechanisms specifically designed for this purpose.

The inherent features of the permanent memory structure that interfere with the searching process are the following:

1. The large-scale structure of the long-term memory is a unilaterally directed graph with the properties of a tree growing from a point (Harary et al., 1965). Associations normally flow in one direction only, away from the origin and toward the periphery. The pathway leading from a super-ordinate nodal point is therefore inaccessible from the subordinate node that terminates the pathway. This restriction can be circumvented only by a special effort to trace the sequence of nodes traversed along the pathway leading to the particular nodal point in question.

2. Individual nodal points do not appear to be distinguished from one another as to type or quality of contents. Thus the contents of any nodal point may be associated with the contents of any other. The basic unit of information appears to be the sensory image. Semantic information appears in nodal points that are subordinated to previously recorded sensory information.

3. Associations are unlabeled—that is, the fact that two associated memory units are linked tells nothing about the syntactic, semantic, or logical relationships between them.

A memory structure with these properties is designed for flexibility of storage rather than the instant availability of its contents for problem-solving activity. It is open to the introduction of new items of experience at any existing location in the structure, but it is notably lacking in rapid access to items already in storage. (This is one reason for the lengthy duration of psychoanalytic treatment.) The structure of the memory tree therefore maximizes the input of new information under the pressure of immediate events and affects, even when the ultimate significance and utility of this information are still uncertain. Lindsay refers to a simple structure of this kind as "the *ingenuous graph* for the given initial data set" (1973, p. 377; Lindsay's italics).

Once the pressure of events and affects has subsided, the ingenuous structure of the memory tree may be enhanced by the development of new linkages during the problem-solving activity of waking consciousness. In this way the more significant branches of the tree develop such features as reversible associations, nodal points addressable by content as well as by location, and a rich elaboration of semantic and logical relationships. These branches constitute what I would call the long-term *working* memory, as distinct from the passive or ingenuous structure of the long-term memory as a whole.

How much of the passive memory structure is ordinarily incorporated into working memory is difficult to estimate, but it must differ considerably from person to person. In the case of the neurotic patient who consults a psychoanalyst, many critical elements of past experience are inaccessible. The presenting complaint and the initial history are drawn from his working memory; the analysis proper involves an extended exploration and activation of his passive memory.

Computer simulations of human memory described in the recent literature tend to be simulations of the long-term *working* memory (Schank, 1973; Simmons, 1973; Wilks, 1973). The success of these models in imitating the performance of human subjects in a limited-task environment is extremely impressive.

One can see that the complexity of the output of an information-processing mechanism (C_0) depends on both its computational power (P) and the internal complexity of the information units which form its input (C_I):

$$C_0 \sim (P)(C_I)$$

It is not surprising, therefore, that a mechanism of relatively limited computational power (a digital computer program in the current state of the art) can simulate the performance of a human subject if its information units are already highly elaborate at the time of input.

A successful program, like the Human Associative Memory of Anderson and Bower (1973), requires an input which is organized at the level of grammatical sentence or logical proposition. It assumes that perceptual information has been translated from sensory images into semantic structures, and that all associations are labeled and reversible. These conditions or their equivalent must certainly be achieved in the human long-term *working* memory, but they cannot be typical of the long-term memory as a whole.

A program that retrieves propositional statements from its memory and makes low-level logical inferences from those statements is a simulated student, not a simulated person. I draw attention to this difference because the information-processing function performed by the human mind in the dreaming state, though in principle quite similar to analogous functions performed by intelligent computer programs, exists on a scale barely contemplated in the current literature of cognitive psychology (Hunt, 1973).

Freud's description of his own associations to the dream of "The Botanical Monograph" in *The Interpretation of Dreams** provides us with an apt illustration of the tree structure:

> Not only the compound idea, "botanical monograph," however, but each of its components, "botanical" and "monograph" separately, led by numerous connecting paths deeper and deeper into the tangle of dream-thoughts. "Botanical" was related to the figure of Professor *Gärtner* [Gardener], the *blooming* looks of his wife, to my patient *Flora* and to the lady [Frau L.] of whom I had told the story of the forgotten flowers. Gärtner led in turn to the laboratory and to my conversation with Konigstein. My two patients [Flora and Frau L.] had been mentioned in the course of this conversation. A train of thought joined the lady with the flowers to my wife's *favourite flowers* and thence to the title of the monograph which I had seen for a moment during the day. In addition to these, "botanical" recalled an episode at my secondary school and an examination while I was at the University. A fresh topic touched upon in my conversation with Dr. Konigstein—my *favourite* hobbies—was joined, through the intermediate link of what I jokingly called my *favourite flower*, the artichoke, with the train of thought proceeding from the forgotten flowers. Behind "artichokes" lay, on the one hand, my thoughts about Italy and, on the other hand, a scene from my childhood which was the opening of what have since become my intimate relations with books. Thus "botanical" was a regular nodal point in the dream. (Pp. 282–83)

The pathway traced by Freud's associations can be designated by a listing of the sequence of nodal points through which it passes: A1–B1–A1–B2–A1–B3–A1–B4–A1–B1–C1–B1–C2–B3–C2–B4–C3–D2–A1–B5–A1–B6–A1–C2–D1–E1–C3–E1–F1–E1–F2. (Because of some ambiguities in Freuds language, several slightly different alternative pathways could be constructed.)

---

* Page references not otherwise identified are to this work (Freud, 1900).

There are three distinct directions of movement relative to the tree structure included in this (or any similar) pathway.

1. Movement from superordinate to subordinate node (indicated by the solid arrows in Figure 2): A1–B1, A1–B2, A1–B3, A1–B4, A1–B1–C1, B1–C2, B4–C3–D2, A1–B5, A1–B6, A1–B1–C2–D1–E1, E1–F1, E1–F2. These are true "free associations," moving downhill along the structural gradient of the memory tree. They reproduce the structure of the tree as it was originally generated by the memory cycle. It is the initial establishment of these connections during the operation of the memory cycle which specifically concerns us here.

2. Movement from subordinate to superordinate node, retracing a recent downhill movement in order to begin a new movement through another branch radiating from the superordinate node. Movement in this direction requires effort. As I have suggested earlier, one of the analyst's functions is to assist the patient in working his way back uphill by keeping a mental record of the significant nodal points through which his associations have passed. Without this uphill work (or working through), the associative pathway would break up into disconnected fragments. In the passage quoted here, the uphill segments of Freud's associative pathway are represented by the segments B1–A1, B2–A1, B3–A1, B4–A1, C1–B1, B5–A1, B6–A1, F1–E1.

3. Movement crossing from one branch to another without first returning to a node superordinate to both. There are four such examples here, C2–B3, C2–B4, E1–C3, D2–A1 (indicated by dashed arrows in Figure 2). Cross-connections like these are the result of problem-solving activity, i.e., not included in the original programming of the memory tree by the operation of the memory cycle. Therefore we cannot fully pursue our interest in them here.

Nevertheless, it should be noted that the establishment of cross-connections creates a variety of associative shortcuts which facilitate many routine and repetitive but absolutely necessary cognitive operations. The analyst plays an important role in helping the patient establish new adaptive cross-connections, as well as in helping him to circumvent existing maladaptive cross-connections (which act as short circuits rather than shortcuts).

The Memory Cycle: Stage I
Collecting and Recording

Freud's analysis of his own dreams forms one of the most fascinating chapters in the history of psychoanalysis. That there is still a great deal more to be learned from them has been demonstrated by such able writers as Erikson (1954), Schur (1966a), and Grinstein (1968).

If it were possible, it would certainly be very useful to trace the part played by a dream of Freud's, such as "The Botanical Monograph," in the memory cycle during which it occured. But to attempt such a project here, with its attendant conjectures and reconstructions, would only direct our attention away from the already sufficient complexities of the memory cycle itself.

For the sake of simplicity, then, we will take as an example the introduction of the impression produced by a gratifying feeding experience with his mother into the permanent memory of a hypothetical infant. We will imagine that the mother has just finished nursing her baby and is now holding him, smiling at him and talking to him.

The human nervous system is designed to take in through its sense organs vastly more information than it can possibly store for an extended period of time. This arrangement permits an optimal response to any immediate danger where the first priority is a maximum of information about the situation of the moment. The complicated procedures required to sort out and evaluate the long-range significance of the experience can be postponed until a time of relative security. This means that there must be available a short-term memory system capable of holding a very large volume of information until this evaluation can take place.

For our infant, the immediate danger compelling his waking attention arises from his dependence on others for the fulfillment of his basic physical needs. The nature of the initial mother-infant relationship is such that the infant's communication of these needs and of his feelings in general can be effective without the integration of his various sensory modalities. Piaget (1954) has described with great sensitivity how this integration takes place slowly and through many very small increments during the first year of life. This suggests that the information transmitted from the sense organs remains segregated according to sensory modality in the short-term memory.

These new sensory impressions arrive in the coded form required for serial transmission. To understand this, we can compare the transformation taking place in the sense organ with the action of a television camera.

The television camera picks up a two-dimensional visual image from the outside world. Through rapid line-by-line scanning, it transforms this image into a one-dimensional sequence of electrical pulses. If this sequence of electrical pulses is stored on a videotape, the physical form it takes has nothing in common with the original image.

For reasons of economy, it is almost certain that the sensory data stored in the short-term memory remains in the coded form in which it arrives. If and when it becomes necessary to make a sensory impression conscious once again, it can be decoded and transformed back into its original sensory form through the use of the sensory projection mechanisms (as signals are transformed back into images by a television receiver). Because we are not conscious of the contents of the short-term memory (except when an individual item is deliberately recalled) it is extremely unlikely that this sensory reconstruction takes place during Stage I.

The information gathered through each of the various sensory modalities is transmitted to the short-term memory in coded form. Are the codes identical? Can a message from the eye be translated into the code ordinarily used for information coming from a joint capsule? The enormous difference in both quality and quantity of information coming from these dissimilar sources argues strongly against this possibility.

If the sensory codes are incompatible, as I believe they must be, then it follows that sensory integration can take place most conveniently when the sensory projection mechanisms are in use and the stored sensory data is decoded and transformed again into images. There are two situations in which sensory integration seems to be mandatory: first, when action is being taken with respect to the environment during waking consciousness, and second, as I will show, when the relationship between present and past experience is being determined and continuity between them established, during Stage III of the memory cycle.

The Memory Cycle: Stage II
Reduction and Evaluation

The mechanisms operating in Stage II function as an information sieve or filter; a rather coarse filter, in fact, for the enormous quantity of information held in the short-term memory must be reduced by several orders of magnitude to be manageable. But the mesh must nevertheless be fine enough to retain all of the sensory impressions which record the significant elements of experience. A graded series of filters would be most likely to give the precision required to achieve the necessary balance.

The Gestalt characteristics of the new sensory impressions and the immediate emotional responses evoked by them must provide the major criteria for these tests of significance. Perhaps later on in life, new methods of discrimination may be learned, but the influence of past experience must be limited in Stage II in order to ensure the retention of experiences which are truly novel.

In all sensory modalities, then, figure will be separated from background and intensely felt experiences from affectively neutral ones. For our infant, this will mean the selecting of those impressions which arise from the experience of pleasurable contact with his mother. Perhaps, as extraneous material is eliminated, these surviving impressions will tend to form aggregates of significant information which are marked off in such a way that they move together through the rest of the system. In this way, the "day residues" described by Freud and familiar to us in our work with dreams would be formed.

The idea that dreaming is associated with the process by which insignificant sensory input is eliminated from the short-term memory is an old one. It was proposed by Robert (1886) and refuted by Freud in *The Interpretation of Dreams* (1900: pp. 79–80). Robert assumed that the contents of dreams are chaotic and argued, in effect, that only a waste-disposal operation could account for such an output. Freud's refutation was based simply on his recognition that the contents of dreams are meaningful and interrelated.

In addition, Robert's theory requires that the very costly procedure of decoding and sensory reconstruction be applied to waste material about to be discarded. Even if it were desirable to do this, the huge volume of nonsignificant sense data would completely swamp the sensory projection mechanisms.

Dreaming is not identifiable with the elimination of extraneous input from the short-term memory. But the separation of useful from superfluous sense data is one of the basic processes of the memory cycle. Robert's synthesis was therefore a step toward the understanding of the larger system of which dreaming forms a part. (The idea that something is discarded in the course of dreaming is one that we will find ourselves returning to later on.)

Interestingly, the earliest suggestion of a relationship between human dreaming and the operations of the computer memory involved a revival of Robert's theory. When a new computer program is to be run, the contents of the computer memory accumulated through the operation of previous programs must be cleared. These leftover contents can be printed out as they are eliminated from the memory, in which case the printout has a typically chaotic appearance. Accordingly, repeating the error of Robert, Evans and Newman (1964) proposed that dreaming is analogous to the clearing of the computer memory.

The dreaming state is reserved for the much more difficult task of matching day residues with the older memories occupying prospective locations in the permanent memory. Stage II, which prepares the day residues for this procedure, must, of course, precede it.

From the viewpoint of economy, it would be preferable to have the day residues sent on to Stage III as soon as they are selected, without further storage. This would place Stage II during the period of non-dreaming sleep which immediately precedes each period of dreaming. This arrangement would have two other advantages. It would effectively close the short-term memory to further input while the sifting and sorting of Stage II is carried out. In addition, it would allow this vast amount of processing to be done under conditions of minimum interference from other cerebral mechanisms (especially the sensory-projection mechanisms, which are in operation at all other times).

When sleeping subjects are awakened during nondreaming sleep, they report "dreams" which consist of single, isolated memories of the previous day, undistorted by the "dreamwork," just as our theory would lead us to expect in Stage II. (The suggestion that these are the "latent dream thoughts" of which Freud speaks is attractive. But we must remember that they merely duplicate the waking experience of the previous day and have no connection with unconscious wishes, past or present).

An ingenious experiment by Greenberg and Pearlman (1975a) provides support for the assumption that Stage II coincides with nondreaming sleep. We would expect that an emotionally charged waking experience would require less effort of discrimination during Stage II in order for it to be selected for transfer to the permanent memory. If it could be shown that the first period of nondreaming sleep following an affect-laden waking experience is significantly shortened compared with the average for a given subject, then we would have reason to believe that Stage II is in operation during nondreaming sleep.

Greenberg and Pearlman were able to demonstrate this relationship. The time of onset of dreaming was measured repeatedly for a subject who came to the sleep laboratory soon after a psychoanalytic hour. Transcriptions of the analytic hours were independently scored for intensity of affect by a team whose ratings were highly reliable. A significant inverse relationship was found between affect-intensity ratings and length of first nondreaming sleep period (REM latency).

We must now return to the "elimination" of sense data from the short-term memory. According to the model originally suggested by Greenberg and Leiderman (1966), once the selection of day residues has taken place, the contents of the short-term memory have no further use and can be cleared, just as the computer memory is. Since the day residues have been transferred to the long-term memory, the remainder is simply occupying valuable space in the short-term memory.

It might follow that if a subject were allowed to sleep through a night but were prevented from dreaming, he would empty his short-term memory without having transferred any of its contents to his permanent memory. Greenberg, Pearlman, Fingar, Kantrowitz, and Kawliche (1970) tested this hypothesis. They had four subjects learn and memorize six lists of paired word associates. After various (brief) periods of dream-deprived sleep, they were tested for retention of the memorized word associates. They were found to have no memory deficit when compared with control subjects who had slept normally.

According to Greenberg and his associates in this experiment, these results are incompatible with the hypothesis that during dreaming sleep the contents of the short-term memory are transferred to the long-term memory. They appear to reach this conclusion by assuming that in their experiment the short-term memory has in fact been emptied, but that despite dream deprivation, its contents have been transferred to the permanent memory.

An alternative—and, in my opinion, much more reasonable—explanation of their results is that the short-term memory is not emptied during nondreaming sleep. There is no evidence to suggest that when a day residue is transferred to the permanent memory, it must also be removed from the short-term memory. It would be more economical simply to copy the memory trace into the new system than to remove it physically from the old. (Compare a sequence of signals on a magnetic tape. It is much easier to copy this sequence electronically onto another tape than to cut it out of the first and splice it into the second.)

There are also considerations of safety. The information being held in the short-term memory is potentially very valuable. The mechanisms which sort it out in Stage II function by looking for closer and closer approximations to their generalized image of a significant experience. A new sensory impression may be overlooked if it is sufficiently divergent from what is expected. If the coded sensory input were retained in the short-term memory through several periods of nondreaming sleep, the chances of accidentally losing it in this way would be minimized.

The same argument applies with even more force to Stage III. The uncertainty inherent in the process by which day residues are matched with older memories is such that it would be very risky to have a day residue run through it only once before being destroyed. The structure of the permanent memory is designed to forever retain each item of information introduced into it, no matter how that item is superseded by later experience. The time during which a sensory impression can be retained in the short-term memory is, of course, limited, but it must be long relative to the time required to process it in Stages II and III.

How, then, is the short-term memory cleared? Experience suggests that new memories may be held in the short-term memory for several days before being transferred to the permanent memory. Retroactive amnesia after acute brain injury involves a loss to the permanent memory of material several days old which would have been available to it under normal circumstances. A given waking experience may reappear in successive dreaming periods or in successive nights of dreaming. It is not cleared in a single night.

But it is apparent that there is a progressive falling-off in the likelihood that an experience will remain in the short-term memory after intervening periods of sleep. When a student preparing for an examination postpones studying the material until the last minute, the student is taking advantage of the greater ease of recall from the short-term memory. By staying up all night before the exam, he is not only giving himself more time in which to cram his short-term memory with facts, but is also preventing the relative loss in his power of recall which would be caused by a period of sleep.

In so doing, he makes certain sacrifices. Only a small proportion of the contents crammed into his short-term memory will become permanently available to him. Learning the same material over a period of many days separated by adequate intervals of sleep would have allowed more of it to enter his permanent memory. On the day of the examination, the crammed material in his short-term memory, although easier to recall, will be much more difficult to relate to the rest of his store of experience— i.e., the contents of his permanent memory system.

We must therefore think of the clearing of the short-term memory as a gradual and continuous process of decay, with new experiences fading away over a period of several days. In this way, sufficient redundancy is introduced into the memory cycle to counteract much of the uncertainty inherent in its operations.

The Memory Cycle: Stage III
The Matching Process

We have followed a new sensory impression—now a day residue—to the point at which it is ready to be evaluated for its relationship to the contents of the permanent memory store. Having survived the sorting of Stage II, its significance has been attested and the desirability of its being represented in the permanent memory established.

The day residue must be located where it will be connected with the past memories which are most closely related to it, both cognitively and affectively. This is certain to mean that it will be represented at many locations in the memory tree. I shall assume throughout that the process by which the representation of the day residue is introduced is the same for each new location, however many there may be.

Until this point, the major constraints on the process of memorization have been biological. The manner in which the organism maintains contact with and gathers information from the environment has determined the nature of the collecting and sorting stages of the process. In Stage III, the limiting factors arise from the properties of the associative memory tree which have been described in the introductory sections.

The structure of the memory tree permits the introduction of any new item of experience at any point in the tree judged to be appropriate. Only a structure which is open and inclusive in this way can take full advantage of the information conveyed by a new experience.

An open associative structure, however, has no built-in cross-referencing system. If the location into which the day residue is to be inserted were specified in advance—i.e., indexed according to a prearranged system of coordinates—it would be easy to trace and recover. In the memory tree, only the connection between a given node and its superordinate node can be used as an indicator. And from the contents of its superordinate node, it is not possible to predict the contents of the given node except in the most general way (as demonstrated regularly by free association during psychoanalysis).

This situation introduces a considerable degree of uncertainty into the operations of Stage III, in which those nodal points in the permanent structure whose contents most closely match the day residues must be located. For this to be accomplished in a practical way, (a) a great expenditure of effort is required, (b) a relatively modest degree of success must be accepted, and (c) the existing structure must be subject to continual review and revision. Dreaming provides a technique which minimizes these difficulties.

Freud attributed the fact that dreams are capable of becoming conscious—i.e., displayed in the sensory-projection system of the brain as if they were actual events being perceived by the dreamer—to a need for substitute satisfactions to replace the satisfactions not available during sleep. Although I have no doubt that the reproduction of sensory imagery in dreams creates the opportunity for using them in this way, the extended and almost invariable pattern of nightly dreaming indicates that dreams have a more primary function which is not subject to the inconsistencies of wishing. But this does not mean that emotion plays an incidental role in dreaming.

Rapaport (1961) is certainly correct that affects have the first priority in determining what is remembered and how the memory is organized. The earliest experiences in life introduced into the permanent memory are experiences of bodily satisfaction and frustration. The affective values assigned to these experiences must be very high, both absolutely and relative to experiences later in life. As the memory tree branches from its point of origin, these affect-laden memories become the contents of the first set of subordinate nodal points to be established. New memories which are added later are subordinated in the structure to these earlier ones.

If we assume, as Freud suggested and observation confirms, that as the infant matures, his attention is directed away from bodily satisfaction and toward the detailed exploration of his environment, then the memory tree will develop a gradient of affective loading such that throughout the tree a given nodal point will tend to contain material with a higher affective value than the points subordinate to it. This gradient will be steepest near the origin of the tree, at the beginning of life, and flatter as reality supersedes immediate pleasure as the criterion for evaluating new experiences. (It should be noted that dreaming time is extremely high in the newborn and decreases, at first rapidly and then more gradually, throughout the remainder of life.)

How does affect enter into the matching process during Stage III? We have a day residue to be matched with closely related memories in the permanent store. But only a reasonably small set of older memories can be selected for comparison with the new experience.

The day residues must be scanned with the purpose of defining criteria for making this preliminary selection. Older memories chosen by these criteria will match the day residues only to a first approximation, with a more detailed method of comparison to follow. The day residues might be scanned one at a time, followed by detailed comparison with the evoked older memories. Or else the initial scanning might cover a series of day residues, followed by detailed comparison of the whole series with their corresponding older memories.

The latter of these procedures would require less switching back and forth and would also preserve any relationships which already exist among the day residues in the series. Several investigators have found that when a sleeping subject is awakened near the beginning of a dream period, the dreams he describes are relatively undistorted, affectively neutral memories of the preceding day's events. If the same subject is awakened later in the dream period, he will report dream contents which are less coherent, less clearly related to the events of the previous day, and more affectively charged (Hartmann, 1967).

These findings suggest that an extended series of day residues is first displayed in the sensory-projection system. Only after this series has been scanned would the older memories be introduced into the projection system, together with a second display of the day residues. (The day residues remain registered in coded form during the display; otherwise they would be lost when the display ended.)

We must remember that a trial-and-error search of the entire tree in the time available for the matching process is quite impossible. Two ways of minimizing the time required for the location of related older memories after the preliminary scanning suggest themselves. One obvious procedure would be to begin the search with those older memories which have the same quality of affect as the new memory and the greatest intensity of this affect. The second approach would be to begin the search for related older memories at or near the origin of the memory tree. This would direct the search from superordinate to subordinate nodal points all along the way. The search would then be following a path of least resistance toward the desired location. It would also guarantee that if the search were broken off prematurely, the nodal points already recovered, to which the day residue might then be attached, would be those which have a higher affective value than the more precise memory actually being sought.

The manner in which the structure of the tree develops over time determines that the nodal points with the highest affective value tend also to be those which are nearest the origin of the tree. Therefore the two methods mentioned above for minimizing the searching time will have identical results in practice. It is the earliest of the older memories recovered during Stage III in the search for the nearest matching memories which correspond to the latent dream thoughts described by Freud as "unconscious infantile wishes."* We have seen why these memories in particular are highly charged with affect, and why they are likely to be recovered during dreaming.

Two salient phenomena must be accounted for as we describe in detail how the matching takes place. (1) The dream is a display in the sensory projection systems. (2) The contents of the dream appear to be distorted, irrational, arbitrary.

What is the reason for the sensory display? Why should the matching of the day residues and older memories require a transformation from the coded signal mode to the reconstructed sensory mode? One might imagine that the day residue could be introduced into the permanent structure by a simple procedure like the copying of the signal recorded on a videotape. Instead we find the day residue, together with the older memory which has been evoked by the preliminary scanning, simultaneously displayed in the sensory projection system, their images superimposed in a kind of montage.

The montage appears as if on a television set which is receiving signals from two different transmitters and displaying the images reconstituted from these signals in a composite picture on a single screen. It is the character of this composite image in the sensory projection mechanism during Stage III which determines whether a valid match has been made between the day residue and the older memory.

If the component images are similar, they reinforce each other and combine to form a relatively coherent composite. If they are dissimilar, the composite will appear to be chaotic. Whenever the combined images are judged to be coherent, the day residue in question is marked for

---

* Freud often uses the term "latent dream thoughts" to refer to any material of emotional significance which emerges in the associations to a dream. This would include, for instance, "a second source of the dream . . . in another experience of the same day." (P. 174) At other times he indicates that the latent content is connected in a special way with more remote experience: "Stated in general terms, this would imply that every dream was linked in its manifest content with recent experiences and in its latent content with the most ancient experiences." (P. 218)

The evoked older memories in Stage III of the memory cycle correspond to the "latent dream content" in this latter, more restricted sense. These evoked memories are not necessarily ancient, but they have already entered the permanent memory where they have been located and connected according to their relationship with other past memories. (See chapter 5 for a detailed discussion of Freud's usage.)

introduction into the permanent memory structure in a new node subordinate to the one containing the older memory.

The principle of identification by superimposition is illustrated in a simple way by the operation of the blink comparator, a standard instrument of the astronomer with which the planet Pluto was discovered. Two photographic plates of the same region of the sky, taken several days to a few weeks apart, are mounted in the comparator so that their images coincide exactly when projected on a ground-glass screen. The two plates are projected alternately several times a second. An ordinary star, whose image is the same on both plates, appears on the screen as a steady, unchanging point of light. An object whose intensity is not constant (for example, a nova or variable star) appears to flash and fade alternately.

The smaller and more distant members of the solar system, like Pluto and the tiny asteroids, appear on a single plate to be indistinguishable from faint stars. But since they are moving slowly with respect to the fixed stellar background, their images in the comparator jump back and forth between their distinct locations on the two plates. By superimposing the two plates in this way any unusual activity taking place in an area containing many hundreds of stars can be detected within a few seconds.

Conditions are much more complex in the human memory apparatus, of course, where simultaneously projected images in several sensory modalities change continuously over time. Moreover, in using the blink comparator, the astronomer is interested in detecting instances of difference against a background of uniformity. In Stage III, what is required is the recognition of moments of similarity in an indeterminate flux.

Despite these differences, Freud was able to develop the idea of superimposed photographs to exemplify the more complex matching procedure observable in dreams.

In *The Interpretation of Dreams,* he gives these characteristic illustrations (among many others):

1. The face that I saw in the dream was at once my friend R.'s and my uncle's. It was like one of Galton's composite photographs. (In order to bring out family likenesses, Galton used to photograph several faces on the same plate. So there could be no doubt that I really did mean that my friend R. was a simpleton—like my Uncle Josef. (P. 139)

2. None of these figures whom I lighted upon by following up "Irma" appeared in the dream in bodily shape. They were concealed behind the dream figure of "Irma," which was thus turned into a collective image with, it must be admitted, a number of contradictory characteristics. Irma became the representative of all these other figures which had been sacrificed to the work of condensation, since I passed over to her, point by point, everything that

reminded me of *them*. There is another way in which a "collective figure" can be produced for purposes of dream-condensation, namely by uniting the actual features of two or more people into a single dream-image. It was in this way that the Dr. M. of my dream was constructed. He bore the name of Dr. M., he spoke and acted like him; but his physical characteristics and his malady belonged to someone else, namely to my eldest brother. One single feature, his pale appearance, was doubly determined, since it was common to both of them in real life.

Dr. R. in my dream about my uncle with the yellow beard was a similar composite figure. But in his case the dream-image was constructed in yet another way. I did not combine the features of one person with those of another and in the process omit from the memory-picture certain features of each of them. What I did was to adopt the procedure by means of which Galton produced family portraits: namely by projecting two images on to a single plate, so that certain features common to both are emphasized, while those which fail to fit in with one another cancel one another out and are indistinct in the picture. In my dream about my uncle the fair beard emerged prominently from a face which belonged to two people and which was consequently blurred; incidentally, the beard further involved an allusion to my father and myself through the intermediate idea of growing grey. (P. 293)

3. If the objects which are to be condensed into a single unity are much too incongruous, the dream-work is often content with creating a composite structure with a comparatively distinct nucleus, accompanied by a number of less distinct features. In that case the process of unification into a single image may be said to have failed. The two representations are superimposed and produce something in the nature of a contest between the two visual images. One might arrive at similar representations in a drawing, if one tried to illustrate the way in which a general concept is formed from a number of individual perceptual images. (P. 324)

4. I will therefore quote one more dream, which seems to be composed of two different and opposing phantasies which coincide with each other at a few points and of which one is superficial while the second is, as it were an interpretation of the first. . . . Here there is no difficulty in separating the two components. The superficial one was a *phantasy of* arrest which appears as though it had been freshly constructed by the dream-work. But behind it some material is visible which had been only slightly re-shaped by the dream-work: *a phantasy of marriage*. Those features which were common to both phantasies emerge with special clarity, in the same way as in one of Galton's composite photographs. (Pp. 493–94)

In this series of observations we see Freud's awareness of the super-imposition of dream materials expanding. From the two-dimensional photographic image of (1), he moves to the "composite persons" of (2). These composite persons can be three-dimensional, represented in any or all sensory modalities, by speech, behavior, or abstract characterizations. They can also reveal themselves through changes in representation during the course of the dream, "point by point."

The static photograph of (1) is developed in (3) into a dynamic interactional process, a "contest" between disparate perceptions. In (4) it is not only a set of objects which are superimposed, but entire fantasied experiences. In most of this material, the superimposed elements clearly retain their identities either as day residue, for example, Dr. R., Dr. M., Irma, the "superficial phantasy" of (4), or as affect-laden older memory, e.g. the uncle, the brother, the eldest daughter who is in danger, the "interpretive phantasy" of marriage.

Example (3) is especially interesting, for it records an instance where the matching process has failed within the dream itself. The traditional psychoanalytic theory of dream construction implies the existence of a similar test situation in which a decision is made before the materials of the dream enter consciousness; that is, before they achieve representation in the sensory projection mechanisms. This test must determine the "suitability" of a given day residue to act as the vehicle for carrying a particular infantile impulse into consciousness.

Freud makes it plain that not every day residue is qualified to serve as the vehicle for every impulse. Therefore a process of selection is necessary, during which any proposed combinations of residue and impulse must be judged to be "suitable" or not. According to this theory, a positive outcome of the selection process will lead to the emergence into consciousness of the "suitable" combination. A negative outcome of this determination would have to mean that the mismatched dream materials could not enter consciousness at all; that is, they could not achieve representation in the sensory-projection mechanisms if, in Freud's words, "the process of unification into a single image may be said to have failed." But this is exactly what happened in Example (3).

For the model being presented here, the dream itself is the test situation in which the congruence between images of the present and the past are determined. Moreover, given the possibility of disruptive interventions by the censorship mechanisms, we would expect to find the full range of chaotic to coherent matchings appearing in the dreams that actually take place—as, in fact, we do.

Arlow takes the analogy of Galton's procedure a step further than Freud. He postulates (1961, 1969a, 1969b) that a continual confrontation takes place (normally outside conscious awareness) between parallel sequences of imagery derived from current experience and from the hierarchical memory structures in which the dominant fantasy representations of the past are stored and organized. For Arlow this procedure is clearly an integrative process. The fantasy material from the past is primarily instinctual in nature, but the process of bringing it into an ordered relationship with new experience is an adaptive device for maximizing the opportunities for instinctual gratification under currently existing circumstances. Arlow says (1961):

There is a hierarchy in the fantasy life of each individual, a hierarchy which reflects the vicissitudes of individual experience as well as the influence of psychic differentiation and ego development. To use a very static analogy for a highly dynamic state of affairs, we may say that unconscious fantasies have a systematic relation to each other. Fantasies are grouped around certain basic instinctual wishes, and such a group is composed of different versions or different editions of attempts to resolve the intrapsychic conflicts over these wishes. Each version corresponds to a different "psychic moment" in the history of the individual's development. It expresses the forces at play at a particular time in the person's life when the ego integrated the demands of the instinctual wishes in keeping with its growing adaptive and defensive responsibilities. To continue with a static analogy, we may conceive of the interrelationship between unconscious fantasies in terms of a series of superimposed photographic transparencies in which at different times and under different psychic conditions one or more of these organized images may be projected and brought into focus. (P. 377)

The "static analogy" derived from Galton was later modified by Arlow in this interesting passage (1969a):

The contribution that unconscious fantasy makes to conscious experience may be expressed illustratively through the use of a visual model. The idea for such a model occurred to me several years ago. It was after Thanksgiving dinner and a friend had brought a movie projector to show the children some animated cartoons. Since we did not have a regulation type movie screen, we used a translucent white window shade instead. During the showing of the cartoons, I had occasion to go outdoors. To my amusement, I noted that I could watch the animated cartoons through the window on the obverse side of the window shade. It occurred to me that an interesting effect could be obtained if another movie projector were used to flash another set of images from the opposite side of the screen. If the second set of images were of equal intensity to the first and had a totally unrelated content, the effect of fusing the two images would, of course, be chaotic. On the other hand, however, if the material and the essential characters which were being projected from the outside and the inside were appropriately synchronized according to time and content, all sorts of final effects could be achieved, depending upon the relative intensity of the contribution from the two sources." (Pp. 23–24)

Arlow is describing the process of comparison by superimposition, a testing procedure whose outcome has a significant adaptive value. If the test result is positive, then the current situation may be responded to with a plan of action similar to that which accompanied the past experience with which it has been successfully matched. This plan of action may involve either the active pursuit of the wished-for gratification or the avoidance of danger associated with previous attempts to achieve the instinctual goal in question. If the test is negative, then a new plan of action must be devised, perhaps with contributions from other past experiences which may then be tested for congruence with the current situation.

Arlow's model applies to the process of dreaming as well as to unconscious fantasy during the waking state. Moreover, it is possible to observe the process of comparison by superimposition at work in dreams with unusual clarity, since the sensory projection mechanisms are available to it without the distractions of incoming sensory data which normally take precedence in the use of these mechanisms.

But we must expect a difference in the adaptive purpose of the matching process when it takes place in the dreaming state. During waking consciousness, the immediate adaptive issue is the quality of the ongoing interaction with the environment. Comparison of current sensory data with representations from the past is necessary to facilitate this interaction, i.e., to maximize the available opportunities for gratification and to minimize the vulnerability to external dangers. Since interaction with the environment is suspended during dreaming sleep, the adaptive purpose of the matching procedure must have to do with an internal reordering and updating of experiential information which has already been registered in previous waking experience.

However, while Freud's observations were approaching the idea of superimposed day residue and past memory experiences, his theoretical interests were taking him in another direction. In his clinical work as a psychoanalyst, his attention had been focused on the Unconscious and the barriers which appear to surround it. He was seeking an explanation for what appeared to be the sudden penetration of these boundaries in dreaming, and he thought he had found it in the concept of condensation. He postulated that while cognitive elements are deleted when two images are condensed, their affective charges are nevertheless added together. In this way he thought he could account for the buildup of high levels of affective pressure behind apparently insignificant cognitive materials.

In accordance with this view, Freud considered superimposition to be either one of several alternative techniques employed to achieve the effect of condensation of affects or else as the mere appearance produced by the action of a procedure whose aim was the condensation of affects.

We can now understand the display of affect-laden early memories in the dreaming state as something essential to the adaptive purposes of the memory cycle. There is therefore no necessity to postulate a difference between the way in which cognitive elements interact in the dream (by cancellation) and the way in which affective charges interact (by addition). The buildup of affective pressure in pathological conditions can be explained more simply as the effect of pathological defensive operations which prevent the emergence of forbidden infantile wishes.

Furthermore, it seems highly improbable to me that the extensive manipulation of cognitive elements during the dreaming state serves merely as a vehicle for the accumulation of affects. Not only would such a situation be economically very wasteful, but it would actively interfere with the essential procedures for updating the memory structure, which require that existing structure be preserved and expanded, not broken up and disposed of.

As it is, the matching procedure is very costly. It ties up the sensory-projection mechanisms which are essential to waking consciousness. It consumes more biochemical energy, as measured by cerebral blood flow and oxygen intake, than any other activity of the brain. And it incapacitates the dreamer for bodily activity of all kinds.

My belief is that only a transformation of memories into the sensory mode during dreaming, making them as close as possible to the form they had during waking consciousness, will permit their affective value to be determined. The various sensory components of the memory must be integrated: visceral, proprioceptive, tactile, olfactory, auditory, visual, and spatial. Our dreaming infant must be able to reexperience the sensation of a full stomach, the comfort of his mother's touch, her smell, the sound of her voice, the look on her face, the sense of being enclosed by her arms and her body. The experience of his mother in this fully integrated form promises safety and satisfaction in a way that a simple sum of the component memories could never do.

The older memories with which these day residues are to be compared must also be present in the matching mechanism in an integrated sensory form. Otherwise the matching could not take place at the level of affective significance with which the day residue was actually endowed.

The muscular inhibition which occurs during dreaming sleep is necessary because the affective response to a display in the sensory-projection mechanisms does not distinguish either the source or the purpose of the display. The same feelings are aroused by memories of the distant past evoked during Stage III as by the sensory display of ongoing waking experience. What is required by the memory cycle is the information conveyed by the fact that a particular affective response is aroused by a set of day residues and older memories on display at a given time. The bodily activity which ordinarily follows the arousal of affect is not only superfluous during Stage III, but would be severely disruptive to it. Since the information-carrying function of the affective response cannot be separated from its action-initiating function, the strictest measures must be taken to prevent the action from taking place. This is done through the immobilization of the voluntary muscular system.

In Stage III, a day residue is delivered in signal mode to the matching mechanism for memorization. It is transformed into the sensory mode and scanned for characteristics to be used in making a preliminary selection of the older memories to be matched with it. The memory tree is entered at or near its origin, and the early nodal points which are most nearly related to the new memory are selected. The contents of these nodal points, and of as many of their subordinate nodal points as is practical, are also transformed into the sensory mode and superimposed on the day residue in the sensory-projection mechanisms. A decision is made as the composite image is run through as to which of the older memories will have the day residue subordinated to it in the memory tree.

The Memory Cycle: Stage IV   Insertion of the Day Residue into the Memory Tree

Stage IV, in which the day residue is introduced into the locations determined in Stage III, follows immediately. The day residue, its original coded signal unaltered by the fact that it was temporarily transformed into the sensory mode during the dream, is inserted into a nodal point immediately subordinate to the nodal point whose contents were successfully matched with it.

The day residue may be introduced into more than one location in the memory tree—i.e., subordinated to more than one nodal point already part of the tree structure. We must now ask whether there is more than one possible point of attachment on the day residue itself. This would suggest that the day residue might have its own internal structure, a complication we have not yet considered.

Since the day residue is destined to become an element in the structure of the memory tree, its own internal structure would have to be compatible with the overall structure of the tree. In the simplest case, this requirement would be satisfied if the day residue were itself a tree. Such a tree might consist of a single nodal point, of a point with several other points subordinated to it, of a slightly more complicated structure like the one illustrated by the solid lines in Figure 2, or of a structure of indefinite size and complexity.

The memory cycle would have maximum flexibility if the day residues were themselves tree structures of indeterminate size. In practice, some limit must be imposed by the necessity of reducing the mass of sensory input to manageable proportions in Stage II. Nevertheless, the presence of preexisting structure in a set of sensory impressions must strongly favor their retention in one of the day residues when the sorting process has been completed. The human capacity for learning indicates that the practical limit to the size of a day residue is actually very large.

The point of attachment in a given day residue must be a nodal point which is superordinate to all the nodal points contained in its structure. If that structure is simply a tree (no matter how large a tree), the nodal point in it which has this property is unique. However, the problem-solving activity of waking consciousness is not restricted to the construction of unilateral superordinate/subordinate linkages, as is the Stage IV mechanism of the memory cycle. The structure preserved in the day residue may therefore contain enough cross-connections (see p. 36) to convert the basic tree structure of the residue into a more highly articulated mathematical structure containing several points each of which has the property of being superordinate to all other points.

Each one of the maximally superordinate points in a highly articulated day residue may (and perhaps must) become a point of attachment to the permanent memory structure in Stage IV. This, in turn, would require that each of these points be capable of evoking its own set of related older memories during the scanning phase of Stage III. We would expect these sets of evoked memories to overlap considerably but not to be identical.

It follows that the more highly articulated the day residue is, the greater will be the number of locations in the memory tree into which it is introduced and consequently the greater will be its capacity to bring the permanent memory into alignment with current reality. The efficacy of the analyst's interpretations is enhanced by their ability to extend the articulation of the day residues which evolve from the patient's experience in analysis.

Figure 2 provides an example of a tree structure converted into a structure with several point sources by its cross-connections. The solid lines indicate the original tree which had a unique source in A1. Because of the cross-connections, every nodal point in the structure can be reached from (i.e., is subordinate to) the set of points consisting of A1, B1, B4, C2, D1, D2, and E1. The critical connection is D2–A1, without which the structure would remain a tree with only one source. This is probably what Freud had in mind when he wrote the first sentence of the passage quoted (p. 35). Although the element "monograph" is on the third level of subordination to "botanical" in the original tree, its cross-connection with "botanical" is responsible for the fuller articulation of the structure.

There is an interesting alternative possibility for the process of memory insertion in Stage IV. One might imagine that the day residue alone is a less likely candidate for introduction into the permanent memory than the more complex amalgam of the dream which incorporates it. The dream, after all, contains all the information present in the day residue plus the additional information which pertains to its relationship with the contents of the permanent memory.

However, the adaptational reasons for rejecting this alternative are clear and compelling. The permanent memory needs information about the real world. The dream is a means to this end, an intermediate result in the processing of sensory input. It is not itself a report about the world and is not regarded as such by the mechanisms of the memory cycle. For this reason dreams are ordinarily prohibited from entry into the memory store.

In the sense that they are not remembered, the reconstructed contents of the dream may be said to be discarded or eliminated during the operation of the memory cycle. Robert (1886) and Evans and Newman (1964) may have been responding to this phenomenon when they mistakenly assigned dreaming to Stage II.

Nevertheless, there are circumstances in which the dream actually functions as a report about the subject's experience in the world. This is what happens whenever the matching mechanism of Stage III fails to find a reasonably close fit between the day residue and the contents of the permanent memory, and especially when the affective charge carried by the evoked older memories indicates a danger situation which appears to have been overlooked during the previous period of waking consciousness.

It is necessary for the dreamer to know that this discrepancy exists between his waking judgment and the picture of the world implied by the contents of his memory store. Because of the exclusion of dream contents from direct access to the permanent memory, however, the evidence that the matching mechanism has failed to accomplish its task must be conveyed to the permanent memory by a circuitous secondary route.

The contents of the dream can reach the permanent memory only by being introduced into the waking consciousness of the dreamer. The dreamer must therefore be awakened while the dream is in progress. It is then possible for the contents of the now-"remembered" dream to be incorporated into the day residues which will form during the next period of nondreaming sleep.

The contents of the original dream will then constitute the day residue which becomes the basis of a second dream. Through the action of this second dream, which will itself most probably be completed without awakening the dreamer, the contents of the original dream will be introduced into the permanent memory. The discrepancy between waking experience and memory store revealed in the original dream has now become a matter of record, available as a reference point for problem-solving activity aimed at resolving the mismatch.

The sequence just described through which a dream can circumvent the usual barrier against its entering the permanent memory provides the memory cycle with a feedback mechanism—the correction dream—which greatly assists its task of keeping the memory structure up to date. How this feedback mechanism facilitates the work of psychoanalysis will be the subject of chapter 3.

By now the operations of the memory cycle will have introduced a new memory of his mother into the permanent memory store of our infant. This new memory will be located in a set of nodal points subordinate to the nodes containing earlier memories of gratifying interaction with her.* Along the way, the infant will have fallen asleep and had a dream in which the complex image of his new experience was superimposed on and combined with a variety of images derived from closely related memories of the past.

---

* Neither is it required that a single representation be stored in a unique location. The elements of the representation may be distributed in a holographic pattern over a large area of the brain. But the mechanism which triggers the joint activation of these elements must have a unique address (Kohonen 1977). We might wish to say that the nodes of the memory structure contain the addresses of the triggering mechanisms, but this modification does not alter the argument that follows.

CHAPTER 3

Interpretation and Adaptation

The Complete Dream Analysis

Freud warned against the attempt to interpret dreams without taking into full account the clinical context in which the report of the dream occurred. For our purposes, too, the full meaning of the dreams we will examine can be appreciated only when the concurrent therapeutic inter-action between patient and analyst is known in detail.

For this reason I have chosen to present the data as they emerge in the course of the ongoing psychoanalytic process. This procedure will permit us to evaluate each piece of evidence as it emerges, in terms of the information available to the analyst at that moment. Each of these moment-to-moment evaluations will necessarily be incomplete. They will illustrate the many problems which arise when we attempt to understand dreams on the basis of insufficient evidence, as the analyst is routinely forced to do in the course of his work with patients.

Two dreams were reported at the beginning of the Thursday analytic hour, both of which took place on Tuesday night. These are the *index* dreams, which will be designated IA and IB. In the sleep laboratory on Thursday night, three dreams were recorded when the patient was awakened at the conclusion of each REM cycle. The Thursday-night dreams will be designated IIA, IIB and IIC. Dreams IIA and IIB are the *correction* dreams for IA and IB, respectively. In chapter 4 we shall bring together the material of Dream IA from its initial report at the beginning of the Thursday hour through its incorporation into Dream IIA on Thursday night, and then its associative elaboration during the Friday hour. This sequence will then be repeated for Dreams IB and IIB.

The memory-cycle model provides us with a criterion for determining whether the analysis of a dream is *complete*. Complete cannot mean exhaustive; it means that both of the experiences of present and past whose representations are superimposed in the manifest content of the dream have been identified. The dream itself is a bridge between the present and the past, between the transference neurosis and the infantile neurosis in the analytic situation. The analysis of the dream is *complete* when the individual experiences which anchor the time span of the dream are known.

Many associative pathways lead to and from each of these anchoring experiences, which constitute the present and past components of the latent content of the dream. An exhaustive analysis of the dream would take in these associative pathways as well, but we know from clinical experience that no dream analysis can be fully exhaustive. The complete dream analysis, though seldom attained in practice, is clearly within our reach, however. In our examples here, the analysis of Dreams IA and IIA is essentially complete, and that of IB and IIB close enough to reveal their underlying structures.

Where elements of the past components of IB and IIB were still missing, we are able to fill in, as Freud did, with developmental re-constructions based on the instinctual themes and cognitive forms implicit in their manifest contents. Unlike Freud, however, we would not consider these approximations to be the latent contents of the dreams, but rather an interpretive scaffolding ready to be dismantled when the actual experiences which contributed to the dream have been discovered.

In this chapter, the approach will be predominantly clinical. I will try to explore and describe the dominant associative pathway leading from the patient's first utterance at the beginning of the Thursday analytic hour to his last utterance on Friday morning. By following this pathway, we shall have the opportunity to observe the nature and variety of associative contexts in which the component elements of the reported dreams emerged.

As we would expect, the pathway is not a straight line, but a complex counterpoint between the patient's experience in the present (the transference neurosis) and the shaping experience of his past. The important movements along the pathway are those which bring about the transition from present to past and from past to present.

The impetus for these transitions comes from two independent sources: the interpretations of the analyst during the hour and the matching process of the memory cycle in the dreams between the analytic hours. The importance of the complementarity between the analyst's interpretations and the integrative work of the memory cycle can hardly be overestimated. In particular, we shall find that the action of the memory cycle is not imitative of the analyst's work, but often carries it forward in a way that the analyst could not possibly have anticipated. The fact that this observation runs counter to a long-standing belief on the part of many analysts provides one reason for my wishing to illustrate it as thoroughly as possible.

My principal justification for asking the reader to pay such close attention to the details of the analytic hours is, of course, that this procedure will give him the best opportunity to determine for himself that the dream material on which this study is based emerged from the natural flow of associations in the service of the conventional therapeutic goals of psychoanalysis.

More important in the long run, however, may be the descriptive power of the memory-cycle model in demonstrating the fine structure of the psychoanalytic process. Riding a bicycle is one thing; explaining just how it is done quite another. Our efforts to describe how an activity as complex as psychoanalysis can be done have lagged far behind our ability to treat patients successfully with it. I believe that by bringing the memory-cycle model and the correction dream into our picture of patient and analyst at work we can markedly improve the resolving power of our theoretical instrument.

For all these reasons, our treatment of the dream material in this chapter will follow the chronological sequence of the analytic hours. It will be assumed throughout that the reader, like the analyst, has no knowledge of subsequent events, either in the analytic office or in the sleep laboratory.

The Elements of the Dream

In a moment we shall go on to examine the interaction between patient and analyst initiated in the Thursday hour by the first dream report. Before doing that, however, we must stop to ask how the memory-cycle model approaches the text of the dream as reported by the patient. We would expect the process through which a dream is constructed to leave the stamp of its work on its final product, the reported dream. How does the memory-cycle model make use of this evidence in its attempt to understand the details of the process of construction?

Traditional psychoanalytic theory analyzes the dream along a single critical dimension; the dimension of psychological depth, or accessibility to consciousness. The elements of the dream are divided into those which are visible on the surface of the dream, called by Freud the "manifest content," and those whose meaning is more deeply hidden, the "latent content." Since the latent content is usually revealed in analysis through the patient's associations to the manifest content, Freud made the reasonable assumption that the dream is constructed by a reversal of this process, a transformation of latent content into manifest content.

Because the latent content often includes impulses experienced as threatening or shameful by the waking ego of the patient, Freud assumed that the motive for the transformation from latent to manifest content was the wish to keep these impulses out of consciousness. The construction of the dream was therefore the work of a censorship mechanism which disguised the latent content through a variety of procedures, the most important of which he called "condensation" and "displacement."

From the traditional point of view, then, what is significant about the manifest dream is primarily the evidence it gives of its underlying latent content. The memory-cycle model adds another critical dimension to the analysis of the dream; the historical dimension. It suggests that every element of the manifest content is ultimately derived either from an experience of the present, the day residue, or from a memory of the past stored in the permanent memory structure, and that every dream contains both of these. If the manifest content results from a transformation of the latent content, then there must be one component of the latent content derived from present experience and another component of the latent content derived from the past.

For Freud, the concept of "latent content" was quite elastic. It could refer to everything relating to the dream uncovered by the patient's associations, but it could also designate a single meaning attaching to the specific impulse which Freud believed had given rise to the dream. With respect to the time dimension, his usage was not consistent. At various points in his writing, "latent content" refers exclusively to the thoughts connected with the day residue but not represented directly in the dream. At other points, "latent content" can mean only the repressed wishes of childhood. Although his position on this issue shifted continually, at no time did he suggest that both the past and the present must contribute equally to the hidden meaning of every dream. (See chapter 5 for a review of Freud's remarks on this topic.)

The logical structure of the memory-cycle model requires that we recognize one component of the latent content derived from present experience and another derived symmetrically from the past. We may now ask how inclusive each of these temporal components of the latent content can be.

For Freud, the distinction between a single meaning associated with a given repressed impulse and the possibly vast array of associated meanings was not crucial. For him, the specific meaning is only one of many which might have "represented" the impulse; the choice was an arbitrary one from the beginning. Therefore he could have seen little harm in using the term "latent content" to include both a specific meaning and the many possible alternatives to it.

For the memory-cycle model, the distinction has a different significance. The representations matched in the dream are the records of actual individual experiences. They do not "represent" the generalized drive-determined impulses which may be associated with them. The dream originates with the matching of a specific pair of these recordings of experience in order to reach an adaptational goal, the introduction of the new experience into a suitable location in the permanent memory.

The dream censor may interfere with this adaptive process by substituting closely associated memory representations for the original ones in the matching process. This is the mechanism of displacement described by Freud. While the original choice of representations is adaptive, the substitution of associated meanings is defensive and maladaptive.

Because of this difference, I will restrict my use of the term "latent content" to the original representations of present and past experience brought together for matching by the memory cycle. I will refer to other memories closely associated with the original latent contents in the short-term memory or the permanent memory as "associated latent contents" or as "associations." When an associated memory representation is substituted for the original latent content in the construction of a dream, this representation will be called simply the "substituted latent content."

The latent contents in the memory-cycle model are representations of actual events (including, of course, intrapsychic events). Thoughts, feelings, wishes, and impulses may be embodied in or exemplified by these events, or secondarily associated with them, but they are not in themselves the building blocks of dream construction.

The distinction between the original latent content and the substituted latent content helps to clarify the difference between the two primary characteristics of dream distortion described by Freud. As our data will show, condensation is the effect of the superimposition of the two temporal components of the latent content during the matching process. It is caused by the adaptive function of the dream; that is, the function of the dream in the memory cycle, and is present in every dream.*

Displacement, on the other hand, results from a defensive interference with the memory cycle. As Freud pointed out (1901, p. 655), "There are dreams which come about almost without any displacement." For the memory-cycle model there is no requirement for the censorship mechanism to interfere with the construction of a given dream. An associated latent content which is substituted for the original is present only in those dreams which have been censored.

When a censored dream has been successfully analyzed, as we shall see in the case of the dreams to be presented here, the substituted latent content, both present and past, is likely to be discovered relatively early in the associative work and the original latent content much later. In all cases, of course, we would expect the affective charge of the original latent content to be greater than that of the substituted latent content. We would also expect the past component of the original latent content to date from an earlier developmental phase and to be cognitively more primitive than the substituted past component.

In what follows, the events of each analytic hour are referred to in consecutive order. The speech segments of patient and analyst during the Thursday hour are numbered T1–T83, and during the Friday hour F1–F84. In each case, patient utterances are odd-numbered and analyst utterances even-numbered. Dream material is recorded verbatim, except when the patient is simply repeating what he has already reported previously during the hour. Associative connections may be indicated

---

* In his *Introductory Lectures* (1916, p. 173), Freud says: "But although condensation makes dreams obscure, it does not give one the impression of being an effect of the dream-censorship. It seems traceable rather to some mechanical or economic factor. . . ."

by quotation, paraphrase, or description, as each instance requires. Identifying material has been altered throughout to preserve the patient's confidentiality.

The Thursday Hour 1 : Report of the Tuesday-Night Dreams*

The Tuesday-night dreams were reported at the beginning of the Thursday analytic hour in the following exchange:

T1   PT: Today I am disturbed about my throat and my chest—that I think this cold or whatever it is has settled in my chest—I have pains here and there. When I breathe I feel cold air that causes me to cough. So I'm getting these allusions that I am developing lung cancer—this sort of thing. Thinking about it, I am saying to hell with it—I am not going to let it get control of me, but I did think about it seven or eight times today. Just this whole syndrome of nose, throat, and down the chest. I suppose it is the logical place for the phlegm to go if I have an infection down there, but that is what comes to mind. I had a dream two nights ago—I wrote it down. It is a long long dream, and this is Tuesday—this is what I wrote down—just the items, I probably have to fill in as I look over the notes. A rooming house.

T2   DR: This was Tuesday night?

T3-T7 PT: Yes, not last night—it was Tuesday night. Tuesday night—where was I Tuesday night? I was in Richmond Tuesday night? Right—and I had just finished reading a couple of chapters of that book—*Reality Therapy*, if that means anything. There was something about a horse show—I will go back to that in a minute. Rooming house: A large bathtub, big tub, different one—first large room, second large tub, in other words somewhere in this dream I saw a bathroom, a large bathroom with a large tub. And when I got back towards the end of the dream I saw a small bathroom with a very large tub. I remember that distinctly. Where have I seen tubs like this before? Well, in Judith's house—both in Atlanta and in Richmond. That is what it reminds me of. The only place I have seen large tubs. And then I put down married. What? Kate Davis instead of Ellen Thornwald. Now, did I ever mention the name Thornwald? . . .

What a knockout she was. Anyway, this was an unattractive, bright, nice Goucher girl who works as Senator Smithfield's secretary, a real nice person. I had not mentioned her before. So something else hap-

* The abbreviation DR signifies doctor's portion of the dialogue; PT indicates the patient's response.

pened. So decided—something consecutive—drop her off and make a mistake. I decided something and I dropped her off because I made a mistake. I married one instead of the other. Now . . . a wife in here— I don't know what the hell she is doing in this dream, and I got a Fairfax—and a local church—I was writing this in the morning and have not looked at it since then. And I go there or to an antique shop or a garden—I am not sure what—and I was single when I went there. This is quite a dream. I was making a film and I was also looking for girls at parties where I was making the film, and I was single. I had to get married in a church or a garden or an antique shop. And Ellen looked much better in the dream than she looks in reality. And I was confused, and maybe it was not her, and I could have married her, and, I said, I could have married her and not Kate.

In this material we have the initial reports of Dream IA (the bathtub dream, T3) and Dream IB (the photographer dream, T7). T3 also includes the "Reality Therapy" residue of Dream IB, preceding the report of the dream, and the reference to Judith's bathtubs and houses. Since M. A. was preoccupied at the time of this hour with his inability to decide whether or not to marry Judith, it is likely that the association to her bathtubs represents something on his mind during the dream day, therefore another day residue.

The hour began with an identification of his chest cold with the lung cancer which killed his father. Ambivalence about M. A.'s identification with his father will be the major theme of this analytic hour and the next. Since the statement of this theme *immediately precedes* the report of the Tuesday-night dreams, we must be especially alert to the absence of his father or any adult male figure who might represent him from the manifest content of the dreams.

The Tuesday-Night Dreams: First Approximations

Dream IA

Is it possible to distinguish the components of the manifest content derived from present and past experience without further data? In part, the answer to this question must be "no," since the condensed imagery of the manifest dream emphasizes what is common to both present and past. There are often references to specific events which, when recognized, can determine the time of origin of the images that contain them. I have found that more often than not, in response to a direct inquiry, the patient can recall the specific memory of his early years from which a component of the manifest dream content is derived. However, it is much more likely that a specific event of the dream day will be recognized than an event in the remote past when the structure of the dream has been altered by the censorship.

The manifest content of Dream IA is entirely ambiguous with respect to time. It consists of a single scene whose images reflect events which could have taken place during the dreamer's childhood or at any time after it.

The memory of Judith's bathtubs appears to be the latent content of the dream derived from present experience; that is, the day residue. We do not know yet whether it is the original latent content or a substitution. The obscurity of the reference and the lack of associated affect suggest, however tentatively, that the image of Judith's bathtubs has been substituted in the dream for the representation of a more important experience on the dream day.

Thus far we are still fairly close to the traditional psychoanalytic view of the dream. Both theories allow for a less significant experience of the dream day to be substituted for a conflict-laden psychic representation. However, the traditional view would suggest that without this substitution no dream at all would have occurred. The memory-cycle model requires that the dream resulting from this substitution be taking the place of another more emotionally explicit dream whose construction was interrupted by the censorship.

We have been able to identify the bathtub imagery as the component of the manifest content derived from present experience only through our independent knowledge of the day residue itself. Moreover, we suspect that we are dealing with a substituted latent content, and that the original latent content has yet to be discovered. The precise identification of the component of the manifest content derived from the past without additional evidence is ordinarily even more difficult.

In clinical practice, this problem is not particularly burdensome, since the analyst's interest in the past component of the dream rests primarily on what it can tell him about the drive-related conflicts which interfered with the patient's development. Freud's discovery of the stages of psychosexual maturation provided a method for approximating the time of origin of incapacitating conflicts. The analyst can use these approximations to stimulate the recovery of more exact historical material during the patient's further associations.

In the absence of such associative material, we can make use of Freud's method of approximation as a first step in identifying the past component of Dream IA. Since nothing in the manifest content is exclusively related to the dreamer's present experience, we can begin by assuming that all of the manifest content is derived, at least in part, from the past. What we will reconstruct in this way is not the past component of the latent content itself, but a series of instinctual themes which are likely to be closely associated in the permanent memory store with the specific past memory we are seeking.

The setting of Dream IA is a series of concentric spaces (house, bathroom, bathtub) which ordinarily contain people and derive their significance from the activities of these people. In the case of bathroom and bathtub, the expected activities are quite intimate ones, yet in the dream the people in question are conspicuously absent. In fact, the house is a rooming house, where one might expect to meet only strangers.

Spaces which ordinarily contain people are often symbolic of the female genitals, and this meaning is likely to be important here. Imagery of this kind often has it origin very early in life, however, before object constancy has been established, when the appearance of a libidinal object in the perceptual field is not yet a predictable event (Palombo and Bruch, 1964). In the case of a neurotic patient, difficulties with Mother in the oral or intake stage of development naturally do not represent the major source of conflict, but will have been reactivated as a defense against positive Oedipal strivings.

The large and small bathrooms, each containing a large bathtub, might suggest a competition between the patient and his father as to which of them will contain Mother in his sphere of influence, but at the same time be contained within her protective and gratifying body. In spite of this hint of the Oedipal rivalry, however, the historical component of the manifest content is primarily pre-Oedipal. The presence—even the existence—of a gratifying object is uncertain. The dreamer is purely an external observer, without representation in the dream and without the power to influence what happens in it. There are suggestions of intimate human activities, but these would be autoerotic, related to body surfaces and excretory orifices.

On the question of substitutions in the past component of the latent content, we are as yet completely uninformed. Freud's method reconstructs a developmental history for every element in the dream, including those which have been substituted for the original past memories deleted by the censor.

Dream IA is therefore a difficult one to interpret without further data. Its present and past components are not distinct in the manifest content, and the possibility of widespread substitution must be kept in mind.

Dream IB is quite different. The dreamer is a participant and himself the source of action in the dream. This action is typically adult, and we can begin by provisionally assigning it to the dreamer's present experience and thus to the day residues. In doing so, we make the assumption that looking for girls at parties and getting married are topics which cross M. A.'s mind with a certain regularity. Making a film probably does not— it is an uncommon adult activity with obvious connections to the scoptophilic interests of childhood. The double ambiguity about marriage, whether or not the dreamer is actually married and to which of the women in the dream, is clearly the result of a defensive operation aimed at reducing guilt feelings arising from the Oedipal conflict.

M. A.'s reading of *Reality Therapy* on the evening of the dream day is no doubt connected with this ambiguity. The analyst is to have the responsibility for deciding what is real and what is fantasy in the patient's relations with women, leaving him free to plead to his superego that he is not responsible for what happens in this area.

The obvious Oedipal content of Dream IB serves to date the historical component of the dream to the phallic/Oedipal period. Although the aim of the action is explicitly sexual in the adult sense, the importance of the sexual partner is minimized, most likely as a defense against castration anxiety. Unlike the situation in Dream IA, potential libidinal objects exist and are present, but their identities are blurred, and the problem of finding the right one is apparently insoluble.

In separating the manifest contents of the two dreams into present and past components, we are faced directly with the problem of identifying the actual experiences of present and past, whose representations are combined in the dream. Lacking more detailed information, we tend to make use of fragmentary associations in reconstructing the present experience and of psychosexual approximations in reconstructing the past.

As our information becomes more complete, we shall see this asymmetry vanish. Even now we notice that in the case of the day residue, there has been no difficulty in connecting long-term motivational trends, drives, and their affective derivatives, with specific thoughts, fantasies, and memories of the dream day. What prevents us from doing the same for the component of the dream derived from much earlier experience is the practical problem of identifying and dating the specific psychic events of the past.

In addition, we must consider the uncertainties created by possible deletions and substitutions, which interpose themselves between the original experiences of either the present or the past and the final imagery of the dream. All of these uncertainties must be resolved as we continue our investigation.

The Thursday Hour: Interpretations

The analyst's immediate goal must be to set the associative process in motion. The remoteness of the patient's parental figures in the dreams makes it unlikely that an approach through the historical antecedents of the manifest content would be fruitful. Moreover, the patient's incidental remarks before and after the dream report indicate that he considers the dreams to be an offering to the analyst as much as the object of his own curiosity. The practical issue then is not so much the content of the dreams as the manner and meaning of their presentation to the analyst.

We are now about ten minutes into the Thursday hour. The patient closes his dream report with an offhand remark to the effect that he had forgotten the dreams until a stray thought while driving to work that morning had reminded him of them. The analyst points out his ambivalence about remembering dreams and suggests that this is due to his fear of opening up "some inner side of yourself."

I think it should be clear that this interpretation, although it makes no reference to the manifest content of the dreams, is in fact a dream interpretation, and specifically an interpretation of the dreams reported by the patient in this instance.

The patient responds to the interpretation in a superficially compliant way, saying, "Let's bang away at this thing—maybe I can recall something." He repeats the report of Dream IA with slight variations, adding that he has had dreams about rooming houses before, that the scene of the dream is on the second floor of the rooming house, and that the small bathroom, "was almost cut right in half" (T13–T15).

Then he adds a little more about Dream IB:

T15   Now, I don't remember anything about this marrying Kate Davis versus this Ellen Thornwald except again in the dream I remember Ellen was a hell of a lot better-looking in the dream than she is in reality. And describe—I still can't recall—I can't see what . . . wife is doing here—I don't know except she is a real good-looking girl, and as far as I am concerned, a nice girl. And this Fairfax and church—well, I think in the Fairfax church all my friends have gotten married—relatives, friends—John Mason just recently got married, Bill got—no, he did not get married there—but Jim Spence—oh, God, there is a slew of them got married there. And I was single, I am still single, I am making a film. I am always running around taking pictures of everybody, everybody's family, and this and that—I am the historian, the photographer.

The related themes of competition with men and anxiety about castration are beginning to come more clearly into view. The patient next admits to some curiosity about his difficulty in remembering dreams. He notes that his forgetting is selective and that his memory is generally good. The analyst asks why he would want to forget dreams.

T17–T27

         PT: "Oh, I am probably embarrassed, afraid.

         DR: Embarrassed?

         PT: Embarrassed about something that might come up. Might be something sissy in the dreams, scary, effeminate.

         DR: Embarrassed that something might come up? What else does that . . .

         DR: I am trying to think now what I could be embarrassed about. The only thing that would probably embarrass me to dream—well, I was about to say a sexual perversion or something like that—but something else, a weakness, on my part—me being awakened in a dream might embarrass me.

         DR: But those are all the same.

         PT: They are?

         DR: One sign of weakness and that means that you are a pervert. One sign of gentleness or tenderness and that means that you are feminine—which also means that you are a pervert. Any sign of closeness to a man—that means that you are strong, that you are virile.

         PT: Fairy type. Well, that is probably what is holding me back, as far as—or can my intellect convince myself that I should not forget it? Or is intellect not to be dealt with?

         DR: I thought maybe we could work at some of these fears. Where did this fear of weakness, this fear of femininity, this fear of passivity towards a man—where did it all come from?

         PT: I can think of only—it has to be again back to the family. I didn't have any brothers, so there is no problem there. And the only male that I came across, of course, was my father—who was never around. I'd say I had in my mind the impression he was a superhuman, you know, a great bull of a man, therefore try to emulate him. And the only way how—you got to be tough, you have to be distant—I can't do any of the things he did. I suppose I was afraid of getting steam-rolled all the time. It is a possibility. Mother was always telling me what a marvelous person he is, was.

The Thursday Hour: Associations

With this interchange, a breakthrough is effected which establishes the impetus for the associative work of the hour as well as its theme: namely, the patient's ambivalence toward his father as it is reflected in the transference. For the remainder of the session, the patient's tone is animated, often excited. We see him torn between the wish to conquer and replace his father, associated with the fear of retaliatory castration, and the wish to become the passive object of Father's attentions, threatening castration by another route.

Father's absence, temporal and emotional, appears to the patient to deprive him of the opportunity to become a man himself by identification with Father. But it also increases the temptation to poach on Father's territory, with imagined consequences.

T25–T27

> PT: Someone will see me in privates walking around—who the hell knows. I don't know if someone is going to grab me or anything. I always was very careful to cover up my body, and not walk around naked. I sort of mention again—I recall now that one day I saw Alice whisk by in the nude—oh, boy, that sort of thing—whereas in Mark and Alice's home the kids run around naked. I think that is overdoing it.
> DR: But you say you don't know if somebody was going to grab you.
> PT: Yes. I was figuring I had better keep going, somebody is going to grab me down here.

His imagery becomes spontaneous and vivid (despite obsessive undoing):

T39–T41

> PT: A horse (or a hearse). I don't know, the next image? Now this is something I have seen—just a big man, you know, and a little boy. The big man is wrestling this little boy on the ground. I don't know if I am just conjuring up something because it sounds good, but I close my eyes and I see that image.
> DR: Yes?

PT: It is an outline of a man, he is in gray, the gray ghostlike stonish effect, you know, not really living, but a human body. I don't know why I am so afraid of a human body. Thinking back, is there anything in my past family life—the human body—naked body—that was significant, scary, or affected me—happened? Now, looking at my father again, if I have to, he was always you know, a very muscular person. I was always very thin.

The only alternative to a direct and literal identification with Father's physical appearance is castration. The analyst asks whether the patient had seen his sister in the nude on other occasions.

T51   PT: Oh, I think I might have—I might recall two or three other times, but that was about it—I was in my world and she in her world—we never really, you know, spent time together. Of course the house was such a small house—no, not really. She was as embarrassed as I. She whisked right through. The female body, from what I know about my own activities, I am not particularly holding as something beautiful. There is something along this naked-body bit—that is why I said a super queen to overcome a natural fear.

The small house that was not really small reminds us of the rooming house in Dream IA and its large and small bathrooms. The spaces which contain people and their intimate activities are not merely spaces, but separate worlds. In the female body, all of the dangers associated with the wish to be close to another person—to be inside the world of another person—converge and culminate. Dream IA is a still life—a *nature morte*—the empty world so frightening to the infant suffering from separation anxiety. Coordinated with this more primitive anxiety is the castration fear represented by M. A.'s identification with his sister.

The memory of Alice "whisking through" appears to be the past component of the latent content of Dream IA. The manifest content of the dream is the product of the superimposition of the two experiences: the recent memory of Judith's bathrooms, probably including Judith in the nude, contributed by the day residue, and the childhood memory of Alice whisking through M. A.'s parental house, probably on her way to or from the bathroom. The match is based on cognitive similarity reinforced by a similarity of affect. Desire for a woman leads to an identification with her, and for M. A. in the present as in the past that can only mean castration.

This interpretation is certainly accurate as far as it goes. But the themes of engulfment and separation, suggested by the spatial qualities of the dream, point more directly toward earlier experience with Mother. We already suspect that Judith's bathtubs were an association substituted in the dream for more intimate maternal enclosures. The appearance of Alice in an Oedipal context suggests another substitution for Mother.

At this point, without the clarification provided by the correction dream, these uncertainties cannot be fully resolved. But we can reasonably expect some help from M. A.'s further associations in the Thursday hour.

T53   PT: Horror and antipathy towards the feminine form—right. Now, where the hell did I get all screwed up about the human body? Something about this obesity, too, is important, because I can't handle a fat person. My mother was plump when I was growing up.

After some rumination about his not liking girls who remind him of his mother, he suddenly interrupts himself.

T55   PT: You know the frustrations and understanding—that is fine—but what do I do with it now? Which leads me on to this reality therapy, which does not seem to be any better sort of approach. Here I understand is reality therapy—the guy says, you know—I'll yak on that for a minute—he says ignore the patient, and live for today, and you relate to a human being. And by relating and getting advice, you learn how to solve your problem. Well, I don't think that is going to work, either. Because if a guy made some mistakes, or was not responsible—as they put it, some person telling him or showing him how is not going to make him more responsible—as they put it—some person telling him or showing him how is not going to make him more responsible if the input has not been changed, if the thing that caused him to be irresponsible is not changed. Just another person telling him to be responsible or showing him how, I don't think is good enough. And I am thinking about myself now.

"Reality" is Father showing and telling you how to succeed with Mother. Adulthood is something conferred from the outside by those who are already adults, rather than something that grows from within. The patient is beginning to see the futility of this formulation, but only beginning to. He still refers to what is inside him as "input." He is still angry with the analyst for not teaching him "how to feel."

T55   PT: You see, my problem as I see it today, is I am unable to love because love is a feeling. That is what is the problem. I really cannot hate—I can just say when I was mad at you two or three sessions ago—instead of pussyfooting around I can't even come out and say, "You son-of-a-bitch" to your face, or somebody else's face. I am kidding myself as well as the next person.

As he goes on, he lapses into his pattern of superficial compliance with the analyst, who brings him back once again to his unexpressed feelings and to the memory of his father.

T55–T59

> PT: I feel as though I should practice having feeling. That is what I should do. Try to understand my feelings, that is what I should do. Try to understand my talk about my feelings each time. Man, enough feeling to fill a book. I will tell you something—if I had feelings, I think I would be embarrassed to tell you. That would be tougher to tell you about than if I had a cold feeling towards you—or is it easier?
>
> DR: Why? . . . Let me say that you do have warm feelings for me. What is this fear about?
>
> PT: Because it is not manly.
>
> DR: Follow that image—where does it lead you?
>
> PT: Here we go again. Crying and collapsing in a heap, you know, that is it—just sobbing—sort of leads me on. Now, I am thinking, have I ever shown any warmth? Have I ever shown any towards my father? Kind of search the past. No, I can't recall ever.

In the associations that follow, the patient indicates that he values the analyst for his "common sense," by which he means that he thinks the analyst will warn him against entanglements with "kooky broads" who might cross his path. This would imply to him that the analyst had no emotion, and that in following his advice, the patient would be come like him. The analyst does not agree.

T66–T68

> DR: You really believe that neither of us has any emotion?
>
> PT: Well, I hope I have got it, and I suppose I hope you do, but I have not seen a demonstration on your part.
>
> DR: I don't think you believe that for a minute. I think you think you are full of emotion and you are scared of it. And I think you think I have a lot of emotion, and you are scared of that, too.

Once again the patient retreats, but this time with a relatively clear view of the imaginary dangers which compel him to do so:

T71
> PT: So, let's say I have emotions and I'm guarding them. Because what kind of emotions could come out of here? Here I am lying on a sterile couch looking at the ceiling—what kind of emotions—I mean, there is laughter and there is crying. Those are the two emotions. Or are they? Yes, there is love. Now, when I say "love" it sort of makes me cringe— How can you love another male? That sort of thing. And that gives me the willies.

The image of the sterile couch recalls us to the human spaces of Dream IA, and especially to the bathtubs. Here the emphasis is on the protection from feeling afforded by their containing walls. But the patient is becoming aware of the narrowness of the world-view from within his defensive system. The hour ends with his fantasy about doing an uncharacteristic act of kindness to Judith's seven-year-old daughter, an intimation that his wish to be a father himself has been aroused by the acknowledgment during the hour of his wish to have an accessible father of his own.

By consistently interpreting the patient's evasion of feelings, the analyst has been able to break through his defensive shell at many points, bringing to light derivatives of the basic libidinal and aggressive strivings and the anxiety-provoking fantasies associated with them.

The conflict between the patient's aggressive and submissive impulses toward his father has emerged with great vividness. His attempt to resolve this conflict by putting as much distance as possible between himself and his father is clear. We see these motives operating in the transference relationship, and we have seen the analyst at work in bringing them to the attention of the patient.

As the patient becomes aware of his hidden feelings, we notice a reduction in the tension between the two parties to the therapeutic interaction. The analyst's willingness to be confronted directly by these feelings creates a sense of trust and collaboration in the patient which was not apparent at the beginning of the hour. Our hypothesis that the absence of any other man in the manifest content of the Tuesday-night dreams resulted from an evasion of the patient's Oedipal feelings toward his father appears to be confirmed.

The work of the hour has greatly expanded our understanding of the patient's experience of his father in the past and of the analyst in the present. There is a striking correspondence between his subjective reactions to each of these important men in his life. The demonstration of this correspondence is one of the principal goals of the analysis—perhaps the single most important goal—and it has been considerably advanced during the Thursday hour.

One clear memory of later childhood was reported, that of the patient's sister "whisking by" in the nude. This memory was very likely one source of the bathroom imagery of Dream IA and perhaps also of the confused and fleeting impressions of the young women in Dream IB. As we have suggested, it most probably serves as a screen for much earlier memories, as must also the brief exposures of the patient wrestling with his "stonish" father and of his repugnance at his mother's obesity.

At the end of the hour, we are in a better position to understand the current experiences represented in the dreams, since we have had an opportunity to observe the transference at work. The connection between the patient's behavior toward the analyst and the meaning of the *Reality Therapy* residue has been explicated successfully. The patient's inability to identify the right woman for himself in Dream IB is clearly related to the analyst's failure to give him the wished-for guidance in making this decision.

We have the clue of the "sterile couch" to suggest how the transference situation contributes to the imagery of Dream IA. The couch, the office, and the outside world form a set of concentric spaces in each of which the patient's relationship to the analyst is rather different. The patient's reliance on obsessional defenses suggests that the innermost of these spaces functions as a protective shell from within which he imagines he can see the outer world without himself being seen. But there are hints of an awareness that this shell is cutting him off from the rest of life, and that to be perfectly safe is to be dead like his "stonish" father.

In summary, we can say that the hour has succeeded where psychoanalysis is generally most successful; in relating the patient's current subjective response to the analyst with a repressed subjective response of childhood to a parental figure. At the same time, we have seen relatively little associative elaboration of the manifest content of the dreams.

This discrepancy suggests that we might look at the hour from an entirely different perspective. Perhaps, contrary to our previous assertions, the interpretations made during the hour were not dream interpretations at all, but rather typical examples of the familiar category of transference interpretation. From this point of view, the dream report at the beginning of the hour would have been little more than an obstacle to the analysis of the transference erected by the patient's system of defenses. Following Freud's advice not to exaggerate the importance of dreams in the therapeutic situation, the analyst would then have succeeded in changing the subject to the more significant issue of the transference.

Are there data which would allow us to decide between this formulation and the one I have been developing? The answer must come from the dreams of the night following the Thursday hour. The memory-cycle model predicts that these dreams will represent a matching between the new day residues, consisting of the originally reported dreams, expanded and enriched by the interpretive work of the hour, and new historical material coming from the same vicinity in the patient's memory structure as the historical component of the original dreams.

The more traditional view might allow for either a defensive return to the material of the earlier dreams in combination with a representation of material derived from the Thursday hour, or else for a reaching forward to previously repressed historical material, also combined with the Thursday residues, but not for both at once. The memory-cycle model predicts a series of dreams in which all three of these elements are present simultaneously, with the material of the earlier dreams providing the means through which the interpretations of the Thursday analytic hour are brought into contact with historical material previously inaccessible.

The Thursday-Night Dreams

Before going directly into the content of the Thursday-night dreams, we have another source of information to report about M. A.'s state of mind when the dreaming took place. The tape recorder in the sleep laboratory was turned on whenever the subject arrived, and his conversations with the lab technician were recorded as she set up the electroencephalograph and the device for monitoring muscle activity.

These conversations consisted for the most part of humorous banter which tended to be quite repetitive. We might expect that some affect-laden transference material would emerge in this setting (the outermost of the concentric transference spaces), while still being subject to repression during the analytic hour. This proves to be the case.

Unlike the patient's productions in the analytic hour, which are highly sensitive to the momentary interaction with the analyst, the transference themes in the laboratory banter are broad in content and rather loosely expressed. For this reason, they can be listed without extensive quotation.

1. M. A. begins by asking the technician if she can do something about the temperature of the laboratory, which he says repeatedly is too cold for him.
2. He mentions a shooting, reported recently in the newspaper, in which a man was murdered by three other men.
3. He mentions Dr. R., who pays him for coming to the sleep lab, and asks if he is listening to the tape.
4. He tells the technician, who does not know his real name, that he is "a man of mystery, a secret agent."
5. He refers repeatedly to the technician as the boss's girlfriend, "the girl who kisses the boss."
6. He suggests to Dr. R., via the tape, that the laboratory procedure could be improved through the use of a cap to which all of the EEG leads might be attached.
7. He declares his displeasure at having to come to "a nut house" and being "strapped in" in order to have the dreams recorded.

8.   He mentions a previous female technician he disliked, who "screwed the whole machine up on me."

9.   He expresses further concern about catching cold and having to remain in the hospital as a patient.

10.   He mentions some Indians on a recent TV Western who were "screwed," as other minorities (including the technician's) frequently are.

We can see in this list a more overt expression of Oedipal derivatives than appeared in the Thursday hour. The preoccupation with the coldness of the laboratory and with the caretaking roles of the technician and Dr. R. closely replicate M. A.'s defenses against Oedipal guilt as revealed in his dreams and free associations. (The murder of one man by three others is an interesting reversal of the battle on the road to Thebes, where Oedipus killed four men who attacked him, including his father.)

We shall find both the instinctual and the defensive elements on this list directly incorporated into the dreams and thereby made available for analytic work in the Friday morning hour.

Three dreams were reported when M. A. was awakened during the night.

Dream IIA

PT: I am not sure what I was dreaming at this point. Oh, yes, I was dreaming I was in the sleep lab, I believe, or I was one of a party of three, and I was a prisoner and the other two people were in charge of a refrigerator. I think I was one of three, and they were in charge of a refrigerator which I had to move—part of the stuff which I had to move along belonged to my father—and I had to move that out of the refrigerator. And it was a big problem how it would go and where it was going—and against my will and against my timing they took his things out. Then I guess they had me locked up somewhere and finally sort of forced me to cooperate, and I ended up on a three-man lift line—we were taking things, like Coca-Cola, out of the bottom shelf of the refrigerator and passing them up lickety-split and efficiently as possible into the other refrigerator, or into another receptacle. I was sort of working efficiently and putting in ice—there was not a bit of waste motion—it was a beautiful operation in symmetry—and moves in the dream—Back to the refrigerator—there were so many objects. I think there was an old hat of some sort, also objects of his clothes and my clothes—refrigerator and clothes—two other people, I think they were two brothers.

Dream IIB

Well, another tough dream to pull out—it is fragments. I dreamed about a police officer named Bill—a school bus—dreamed about running a ranch and Miss Iceland—a beauty queen—and the rancher, his name was King, I guess. The King Ranch. And he married Miss Iceland, and I asked him how he met her, and he said his cousin fixed him up in Iceland. And about the police officer—I guess he was collecting furniture or something. Furniture? As I talk about this dream of a security member mentioning furniture—I see an open casket, an image of an open casket. I don't know any more of the dream right now.

Dream IIC

Just before that, I was also in a bar, I think, and I was waiting for change and there was two dollars, and I got two bills that looked like Richmond certificates. There was some kind of a hassle, and finally the guy gave me two dollar-bills—one was torn and taped up. And passing these back and forth. Finally the guy gave me some correct change and took the two Richmond bills and said he would get change of some sort. I was kind of—I was kind of confused because these were my bills. I shrugged it off and said, "Oh, what the hell, he is going through all the trouble of changing these Mickey Mouse–type of dollar bills." And I sort of walked off.

These dreams have a quality very different from that of the earlier ones. They are filled with activity, activity which in a variety of ways delineates M. A.'s relationship with his father, who, like the dreamer himself, is clearly represented in all of them. This transparency of the Thursday-night dreams is enhanced by our detailed knowledge of the patient's thoughts and feelings on the dream day, but it is without question a salient attribute of the dreams themselves.

In a general way, the difference in quality between the two sets of dreams and the richness of connections linking the Thursday-night dreams with the events of the Thursday hour suggest that the Thursday dreams represent an elaboration of or commentary on the Tuesday dreams presented during the Thursday hour, as we were expecting. But the fact that we know almost nothing about the events which preceded the Tuesday dreams requires more specific evidence to substantiate this hypothesis.

The Friday Hour I:
Report of the Thursday-Night Dreams

The Friday-morning versions of the Thursday-night dreams differed from the original reports in the sleep laboratory for the most part only in details. Unlike the others, Dream IIA was reported at greater length on Friday, and most of the associative material which followed the dream reports during the hour was related to this dream. This is fortunate for our investigation, since IIA appears to be the correction dream for IA, which was by far the more difficult to reconstruct of the Tuesday dreams.

In the original (Thursday night) report of IIA, the refrigerator is always called a refrigerator. In the Friday report, it is first an icebox and then simply a box, a revision which strengthens its connection to Miss Iceland of Dream IIB and the patient's mother. In the first report, Father's belongings are referred to as stuff or things; in the second, on two occasions, as "effects." It is only in the second report that Father's "effects" are removed in order to make room for those of the other two men in the dream.

The physical scene of IIA, reported only sketchily on Thursday night, is given a fuller elaboration on Friday morning:

F5   PT: An icebox, a door open, there was three of us. One at the icebox door, one on a ladder, and one on top of the ladder putting stuff into another icebox. And I was not sure if I was one of those three at this point, but I was watching the way they worked, it was really a—I at first suggested that they work as some kind of a water-bucket brigade. Everybody was putting things out of the box into the other box, but when they were lined up, I started handing things out of the icebox, and I handed them up to the next guy, and he handed it to the next guy and he shoved it in. It was really very efficient—I was marveling at the rhythm of the whole thing. I stepped back, and another person took my place. And then when some person—when the guy down below who would stoop for a second—the second guy reached in and grabbed something and scurried up. The whole thing, the tempo was beautiful— the efficiency was beautiful, and lickety-split everything on the bottom shelf was turned into bottles at this point and came out.

Surprisingly, all of these changes and additions help to clarify the meaning of the dream in relation to the other Thursday-night dreams and to the events of the Thursday hour, especially those events bearing on the transference. This suggests once again that the Thursday-night dreams have a positive relationship to the analytic work lacking in the dreams reported at the beginning of the Thursday hour. A productive phase of the analytic working alliance had been initiated during the Thursday hour, and it appears that the revision of the Thursday-night dream report at the beginning of the Friday hour was made in the services of this alliance.

The difference in tone and content between IA and IIA are clearly visible. Can we say the same for the similarities? Is it certain that IIA is a variation of the theme of IA, and that the variation represents a correction or expansion of it?

The evidence at this point in our investigation is strongly in favor of this interpretation, but not yet conclusive. The central image in each of the dreams is a set of enclosed but accessible spaces closely associated with the gratification of pregenital impulses. In one dream, there are a larger and a smaller of these spaces; in the other, a higher and a lower. The bathrooms and bathtubs are spaces which ordinarily enclose people; the refrigerators explicitly contain the things or effects of a person, the remains of M. A.'s father.

Furthermore, the potential elaboration of these pregenital spaces into settings for the Oedipal conflict is inherent in the content of both dreams, though much more explicitly so in IIA. We see the overall sterility of the scene in IA replaced by the more specific inertness and lifelessness of Father's "effects" in IIA. The penetration of the maternal enclosure by Father's "things" is made tangible in IIA, but equally so is the deadening effect of his presence on Mother's capacity to act as a libidinal object for M. A. (represented in infantile form by the bottles in the refrigerator).

The content of the two dreams is also linked through a series of receptacle images which have appeared in other dreams and in the patient's associations. I have suggested that the "sterile couch" is one of these, and the icebox–Miss Iceland connection another. We can now add the isolated image of the hearse (T39) and the casket immediately associated to Dream IIB on awakening. There is also a closely related complex of images connected with the sleep lab (actually a converted closet), which M. A. calls "a sweat box" (F3) in introducing the Thursday-night dreams at the beginning of the Friday hour. It is in this sweat box within a "nut house" that M. A. is strapped in and made a prisoner, as represented in Dream IIA. In the following associations of the Friday hour, many similar examples appear.

As an illustration of the memory-cycle model, however, this picture is still incomplete. If we are to be sure that IIA is a correction of IA within the framework of the model, these symbolic transformations are not sufficient. We must also know the latent meanings of the two dreams, i.e., the actual memories of past and present experiences as they existed before they were substituted for by the dream censorship and distorted by the matching operation of the memory cycle.

We can feel fairly confident that the latent contemporary experience is already known to us through our examination of the Thursday hour and M. A.'s presleep banter (e.g., three men killing another) in the laboratory. There is also a good chance that the historical experiences which contributed to the Thursday-night dreams will be revealed by the patient's associations during the remainder of the Friday hour. But the opportunity to recover anything more of the missing elements of Dream IA would appear to have been lost with the passing of the Thursday hour in which the dream was reported.

The likelihood that M. A.'s associations might return in a productive way during the Friday hour to this obscure and difficult-to-interpret dream of three nights past, especially in the face of an abundance of richly meaningful more recent dream material, would seem to be discouragingly small.

But here is the patient's first association to Dream IIA—the refrigerator dream—on Friday morning, following almost immediately after his description of the three Thursday-night dreams:

F7   PT: And my father's possessions? Well, Mother, in fact, Tuesday, wanted me to look through some of his stuff to see whether I could wear it or keep it or what. There were ski boots and overshoes, and this and that. I have been doing that for the last two years—and it reminds me of that. So if there is anything left, I will give it away—for heaven's sake, the ski boots from the year two, they looked like hiking boots, not ski boots.

This is obviously the principal day residue of Dream IIA. However, the event it records took place not on Thursday but on Tuesday, the day of the bathtub dream (IA).

The traditional psychoanalytic theory of dreams regards the choice of the day residue for a given dream to be a matter of convenience only. A day residue which is not employed in a dream the same night would not be preserved for another night, since new day residues equally lacking in emotional significance are sure to be found on every day of the dreamer's life.

For the memory-cycle model, the day residues are chosen because they contain information sufficiently valuable to be conserved in the permanent memory. If a particularly meaningful day residue were removed from a dream by the censorship, there would be every reason for the adaptive mechanisms of the memory cycle to preserve it until another attempt could be made to match it with the past. (As mentioned in chapter 2, the decay time for a representation in the short-term memory appears to be in the range of a week or two.)

Following the memory-cycle model, then, we would designate the representation of this affect-laden interaction on Tuesday as the original Tuesday residue. In our initial examination of Dream IA in its clinical context, we were led to suspect that the image of Judith's bathtubs had been substituted in the construction of the dream for a current experience associated with fantasies of maternal engulfment. The request by Mother to remove a dead Father's "stuff" from her house would seem to supply the powerful stimulus excluded from the manifest content of the original dream.

In Dream IB, the patient "had to get married in a church or a garden or an antique shop." We can now recognize these three locations as part-representations for the cemetery in which "the gray, ghostlike stonish effect" (T41) of Father—i.e., his body—was buried. Hence the casket associated immediately to Dream IIB, the correction dream for IB, and the "horse or a hearse" (T39). The Oedipal wish to enter Mother's intimate inner spaces leads directly to retaliatory destruction via maternal engulfment, i.e., oral incorporation (the refrigerators of Dream IIA).

This internal evidence strongly indicates that the experience with Mother on Tuesday influenced both of the dreams on Tuesday night—that it was, in fact, the most important daytime experience contributing to those dreams. The differences between the representation of this experience in the dreams of Tuesday and Thursday is instructive. On Tuesday night it was represented indirectly through associated material which had been substituted for it. It was "latent" in these dreams in the traditional sense; disguised for defensive purposes by the mechanism of displacement.

In the Thursday-night dream, the conversation with Mother is represented by concrete imagery which is immediately recognized by the patient. The distortion is psychologically transparent, therefore not likely to be defensive in origin. In this case, it is due to the mechanism of condensation; that is, the adaptive process which superimposes representations of present and past experience in order to match them. It is "latent" in the sense that it has been modified by the mechanism of dream construction, but not because it was disguised by the mechanism of the dream censor.

A major difficulty in the original presentation of the memory-cycle model has been resolved. If, as the model requires, the day residues are selected for matching with related memories of the past because of their emotional significance, why is this significance so often extremely difficult to detect? The answer is now clear. The "innocuous" day residue of clinical observation and the traditional theory is the result of substitution or displacement. The original emotionally significant day residue, which forms the present component of the latent content, is still registered in the short-term memory, available for participation in another dream.

Displacement and the Correction Dream

We now have two new observations which, taken together, raise the possibility of a different and simpler explanation for the genesis of the correction dream than the mechanism originally proposed by the memory-cycle model:

1. That the emotionally significant day residue chosen for introduction into the permanent memory may be deleted from the index dream and replaced by another day residue which arouses less anxiety.
2. That the original day residue may nevertheless be preserved and incorporated into the correction dream at a later time.

These observations suggest that the correction dream may simply be a later dream which revives and incorporates the original day residue of the index dream. If this were so, there would no longer be a need for the complicated feedback mechanism through which the index dream awakens the dreamer and enters into a new day residue which is matched in the correction dream with its own past component.

This simpler mechanism becomes especially attractive when we recall that in the index dream a substitute day residue will be successfully matched only with representations of past experience which resemble it— the substitute—rather than the original day residue. The past component of the index dream might then be quite remote in both form and content from the original day residue. If the matching mechanism in the correction dream had available to it both the report of the index dream and the original day residue deleted from it, its own past component could be matched directly with the original day residue and ignore the possibly misleading past component of the index dream report.

It is possible that some dreams we might wish to call correction dreams are constructed in this simpler way. The role of the reported index dream in the day residue of the correction dream would then be limited to the activation of the original day residue in the short-term memory, thereby making possible its participation in the construction of the correction dream.

Correction dreams of this simple type would be difficult to recognize since they would differ from their index dreams in both the present and past components of their latent contents. The only necessary connection between them would be the associative link relating the original day residue with the substituted day residue, and this link might be poorly represented in the imagery of the dreams.

The correction dreams in our study are clearly not of this type; their resemblance to their index dreams is quite vivid. Nevertheless, the presence of the excluded original day residue of Dream IA, the bathtub dream, in the manifest content of the refrigerator dream, IIA, raises an important question about the influence of the deleted day residue on the index dream.

We can imagine two alternative situations. In the first, the displacement of the original day residue by the substituted day residue takes place *before* the selection of past memory representations for the matching process has been made. In this case, the selection of past memories would be based on a scanning of the *substituted* day residue. The resulting index dream would then be identical to the dream that would have been constructed if the substituted day residue had been the original day residue and the actual original day residue had never existed. The past component of this index dream would have no necessary relationship to the past component of the correction dream which matched the revived original day residue directly. Thus, the correction dream would not introduce new information into a location in the permanent memory subordinate to the nodal point in which the past component of the index dream had been stored.

In the second alternative, the displacement of the original day residue by the substituted day residue takes place *after* the selection of past memory representations for the matching process has been made. The selection of the past memories would be based on a scanning of the *original* day residue. The resulting index dream would contain a past component which was closely related to the past component of the correction dream which was matched directly with the revived original day residue. In this case, the matching in the correction dream of the reported index dream and of the revived original day residue would converge on a specific location in the permanent memory. The correction dream would introduce its new information into the location specified by this convergence.

The resemblance between Dreams IA and IIA appears to rule out the first alternative. As we have seen in chapter 2, and will see again later in this chapter, the resemblance is due to the presence of a specific childhood memory in the past components of both dreams. This childhood memory seems much more closely related to the original day residue of the index dream—M. A.'s conversation with his mother about his father's belongings—than it is to the substituted day residue, his fantasy about Judith's bathrooms. However, because the substituted day residue contains libidinally charged receptable imagery, like the childhood memory, there is an outside chance that the substituted day residue could have evoked the identical childhood memory independently of the original day residue. (This possibility is much diminished by the incompleteness of the match between the substituted day residue and the childhood memory.)

Are we able to show that the past components of an index dream may be clearly related to an original day residue which has been deleted from the dream, and at the same time clearly unrelated to the substituted day residue which has replaced it? We have such an example directly at hand in Dream IB, the photographer dream.

We noted earlier that M. A.'s having "to get married in a church or a garden or an antique shop" in Dream IB can be explained as a cryptic reference to the cemetery in which his father was buried. The single entity which shares attributes with a church, a garden, and an antique shop is a cemetery. If it were necessary to represent an item stored in the permanent memory indirectly, a natural way to do it would be to substitute the items contained in a set of nodal points subordinate to the nodal point containing the item to be deleted, which is what appears to have happened here. If the cemetery image had been deleted from a day residue, we would expect the substitution to take a different form; for example, an adjacent item in a narrative sequence, an event rather than a set of static part-representations. The substitution in this case is characteristic of the tree structure of the permanent memory. The cemetery is therefore most likely to be an element in the past component of the dream.

The reference to Father's death in this image must have been evoked by the scanning of the original day residue, M. A.'s conversation with his mother about the disposing of Father's "effects." The substituted day residue, the fantasy of marriage to an indistinctly identified female contemporary, is related to the original day residue through the theme of collaboration with Mother to eliminate a male rival for her favors. But the substituted residue is very carefully restricted to the libidinal aspect of the relationship with Mother. The aggressive elimination of the rival is not represented in the substituted day residue in any recognizable way. The substituted day residue could not have been the basis for the selection of the cemetery image as a past component of the dream, and the match which was attempted between the substituted day residue and the cemetery derivatives failed to the point of almost impenetrable obscurity.

In Dream IIB, the King Ranch dream, the cemetery reference was matched via the image of the antique shop with the furniture collection of the police officer and the open casket. Unlike Dream IIA, the refrigerator dream, in this correction dream the original day residue of the index dream was not revived and reincorporated. The continuity between the two dreams was provided entirely by the matching between the reported manifest content of the index dream, IB, in which the themes of marriage with Mother and death of Father had been dissociated from each other by the action of the censorship, and the new past componen⁺ of Dream IIB.

We conclude that some elements, at least, in the past component of the index dream are selected on the basis of resemblance to the original day residue, even though all traces of the original day residue may be excluded from the process of dream construction before the matching takes place. Moreover, these elements of the past component of the index dream can be matched successfully in the correction dream even if they have not been incorporated into a coherent composite image in the matching process of the index dream.

This conclusion supports our supposition that the childhood memory which forms the major element in the past components of both Dreams IA and IIA was selected for matching in Dream IA on the basis of the excluded original day residue directly rather than on the coincidental resemblance between the original day residue and the substituted day residue. In the correction dream, IIA, the childhood memory could have been selected on the basis either of the reported manifest content of the index dream or the revived original day residue of the index dream. It seems most probable that both of these elements were active in the process of selection.

The memory-cycle model survives intact as the basic mechanism for the construction of the correction dream. The displacement of the original day residue of the index dream may make the construction of the correction dream more difficult than previously assumed, and the possible revival and reincorporation of the original day residue into the correction dream may make it less difficult. But neither of these complications occurs in every dream, while the basic mechanism must be operative at all times.

The new observations therefore indicate that a relationship between the original present and past components of the index dream had been established before the substitution of a less significant day residue for the actual matching process. In the correction dream, both of these elements reappeared in their original form and were successfully matched. In this case, the correction dream completed the matching which would have taken place in the index dream if the censor had not interfered. The information acquired in waking consciousness during the interval between the dreams (including the Thursday analytic hour) made this completion possible.

According to the memory-cycle model, the incompleteness of the original dream is one of the primary factors which is likely to cause the dreamer to awaken and remember his dream. The awakening of the dreamer is ordinarily the first step leading to the solution of the problem presented by the incompleteness of the remembered dream.

It is now clear that the displacement of the original day residue by a substitute acceptable to the censor has the inevitable effect of preventing the adaptive function of the dream from being completed. This raises the possibility that all dreams in which the original day residue is displaced will tend to become awakening dreams. If this were so, the result would be that displacement of the original day residue would be typical of dreams remembered by the dreamer, including those reported to the analyst, but not of dreams in general. I strongly suspect that this is the state of affairs which has prevented psychoanalysis from recognizing the adaptive function of dreaming for so long.

There would exist a continuing struggle in the operation of the patient's memory cycle between the disruption caused by the mechanism of displacement and the reparative effects of the correction dream. Our more usual clinical observations would be strongly biased in favor of half of this struggle—the half in which the defensive interference of the dream censor had been successful. Freud's suggestion that dreams are a "pathological mental activity" (1932, p. 15) would resolve itself into the proposition that the dreams we normally observe tend to be pathological dreams.

A New Model for the Mechanism
of Dream Construction

Following through on the evidence that the substitution in Dream IA took place after the original day residue had influenced the choice of material from the permanent memory, our model for the construction of this dream would involve these steps:

1. In the waking and predreaming evaluation of the day residue (Stage II of the memory cycle), the daytime experience with Mother must have been recognized as an instance of a large class of events whose theme is Mother's belonging to Father and the effects of this arrangement on Mother's availability to the patient.
2. When the day residue was scanned at the beginning of Stage III, this theme evoked a response from a sector in M. A.'s permanent memory structure which contained the record of childhood experience in which libidinal gratification and spatial enclosure were associated.
3. An associated series of these memory representations was transferred to the sensory-projection mechanisms, for comparison by superimposition with the day residue. The series consisted of affectively charged receptacle images clustered together in the permanent memory structure.
4. After the principal Tuesday residue (Mother's request that M. A. remove his father's things) had been scanned in order to recover these representations from the dreamer's permanent memory, but before the matching process itself could begin, the normal process of dream construction was interrupted by the dream censor. The principal day residue was removed from the sensory-projection mechanisms, and another fragment of the dream day's experience which was associated with it in the short-term memory—the imagery of Judith's bathtubs—replaced it.
5. In the dream which resulted from this sequence, IA, the substituted day residue—the image of Judith's bathtubs—was successfully matched with the memory involving the exposure of M. A.'s sister Alice. We know by now that the memory of Alice in the old house is part of a complex of memories and images related to libidinal objects and the spaces which enclose them. A number of them must have been offered for the matching of the day residue in Dream IA, with the memory of Alice providing the best match. Fragments of other, less-well-matched enclosure memories may also have been incorporated into the dream.

We can be quite sure that the interruption at step (4) above was produced deliberately by a defensive operation. In the contents of the Tuesday-night companion dream, IB, we saw the Oedipal conflict clearly represented, but with the figure of the father conspicuously absent. (We can see in retrospect that his "effects" were present in the dreamer's inability to find a suitable woman for himself). We can only conclude that direct references to the patient's father were being systematically excluded from both dreams.

What kind of mechanism would be capable of interrupting the matching process in this way? The least complicated mechanism that could conceivably perform this function would be the one which monitors the affective charge associated with each of the representations introduced into the sensory-projection mechanisms, and then rejects those whose charge exceeds a certain threshold. Such a mechanism would be similar to the one postulated earlier (Palombo, 1973) to direct the associative pathway during free association. The relatively low level of affect associated with each of the Tuesday-night dreams would tend to support the idea that such a simple mechanism was responsible.

Nevertheless, it is clear that the exclusion of the dreamer's father from the Tuesday-night dreams requires a more complicated monitoring device which is capable of recognizing the cognitive elements in the memory contents (the fact that it is Father who is involved) as well as their affective loading. Moreover, a simple affect monitor would not easily account for the suppression of the cognitive portion of the day residue of Dream IA *after* it had made contact with the cluster of related past memories in the permanent memory structure.

The principal Tuesday residue must have been maintained in the short-term memory despite being removed from the sensory projection mechanisms before the matching operation of Dream IA. This sets the stage for the construction of Dream IIA two nights later, in the following steps:

1. During the Thursday analytic hour, a large body of interpreted material relating to the patient's father (in both historical and transference manifestations) was connected with the representation of Dream IA in the patient's short-term memory.

2. On Thursday night, this material was reintegrated with the Tuesday residue of the patient's interaction with his mother. The result of this reintegration was the more complex day residue of Dream IIA, which incorporated material from at least two distinct dream days.

3. This complex Thursday residue made contact during the preliminary scanning of Stage III with the same receptacle cluster in the permanent memory structure from which the bathroom memory of Dream IA was derived.

4. During the matching phase of the new dream, IIA, the complex day residue which incorporated both the report of Dream IA and the principal day residue which had been deleted from the construction of IA was successfully matched with a number of elements in the receptacle cluster.

Dream IIA was not interrupted when the principal Tuesday residue was registered in the sensory-projection mechanisms, and other memory representations containing references to M. A.'s father and M. A.'s wish to replace him were allowed to participate in the matching process. How was this change effected? The most parsimonious explanation would be that the increased connectedness of the interpreted Tuesday/Thursday residue complex was in itself sufficient to bring about this result. If the interrupt mechanism functions by breaking connections between sets of images about to be matched, then conceivably a very strongly (that is, redundantly) connected day-residue structure could survive as a single connected unit despite the breaking of many individual connections among its components.

Less economical but more intuitive would be an explanation which calls for a modification of the interrupt mechanism itself, limiting its capacity to interfere. That such a modification should have been effected by the interpretive work of the Thursday hour seems highly probable. We would expect that the patient had become less afraid of his internal representations of Father in the course of the Thursday hour, and that his dream censor accordingly allowed these representations to be reconstructed in the sensory projection mechanisms during the matching process.

The content of Dream IIA suggests that the change has taken place through the establishment of an object representation intermediate between the polarized extremes of the victorious Oedipal father and the castrated son. This would be the double figure of the analyst, who imprisons the patient and forces him to work "against my will and against my timing," much as the tyrannical Oedipal father might have done; but who at the same time supports his wish to replace Father and allows him to share in the efficiency and exhilaration of the work, as the imagined Oedipal antagonist surely would not have done.

Although this dream image was not constructed in order to be introduced into the patient's permanent memory structure itself, it does provide us with a stop-action view of the process through which modifications of object representations take place. The new experience of the Thursday analytic hour, in which M. A. was able to share feelings with his analyst which he had almost certainly been unable to share with his father, is in the process of being assimilated to that vast assemblage to images which represents Father and all Father-like creatures in his memory. The new experience introduces new information which, in turn, enlarges the possibilities for interaction with Father and his surrogate, the analyst. But it also creates new nodal points and new pathways in the already complex representation of Father, through which dissociated aspects of the older image may become reconnected, or possibly connected for the first time.

Somehow this modification of M. A.'s image of his father was conveyed to the censorship mechanism, lowering its estimate of the danger involved in dealing with issues relating to his death. We know very little about the nature of the censorship mechanism, and the data supplied by dreams tells us more about what the censorship does than how it does it. But we can be sure that one aspect of its operation must include a set of stereotyped representations of early danger situations with which every new experience must be compared before it can be processed further. The events of the Thursday hour must have caused a revision in this set of stereotypes.

Before we go to the new data of the Friday hour, it is worth noting that the mechanism which constructed the Thursday-night correction dreams made use of the analyst's interpretations in a way that the analyst could not possibly have intended or predicted, since he had no knowledge of the original Tuesday residues. Neither coincidence, compliance with the analyst, nor the continuity of the patient's unconscious preoccupations can account for the resulting dreams. Only the adaptive function of the memory cycle could have recovered the originally deleted contents of Dream IA and completed the interrupted index dream. In so doing, it carried forward the analyst's interpretations of the dream into new and as yet analytically unexplored territory. At the same time, it made use of the analyst's interpretations in a way that fully confirms our earlier assumption that they were dream interpretations and not merely interpretations of the transference.

The Friday Hour: Associations

The richness and object-relatedness of the Thursday-night dreams, leading to a complex intertwining of associations during the remainder of the Friday hour, make it difficult to discuss Dreams IIB and IIC separately. An overall pattern can be discerned, however, in which the greater part of the hour was devoted to a working out of the implications of Dream IIA, climaxed by the discovery of the affect-laden childhood memory which gave rise to the receptacle imagery in both IA and IIA.

The explication of Dream IIB, the overtly Oedipal dream, played a relatively subordinate role in this sequence. After the significance of Dream IIA had been worked out, the patient once again became aware of his positive feelings toward the analyst, which led him to the transference implications of Dream IIC, the bartender dream. This dream was the only one of the three which was derived directly from the Thursday hour; that is, which was not a reworking of one of the Tuesday night dreams.

The report of IIB on Friday morning was different from the original report of Thursday night in several respects (F5). The police officer and the school bus were omitted, as were the furniture collected by the officer and the casket image. In the Friday report the patient was initially named Mr. King and identical with him. It was only after his marriage to Miss Iceland that "I stood back and then I become a third person." These changes tend to minimize the superego aspects of the paternal figure in the dream and the dangers inherent in identifying with him. Whereas the secondary elaboration of Dream IIA on Friday morning appeared to advance the working alliance, the changes in IIB seem to have been determined by a defensive transferential pseudocompliance.

Nevertheless, the contrast between IIB and Dream IB, which it corrects, is striking. The patient's father, excluded from the earlier marriage dream, is represented here in his Oedipal majesty, replete with totemic attributes of horse and bull. (The King Ranch breeds racehorses and cattle.) Two unexplained fragments of the Thursday hour are carried forward, the dream about a horse show (T3), which the patient said he would go back to but never did, and the cryptic association, "a horse (or a hearse)" (T39). The mysterious antique shop has been transformed into the policeman's furniture collection (Father's belongings). The school bus hints at a date during the Oedipal period or early latency.

Mother is also given royal status, and the intensity of her conflicting attractiveness and inaccessibility is graphically portrayed. The alternating identities of the woman married by the dreamer in IB have been replaced in IIB by the contrasting feelings aroused in the dreamer by the single figure of his mother. The furniture and the casket, though suppressed in retelling, link Mother with the receptacle imagery of Dreams IA and IIA and underline the double risk of possessing her and being contained by her. The actor/observer ambiguity of IB is replicated almost exactly in IIB, the difference being that the role of the actor is clearly identified with Father in IIB.

In all major respects, then, Dream IIB reworks the conflictual issues presented in IB, and in so doing corrects a variety of omissions and indirections associated with the shallow and disorganized state of the historical material represented in the earlier dream. In the correction dream, the issues are sharply focused, the connections with childhood memories of the dreamer's parents are deepened, and the glaring omission of his father's central role in the conflict is brought to light. In addition, the symbolic and thematic connections between IIA and IIB are made explicit in many ways (primarily but not exclusively concerned with the dominating presence of Father in both). The relationship between IA and IB, about which we speculated in discussing the Thursday hour, was visible for the most part only to the prepared eye of the analytic observer. In this sense, we might say that the *dreaming* of Thursday night as a whole, and not only each of the dreams individually, was the result of a correctional process which developed the cognitive and affective connections between the branches of the memory tree which contributed to the apparently unrelated dreams of Tuesday night. The thematic convergence observed in the manifest content of IIA and IIB is even more apparent in the associations to the dreams, so that it is difficult at times to assign the associative material to one dream or the other. However, there is a sequence of associations quite specific to IIB which does introduce some new ideas about marriage and its effects on women. It begins with what appears to be another Tuesday residue, a residue which was partially deleted by the censor and then matched with the photographer image to form the past components of Dream IB.

F11   PT: Now, this Icelandic beauty queen. I have seen her before. This is really a stunning girl, and Judith showed me a picture when she was married—an entirely different girl than she was now. She is very thin and sort of pale and emaciated-looking. When she got married, she was a very round-faced—not plump, but an extremely blond, blond sort of a girl. If I saw her picture now, I mean, I still would say that is not you, absolutely not you. And there was some similarity between the beauty queen and what Judith used to look like. Maybe there is something there, I don't know—coming from Iceland, there has got to be a relationship there. Mr. King is another one of those characters like Howard Hughes, you know, that I admire—immense wealth—a lot of power—doesn't seem to—well, from what I know, just a recluse in a way. And he got married last in life I noted in the dream. I am sure he would appreciate me marrying a . . . again—whatever it is.

Father's most visible effect on Mother, of course, was his impregnating her. We have had no clear-cut references to this important subject thus far in our sample of M. A.'s conscious thoughts, although the unwanted presence of Father's effects within a maternal receptacle (Dream IIA) is certainly quite suggestive.

M. A. habitually mentions Judith's many children as the major impediment to his taking her seriously as a potential wife, usually with the complaint that they would be an intolerable emotional burden to him. The passage just quoted suggest another reason for his objections: a fantasy that Judith has been physically wasted away by them. Marrying a much younger woman relatively late in life might offer some imaginary protection against this sort of threat.

There is a silence at this point in the hour, and then a comment about the news of the devaluation of the franc heard by the patient on the way to the analyst's office. International finance is "really a discipline," he says, unlike psychiatry, in which there are no experts (F11). The analyst asks about the financial transactions in Dream IIC, the bartender dream. There follows a paraphrase of the dream as it was reported earlier, and then the report of another section, not mentioned before, which links it with IIA and IIB.

F15 PT: The bills? While I was picking up the bills, I saw a desk, an office desk, and I was looking at the desk—a sort of a light walnut, just a commercial job, poorly stained, with streaks of stain and varnish running off it. And I said to myself "Ach, this is not for me." Suppose I was in Washington, I would make, say, an executive desk that would be hand-rubbed, handmade desk, and it would work out personally and would sell for $2,000 to $3,000, make $2000, profit, make, say, one of these a week, and work over it—and when I say "work over it," guarantee it would be absolutely perfect, there would not be a flaw in it. And I am now saying to myself, "Well, why should I do it by hand when I can have it machine-cut, and then finish it up by hand, and accomplish the same thing—put out more desks and still give a personal end product."

This passage suggests a new possibility for solving the receptacle problem, the creation of a new and better one by the patient for his own benefit, as opposed to his appropriation of the used up and booby-trapped belongings of Father or the analyst. The flawless handmade desk mentioned first appears to represent a narcissistically conceived woman of his own, and the machine-made desks which follow possibly her children. Despite the severely obsessional manner with which these wishes are communicated, their being expressed at all marks a significant departure from the passivity we have encountered until now.

With these contributions from Dreams IIB and IIC, we can anticipate the further unfolding of the meanings latent in IIA. In his associations to

IIA, M. A. established the maternal reference of the icebox quite early, immediately after reporting Mother's request that he look through Father's possessions, in fact.

F9   PT: A place to eat good things—an icebox. The image I see now is going to the icebox—I was having a party and picking up the fruit salad, or the cheese tray, or the cakes. And then she . . . there was only one thing missing—no use to get her upset. I had to put in a steak or something for somebody. Then this chain gang or whatever you want to call it—a water gang or a bucket brigade—

This fragment appears to incorporate the memory of a scene in IIA which occurred just prior to the dream as previously reported. M. A. then went on to mention a stomachache that came and went mysteriously on the previous evening, lasting about two hours. He connected the stomachache with his feelings about the girl he was out with, whom he described as "a skinny, sort of nondescript, awkward girl, a social worker, poorly dressed, not particularly personable, not too good-looking, just a waste-of-time sort of thing." (F9).

A few minutes later, after a momentary silence, he says, "I can see the sleep lab right now, tossing and turning in a hot box. Boy!" (F15). The following dialogue takes place.

F16–21
    DR: So you dream of an icebox.
    PT: I was not in it, though.
    DR: What else does icebox mean—your father's and somebody else's?
    PT: Somebody else's what? There was an icebox, right?
    DR: At least his things were in it.
    PT: Things were in it on the bureau. I don't know how it got all confused, but you have to remove it to get the bottles. You can store things in an icebox to keep them fresh, you know, keep them, you know, current—so if you store them—a man's effects in an icebox to keep them current and fresh . . . and you remove them by orders from somebody else. I wish I could have seen the faces of the other two birds.

And then this more open note of triumph:

F25   PT: I never saw three men trying to get things out of the icebox, out of a receptacle, so quickly—man, I was yelling for joy, they were going so quickly. I was happy that they could accomplish this thing. Maybe the guys were happy, or I was happy. I was first unhappy about the things being removed and then, boy, delighted. Let's say that somebody else is helping me get rid of my father's things—the images or controls of what-have-you—out they go, swish. Well, there were two other people. Who could they be? I would say you were one of them, but who was the other one?

95

The "other one" is certainly Dr. R., at whose direction he visits the sleep lab. This is an example of the well-known phenomenon of the split transference: Dr. R. is introduced into the analytic situation in order to reduce the tension of the dyadic relationship. We must not ignore the kernel of reality incorporated into this fantasy, however, for Dr. R.'s arranging that he be awakened during the night and thereby enabled to remember his dreams is actually helping him to "get rid of my father's things." But the danger is clearly expressed in the text of Dream IIA that this is happening too fast to permit him to master the feelings aroused by such possibly premature self-knowledge.

The dialogue continues:

F20–31

> PT: This icebox is higher up, you know—it is about six feet higher than the icebox we are taking the things out of.
> DR: What does that bring to mind?
> PT: A status stature—the higher you are, the higher you are, you know, and the higher you are physically, the higher you are status-wise. Worry about somebody else's icebox—some social plane—or something. I can see the icebox now—a big, wide icebox. I don't know what else an icebox reminds me of. Where do I see iceboxes? There is an icebox in my home in Richmond at 236 Madison Street. It had a bad motor that was always humming at night. I used to get up to close the door to keep it quiet.

No doubt there was a noisy nocturnal activity of Mother's from which he felt excluded by his low physical stature, an activity he associated with something bad in her. And despite his claiming to close the door to keep the refrigerator quiet, his impulse to spy must have been quite intense. His next associations, a series of half-coherent images of hostile enclosing spaces, indicate the devastating retaliation he expected for it (cf. the "bucket brigade" of Dream IIA, reported in F5).

F31   PT: I see a bucket on a string, a chain—a steel bucket on a chain. Now this just might be—I saw this movie, *The Battle of Algiers,* and they have commandos with trapped other French, and they want to send up this note saying to drop a bucket to get this lieutenant colonel . . . written statement that they would get a fair trial. They did drop the bucket, but a bomb was in the bucket, and it blew up. My bucket is a wicker basket on a rope—mine is a steel bucket on a chain coming down—a perforated bucket. I just heard someone say my name—a female voice—in my imagination. I think I was in an air tunnel or something, a bus terminal (cf. Father's terminal illness). Now I picture myself in some kind of terminal. This is crazy—I am having dreams just lying here. Standing in a half-unfinished terminal, and out behind the seats where the ceilings are unfinished—the studding was there, the insulation is not there—but there is a row of lights starting and somebody comes over to me—a workman—and says there is a row of lights starting, and somebody says, "How would you like to start them—this way and that way." And I said, "Just now I am not even a member here—I am not supposed even to be here—don't ask me"—but looking at it, he thinks I know what I want to be done there. *Silence.* Here is a crazy image.

As the associative strands become more and more closely interwoven, it becomes increasingly probable that their eventual point of convergence will be in a representation of the primal scene, an amalgam of vague and fragmentary memories of parental intercourse with fantasy material very high in libidinal content.

However, before this point of convergence is reached, the associative material must be brought into contact with the patient's current feeling state in the transference, which has to do, as we learned toward the end of the Thursday hour, with the homosexual solution to the problem of Father's retaliation. The "crazy image" alluded to at the end of F31:

F33   PT: I don't know, I just lost it—about a book. Can you have two split-images at the same time? I see myself or somebody saying, "Do you hate me?" At least, me saying, "Do you hate me?" A little boy standing there, and then I see the image of a book, and a pile of books, pocket books in front of a bookstore.

The book (singular) is certainly *Reality Therapy,* and the books (plural) most likely those which helped M. A. to surpass his father, both in the promotion of his fantasy life as a child and in his more advanced formal education later. The analyst asks whether M. A. is referring to the past or the present.

F41   PT: I don't know. I suppose—let's say I am a little boy now. I don't know about the little boy. The little boy wanted to know if his parents loved him, I suppose—looking for reassurance. Jesus, I am glad I am not a little girl. I was thinking if I was a little girl and felt that way, I would probably run out and become a nymphomaniac—that is the kind of the kind of interpretation I would put on that. I was seeking love and all that sort of thing. What do little boys do when they seek love?

They withdraw, he says, and seek out other little boys to be friends with. This train of thought reaches its conclusion in the next statement: "I see a sort of Humpty Dumpty–like guy with a pumpkin head" (F45). Like Saturn, Father will eat his child, and that is apparently the worst that can happen. The sleep laboratory with its EEG and its extraction of dreams must be a stimulus to this fantasy.

97

Now there is a silence, and a reference to his dissatisfaction with last night's dinner. Then, without further introduction:

F47   PT: I see a street-corner curb, a washed street, red sidewalk, black street all wet. I could be in Ocean City. The only time I went to Ocean City was—not the only time—but most of the times with my parents as a young kid. I was looking, you know, seeing an Ocean City scene—the Burgundy Hotel I stayed at, and then a floor scene and open box. The open box turns into a smaller box, and suddenly the smaller box turns into a big box of beetles, and they were slithering across the floor and disappearing in the crevices—huge bugs. I started to laugh yesterday. In all the dreams that I ever had, I never laughed in a dream either. I laugh sometimes but, Jesus, images or dreams are usually somber.

This is the primal-scene fantasy toward which so many associative signs have been pointing. Freud's discovery that "vermin" in dreams generally represent younger siblings seems to be fully applicable here, as indicated both by content and context. In this case, there appears to be a more particular reference to the unborn children potential in Father's spermatozoa.

The inspiration for the imagery of dreams and fantasies like this one is, of course, primarily anal. This quality reflects the impregnation and birth fantasies of the child making the transition from anal to phallic/ Oedipal concerns; but also, I believe, the fact that opportunities for discovering the nocturnal activity of parents often come when the child is under pressure from urgent excretory impulses of his own.

It is easy to see how a fixation at the level of this fantasy has had a pervasive influence over M. A.'s emotional life. If the defensive retreat from the Oedipal conflict transforms the rivalry with Father into a re-enactment of the anal struggle with Mother, then sadomasochism, homosexual anxieties, and eventual humiliating defeat become inevitable. The recovery of this primal-scene fantasy, in which the patient assumed his lifelong role as excited but horrified observer of parental sexual activity, initiates a reintegration of the infantile experience from a developmentally more advanced position. Hence the expression of relief at the end of F47 and in the associations which will follow.

The primal-scene fantasy is not simply a fantasy. It is a fantasy firmly attached to a childhood memory—the memory of his staying in a hotel with his parents—where the unusually close quarters would make his awareness of the primal scene especially likely. In fact, the dreamlike structure of the fantasy, together with the remark about dreams which immediately follows it, and M. A.'s slightly earlier comment that "I am having dreams just lying here," indicates to me that the fantasy is actually the memory of a childhood dream in which a fresh encounter with the primal scene was being matched against similar experiences still earlier in his life.

The imagery of this fantasy-memory-dream has a by-now familiar look to it, for it is none other than the past memory which was about to be matched in the bathtub dream of Tuesday night with the representation of Mother's request that M. A. get rid of Father's things. The hotel is the rooming house, the large and small bathrooms are the large and small boxes; the sequence "a large bathroom and then a small bathroom" is the truncated version of "the open box turns into a small box." The boxes do not have the libidinally specialized social functions of the bathrooms or refrigerators, but their derivation from spaces within the human body is that much clearer.

The anatomy of the body spaces in question is not so clear. This is as one would expect, for the images of the dream represent the body as conceived in the naïve sexual theories of a small child. The large/small, high/low dimension suggests a contrast between the Oedipal rivals, the transformation of large into small perhaps representing the substitution of the genitals of the child for those of the father. But there is also a curious symmetry between male and female, little distinction being made between the first "open" box, representing Father, and the second large box, representing Mother, except for the verminous contents of the latter. This might be explained, for example, by an impregnation fantasy involving the transfer of feces from Father's abdomen to Mother's, perhaps through an intermediate transformation of feces into phallus.

Other possibilities exist, for the imagery of the beetle fantasy is itself derivative, probably from an earlier historical component, if it is actually the memory of a dream, certainly from earlier related experiences superordinate to it in the memory tree, whether it is the memory of a childhood dream or not. The importance of this childhood memory lies not in its specifying the historical point at which a pathogenic emotional trauma occurred, but in its specifying a location in the patient's memory structure from which the *accumulated* meanings of the primal-scene experience throughout childhood could become accessible to his executive apparatus in the present. "Accessibility" here must refer both to the devious channels leading to the unconscious acting-out of his neurosis and to the open air of the psychoanalytic process of integration.

Both of the latent contents of Dream IA have now been exposed: the latent content which had its source in an experience of the dream day and the latent content which represented a much earlier experience related to it, an experience with a clear thematic and associative relationship to the overall structure of the patient's neurosis.

The New Model Completed

Our model for the construction of Dreams IA and IIA can now be carried forward. In Dream IA, after the substitution of the bathtub imagery for the original day residue, a number of affect-laden receptacle images from the permanent memory were matched with the substitute day residue. These included both the memory of Alice "whisking by" and the primal-scene memory at the hotel. The experience of visiting bathrooms in two different houses belonging to Judith was represented in the substitute day residue and was matched with the double-receptacle imagery of the primal-scene memory.

The Thursday residue contained both the report of Dream IA during the analytic hour and the recovered original day residue which had been excluded from the earlier dream. Either of these might have been sufficient to re-evoke the primal-scene memory for matching in Dream IIA. It seems quite likely, however, that if only the original day residue by itself had been matched in Dream IIA with the primal-scene memory, the resulting composite image would not have given such prominence to the theme of the two receptacles in the manifest content of the correction dream.

The noisy refrigerators or iceboxes are the most conspicuous examples of new material in the correction dream from the vicinity in the permanent memory of the nodal points previously matched in the earlier dream. Their reference to Mother may have been evoked directly through the revived original day residue, rather than through the report of Dream IA. The refrigerators were then matched in IIA with the representation of the disappointing dinner date earlier on Thursday evening.

New historical material is almost certainly present in the many spatial details of Dream IIA which have no direct correspondence with IA. The interaction in IIA between M. A. and the two male figures must have resulted from a matching between transference material included in the Thursday residue and the representations of various attempts in the past to identify with Father, especially in areas connected with work.

A major methodological issue comes into focus here. When we observe a single dream in isolation, we are often unable either to separate the past and present components of the manifest content or to identify these components with their actual experiential antecedents, the latent contents. Associations to the dream may supply either or both of these missing elements. Our understanding of the significance of the latent contents is much enhanced, however, when we see either component matched in two different dreams. It may also be the case generally, as it was here, that the availability of a dream element to the analytic associative process is greatly facilitated by recovery from two dreams which form part of a corrective sequence.

Having recovered both the present and past components of the latent contents of Dream IA, we now possess what I would call *the technical basis for a complete interpretation* of the dream. It is now possible for the analyst to move with assurance between the transference neurosis and the infantile neurosis. He is no longer dependent on the conjectures and approximations with which we made do in our initial discussion of the Tuesday-night index dreams.

I do not mean to suggest that we can now identify every element of Dreams IA and IIA. Especially in the case of the new historical material matched in IIA, we can see that obscurities necessarily remain. But we now have good reason to expect that these obscurities would be resolved in later dreams which followed in the same sequence, given the further exploration in waking consciousness of the new themes.

This further exploration might begin with a comparison of IIA and IIC. The principal day residue and the primal-scene memory recovered in association to IIA were not original to that dream, but were taken over from IA during the correction process. Since IIC does not correct a previously reported dream, we might assume with some confidence that the day residue for this dream originated in the work of the Thursday analytic hour itself. Whatever we can find in common between IIA and IIC would refer to this new material, and we could then look for parallels in the past events matched with the new material of the Thursday residues of both IIA and IIC. How the analyst approaches this task intuitively will be seen later on.

If a complete dream interpretation must be based on the actual experiences of present and past which have been matched by the patient's memory cycle, does this or a similar formula apply to interpretations in general? I think that the answer can only be affirmative. Every effective psychoanalytic interpretation must include references to a significant event of the past, another significant event taking place in the present, and the fact that the psychic apparatus of the patient reacts to the new event as if it were equivalent in some important respect to the old.

The "crystallization" of the transference neurosis is the phase of analysis in which these events of past and present and the connections between them are brought into view. The "resolution" of the transference neurosis is the phase in which the criteria by which these connections were established are identified and their inappropriateness to current reality clarified. (Of course, these phases overlap considerably in time.)

The explication of dream material in analysis is a microcosmic version of the overall analytic process. The dream presents the experiences of past and present in composite form. The interpretive work must first of all distinguish the experiences from one another and then seek by inference to determine the nature of the equivalence between them assumed by the mechanism of dream construction.

Here, as throughout our investigation, the major emphasis must be placed on the actual experience of the past rather than the impulses which may be associated with it, although these impulses are sure to be influential in the success or failure of the matching process.

For example, without the aid of the memory-cycle model, we would have to account for the fact that *the same infantile wish* achieved "hallucinatory gratification" in Dreams IA and IIA forty-eight hours apart. We are not referring here to a repetitive wish that arises on different occasions from a similar set of biological circumstances, but to two independent contemporary manifestations of a single biological impulse which arose on a specific night twenty-odd years before.

We cannot account for this recurrence with a theory of dream construction based on impulses seeking discharge. If the impulse was discharged in the Tuesday-night dream, why did it reappear on Thursday night? If the impulse was only partially discharged on Tuesday, we would expect what was left of it on Thursday to be relatively weaker. How then can we explain its ability to compete successfully with other, fresher impulses on Thursday night to form Dream IIA? And why would the affective charge of its dream vehicle be so much greater on Thursday than on Tuesday?

These questions lose their force when we realize that the recovery of the primal-scene fantasy resulted from the exploration of an orderly information-conserving structure. It was the culmination of a process of associative triangulation which brought about a convergence of many lines of approach on a particular nodal point in the permanent memory structure.

Dreams often appear in pairs during the early stages of an analysis, one of the pair representing the same conflict or mismatch in pregenital terms, the other in terms of the interpersonal drama of the Oedipus complex, as was the case here with IA and IB. When such a pair of dreams is reported early in analysis, the affective loading is generally much higher in the case of the dream which emphasizes the pregenital. This did not initially appear to be so with Dreams IA and IB, but with the help of the correction dream and the analytic work which followed, we can see that this appearance was due to a defensive interference in the formation of IA. The disentangling of the Oedipal from the pregenital generally precedes the fully experienced and interpretable Oedipal phase of analysis, and the associative movement in the Friday hour bears this out.

Conclusion of the Friday Hour

The analyst's immediate response to the primal-scene fantasy indicates his understanding that it represents the same experience as Dream IIA. The patient has no difficulty with this transition:

F48–51
> DR: But there was a funny sort of exhilaration in this dream. Very efficient bucket brigade doing everything so fast.
> PT: A joyful yell of victory after, you know, we got everything removed at a certain time.
> DR: What does that bring to mind?
> PT: Well, it just brings to mind a yippee—I am rid of my father's stuff—now let somebody else worry about it. All finished, it is all out of my house, it is out of my possession, it is done, swish. I suppose it was probably me at the anchor of that thing, getting that stuff out of there—pushing at this point. First I was pushing it, I was, you know, we just made it in a couple of minutes—time and motion, man.

As suggested earlier, this passage is the emotional climax of the interpretive sequence which began with the reporting of Dream IA at the beginning of the Thursday hour. To be sure, M. A.'s judgment that he has escaped once and for all from his father's influence is premature. But that is not the point. However much longer the analysis will take, this sequence constitutes a genuine initiative on the part of the patient.

The experienced clinician will recognize at this point in the session the danger of a "flight into health," a seizing on the temporary relief of a symptom to deny the need for further analytic work. What appears to be such an impulse now enters the consciousness of the patient, but with it comes a sobering image from the cluster in the memory tree which contained the casket of Dream IIB. (Note also the reference to "birds" in F21, p. 95.)

F51 (continued

>PT: I am looking now at a bird . . . in Norway, in Oslo, Norway—some city by the ocean. This little blue foreign car coming around the bend. It is outside the city though. To translate, I suppose I would like to be far, far away on a trip. Maybe I am not so wild about travel—I don't have to travel now. While I am talking to you, I am seeing images about something quite the contrary. A rug and a floor somewhere, and then a rug rolled up, and enters a man struggling to get out of the rug—struggling—you know he is wrapped up in his rug—that is how it looked lying on the floor. I know the rug—it is a cheap carpet, wool carpet of some sort. While I am talking about birds, etc., and traveling and analyzing this, I see this guy squirming out of the rug he is wrapped up in.

The associations to the rug image develop some of the anally derived significations of the receptacle theme:

F55   PT: Judith spending all her money on rugs, for one thing. I spend a lot of time on the rug in my apartment, handling my—gee, I am really creating rugs. Just made a white circle, a blue circle, and circle rug—brown rugs—like . . . three rings. Mother's white rugs—never walk on them, you know, get very upset about getting them dirty. Had a big oriental rug one time—we sold it to somebody in Richmond. In fact, it was the widow of Dr. Anderson who bought it. Why I remember that so distinctly? It is a funny thing, I sold a lot of things, and I never was interested in furniture then, but I remember the big to-do about it. It was huge, huge, it must have been 30 x 30 oriental rug—I thought anyway, maybe it was 20 x 30—a big one. This was long before I even thought of furniture or anything. I remember that pretty clearly.

The discovery of the experiential sources of the receptacle dreams has climaxed a progression which began with the analyst's interpretations early in the Thursday hour. Thus far in the Friday hour, his activity has been limited to what I have described previously as "monitoring" (Palombo, 1973). He has been keeping track of the nodal points traversed by the patient's associations and has directed him several times to the immediately preceding nodal point in order to support his movement over some rather difficult ground. With this movement completed, we are not clear as to what will come next, and we wonder whether the last quotation indicates another defensive retreat from the Oedipal theme to the anal level.

This transition is important. An enforced retreat at this point might call into question the authenticity of the associative work which preceded it, for we have been warned by the patient's performance at the beginning of the Thursday hour of his tendency to a superficial compliance with what he conceives to be the analyst's expectations.

There is a period of silence, and then a shift into the present with a rather bored reference to his having no date for the coming evening. He wonders how he is going to react to this "gap." He mentions some thing he might do, rather unenthusiastically, and then says that on the way out of the analyst's office on Thursday he was feeling guilty about sug- gesting to him that he read *Reality Therapy*.

The patient has momentarily returned to his state of mind on Tuesday evening, just before he had the index dreams reported at the beginning of the Thursday hour, when he was alone, bored and reading *Reality Therapy* by himself. He is wondering whether he can find an alternative pathway on which to proceed from this repetitive nodal experience. Has anything changed as the result of the Thursday and Friday hours?

The analyst asks how M. A. felt about him as he was leaving.

F59   PT: Well, I thought you were more human, you know, you were, well, another person . . . probably you could learn, you know, had problems like somebody else—more regular.

The analyst now asks what "a bartender" means to him. Dreams IIA and IIB were correction dreams, originating with the experiences of Tuesday and the dreams of Tuesday night. The bartender dream, IIC, appears to have for its day residue the transference relationship directly as it developed during the Thursday hour, without the same derivation from the earlier index dreams. Unlike IIA and IIB, it portrays a relation- ship between two men which appears to sustain itself without the medi- ation of a woman. The relationship is competitive but not destructive. Inequality is still an issue, but differences between the two men are measurable, negotiable, and reversible. Despite the anal derivation of the medium of exchange and the homosexual implications raised by the exclusion of women, the threats to the dreamer's ego identity and autonomy appear to be much reduced when compared with the dangers lurking in the primal-scene fantasy which was recovered by the earlier dreams.

The analyst has correctly picked up the new elements in the bartender dream and related them to the transference. For our purposes, what is important is the progression from the interpretation of the receptacle dreams to a new representation of the patient's relationship with his father/analyst which matches elements of past and present at a developmental level more nearly approaching an adult partnership. Here is the patient's response when he realizes the identity of bartender and analyst:

F67–69

> PT: So he is an analyst. Now what was I doing, giving him one type of money? What type of money? He had no right to keep my phony bill, did you? . . . both of these phony bills are mine—Mickey Mouse Richmond bills. And I would say, "Why would you want one?" In my imagination, if that is what it is. The Richmond bill is very private; it probably belongs to very few, including myself. So let's say you got half of whatever I had there, and I was jabbering because the whole thing was mine. Resentment, the money—it was not a feeling of any sort. So let's say the bills represent my soul, and the hardest thing for me to say is the word "heart."
> DR: Yes?
> PT: Meaning emotion. Just to say it gives me cringes—I cringe when I say it.

The analyst is now in a position to add to the construction he began to build early in the Thursday hour, when he connected the lack of feeling in the initial dream report with the patient's recurrent behavior in presenting his dreams.

F70–72

> DR: Even the icebox, I think, has to do with warmth and coldness. It has to do with you and your father, and your father's effects and things—getting rid of them or putting them somewhere else. As though somehow that is a picture of yourself and your father's self. It fits very beautifully with what you were saying yesterday about your fear of warm emotions. So what do you do? You dream about an icebox. To say some person is an icebox—what does it mean?
> PT: Rigid, cold, aloof, emotional. Now I am not so sure what I do with that—sort of my feelings and emotions.
> DR: It is almost as if you said how do your father's assets become your assets without any warm interchange with another human being. This is M. A. to the nth degree, you know, this high degree of efficiency. Everything is organized, zip, zip, zip—but all cold and efficient without any real personal interchange. In a funny way, that is the personal interchange, but it is with a bartender, sort of a downgrading that was— and there it is all of a sudden, a question of financial transactions and the reluctance to handle the highly personal stuff.

After so much that we have observed, this may seem like relatively little for the analyst to say. But the analyst's job is not to say everything at once. It is, first of all, to point out the direction in which a productive new associative movement is most likely to take place; and second, to fill in connections which the patient cannot yet make for himself but which he can tolerate and utilize when offered to him by another person who is safely outside his self-depreciating neurotic system.

We recognize the nodal point at which this new movement is to originate as identical to the point where the Thursday hour began. The patient is imagining himself to be alone, without the narcissistic supplies provided by working and dating, and he is struggling with his disappointment that his father/analyst has not provided him with more.

With the end of the hour imminent, M. A.'s verbal response is severely curtailed. But his unconscious has the final word—a word unambiguously in the affirmative.

F73   PT: Highly personal and worth not much to anybody else either, say myself or people in Richmond, if that is what you will. You know, very, very personal stuff. Well, again, if I am holding back personal stuff, I don't know what personal stuff I am holding back at this point. The emotion? But that is the toughest for me. I am just thinking about this weekend. I think on Sunday I am going to take it easy, too—instead of knocking myself out, instead of going skiing and . . . the ski conditions—snow conditions. Funny thing, too, all of a sudden I check over my throat, and it has gotten a lot better.

We remember that the Thursday hour had begun with a complaint about this same sore throat, the symptom of a cold which had reminded him immediately of his father's fatal lung cancer.

The Analytic Hour and the Analysis

Before closing the descriptive section of this study, I think something further must be said about the relationship between the fragment we have examined and the analysis as a whole. Without knowing what has happened prior to the Thursday hour, it might appear to the observer that the analyst's interpretations after the initial dream report contain an element of unconscious reenactment of Father's authoritarian role in the patient's fantasy world. Is the analyst re-creating the father's role because of an unresolved countertransference problem, or is he simply bringing into the open a struggle which the patient has covertly but consistently imposed on their relationship?

The evidence internal to these two hours is sufficient to persuade me that the analyst is confronting the patient with a long-standing pattern of denial which could be brought to his attention in no other way. The exclusion of Father from the Tuesday-night dreams is part of this pattern. The associations which follow the confrontation show the real reason for the denial. The patient tries to deal with his Oedipal guilt by adopting an attitude of submissiveness to Father's overwhelming power as he perceived it when he was a small child. But this stratagem will succeed only if the conflict is kept out of awareness.

When the patient openly acknowledges the struggle with Father, there are two painful consequences. First, the frustration and anger which must accompany the conscious awareness of his psychically emasculated condition must be quite damaging to his conviction that he can get what he wants from life without giving up his passive defenses. Second, by acknowledging the reenactment of his struggle with Father in the contemporary setting of the analysis, he would open himself to the discovery that defeat is not inevitable, with the result that he must come face to face both with his Oedipal guilt and the sadness over lost opportunities in the actual relationship with his father.

A less neurotic resolution of the Oedipal conflict will depend on his realizing that the rivalry with his father, though inevitable, is not necessarily destructive to either of them. The overall movement of the two hours is very plainly in the direction of this realization. Father's presence in the Thursday-night dreams demonstrates M. A.'s increased tolerance for his own assumption of an active role in the struggle. To be sure, in Dream IIA he is a prisoner, acting against his will and on somebody else's schedule, and this feeling is closely linked with his adopted attitude of impotence in relation to his father. But the dream also expresses his admiration for what the others are doing, and the sense that he is capable of participating in it more or less as an equal. The discovery of the primal-scene memory allows him momentarily to experience his identification with the analyst as a voluntary and fully ego-syntonic triumph over his neurotic inhibitions.

The development of a coherent linear narrative which links together a representative sampling of memory contents at critical points in the life cycle, what we usually call "insight," is not the entirety of psychoanalytic work. The work which leads to lasting improvement involves an investigation of all the affect-laden branches of the memory tree which radiate from these representative points, and which lead to the discovery of still other significant nodal points and to others beyond them, until the fully three-dimensional structure of the permanent memory has been revealed and made accessible. During this investigation, each important nodal memory will have to be revisited as many times as there are branches radiating from it. Each new arrival at a given nodal point will appear to be a return to something already "known," but each new departure from it will lead to fresh discoveries.

Our two-hour fragment of M. A.'s analysis fits precisely into this pattern. The sequence of the patient's associations traverses many nodal points already familiar to both patient and analyst, but the pathways leading away from these familiar points appear often to be new ones, leading, in many cases, to the recovery of new nodes whose contents have not previously been accessible to analytic exploration. The special role of dreams and dream interpretations in this process has been our chief concern.

CHAPTER 4

The Mechanism of Dream Construction

Dream IA: The Bathtub Dream

In chapter 3, we had the opportunity to observe the critical role of M. A.'s dreams in the unfolding of the associative pathway during the Thursday and Friday analytic hours. Here we will concentrate our attention on the dream elements as they emerged from the associative flow. This procedure will highlight the relationships among the various elements and show how they can be assembled according to the memory-cycle model to provide a detailed understanding of the process of dream construction.

We will begin with Dream IA:

Manifest Content

T3   Rooming house: A large bathtub, big tub, different one—first large room, second large tub. In other words, somewhere in this dream, I saw a bathroom—a large bathroom with a large tub. And when I got back towards the end of the dream, I saw a small bathroom with a very large tub. I remember that distinctly.

T15   This was on the second floor, this rooming house. I remember at the beginning of the dream I saw the large bathroom with a large tub, and at the end of the dream I saw the large tub and the small bathroom—it was almost cut right in half.

Present Component of the Latent Content (Substituted)

T3   Where have I seen tubs like this before? Well, in Judith's house—both in Atlanta and in Richmond—that is what it reminds me of. The only place I have seen large tubs.

Judith is M. A.'s current steady girlfriend, the subject of much preoccupation at this time. This is what would ordinarily be called the "day residue."

Past Component of the Latent Content (Substituted)

T35   I recall now that one day I saw Alice whisk by in the nude, "oh boy," that sort of thing.

T51   I might recall two or three other times, but that was about it—I was in my world and she was in her world—we never really, you know, spent time together. Of course, the house was such a small house—no, not really. She was as embarrassed as I. She whisked right through.

This memory of M. A.'s seeing his sister Alice in the nude can be dated closely. In response to the analyst's question he replied:

> PT: I know exactly. It was two or three years after I moved to Richmond, so I was thirteen or fourteen.

Although there is no explicit mention of a bathroom connected with this memory, it appears likely that a bathroom was part of the original scene.

The Matching of the Latent Contents of Dream IA

The manifest content of Dream IA would appear to be a composite image formed by the superimposition of the two components of the latent content identified above. The report of the day residue emphasizes the bathroom scene rather than the attractive woman associated with it; while in the report of the past memory, the emphasis appears to be reversed. The composite image reinforces the bathroom scenery but eliminates the attractive woman. It appears to concentrate on those concerns of the patient, represented in both the past and present components, which have to do with the number, size, and identities of the various houses and rooms in which such libidinally arousing experiences took place.

Dream IA as described above is fairly typical of dreams as they are reported in psychoanalysis. We see evidence of early libidinal interests of a scoptophilic character, and of censorship activity which removes direct references to the human body but allows it to be represented by a series of containers (houses, bathrooms, bathtubs).

In this case, the censorship appears to have been active *after* the past and present components of the latent contents had been superimposed and successively matched. Both components included images of attractive women and images of containing spaces associated with them. Each of these pairs of images would have been reinforced by the superimposition, and the composite image would have retained both. But the composite image of the attractive women was suppressed, leaving the composite image of the containing spaces as the manifest content of the dream.

It is possible, though I think unlikely, that the images of the attractive women were each deleted separately before the matching took place. What is clearly impossible in this example is that the censorship acted directly through the mechanism of superimposition to delete *unmatched* significant elements while retaining successfully matched insignificant elements. The latter was Freud's explanation for the role played by condensation in the activity of the dream censor.

Here it is clear that the mechanism of superimposition played no direct role in the censorship. The elimination of the attractive women from the dream was accomplished by part-for-whole substitution. This conclusion is unaltered whether the substitution took place in each component of the latent content before superimposition or, as appears more likely, in the composite image after superimposition.

Missing Elements in Dream IA

According to the memory-cycle model, the reported anxiety dream is unlikely to include the undistorted experiential elements which must have played a role in its construction. From the traditional psychoanalytic point of view, what is missing from Dream IA is primarily the direct, affect-laden representation of drive-related wishes and impulses. We have already made some conjectures about the exclusion of such material by a censorship mechanism operating during the formation of the dreams.

In addition to these excluded wishes, the memory-cycle model would identify the following missing elements:

1. For Dream IA, we would expect to find a day residue of considerably greater emotional significance than the passing thought of Judith's bathtubs. This would be the present component of the latent content which had been purposefully selected from the previous day's experience for introduction into the permanent memory, but then excluded by the dream censor.

2. We would also expect to find a specific memory of childhood which was to have been matched with the censored day residue. This would be a memory from much earlier in childhood than the memory of Alice "whisking by," a memory whose emotional significance was commensurate with that of the excluded day residue. Such a memory representation would be designated as the original past component of the latent content.

3. We would expect a clear-cut associative link between the substituted day residue and the original but censored day residue which it replaced. The imagery of containing spaces suggested by the rooming house, bathrooms, and bathtubs is likely to be involved in this linkage.

4. We might also expect to find some evidence of the original past component of the latent content in the manifest imagery of the dream. The sequence leading to this effect would be as follows: The series of past memories chosen to be matched with the original day residue would have included the as-yet-hypothetical original past component. After the substitution of the bathtub residue, the match with the original past component would have been unsuccessful. But some evidence of this failed match might still appear in the less-coherent details of the dream.

5. We are suggesting, in effect, that Dream IA is a *substitute* dream, and that the memory-cycle model predicts the existence of an original dream whose present and past components were linked associatively with the substituted components which appeared in the manifest content of the Bathtub Dream.

No evidence, either of this original dream or of its present and past components, emerged during the Thursday analytic hour in which Dream IA was reported.

The Thursday-Hour Interpretations

The major theme of the Thursday analytic hour was M. A.'s feeling of remoteness from his father, who in life was "a great bull of a man" (T27) and now in death created a "gray, ghostlike, stonish effect" (T41) in his mind. The transference of this feeling to the analyst was the subject of most of the interpretive work carried on during the hour.

By the end of the hour, it appeared that M. A.'s stereotyped image of his father had softened. The interpretations had provided him with an opporunity to compare his expectation that the analyst would respond to him like the rigid childhood representation of his father with the reality of the psychoanalytic situation. M. A. could now attempt an identification with the analyst which permitted an exchange of feelings impossible when the hour began.

The memory-cycle model predicts that in M. A.'s dreaming on Thursday night:

1. The positive experience of the analytic hour would be selected as a day residue for the dreams of the following night.
2. This new experience would be linked with the report of Dream IA in the new day residue.
3. The complex day residue formed in steps (1) and (2) would be matched during the dreaming of the following night with (a) the identical past memories which had contributed to the original dream, and with (b) new historical material from the same vicinity of the permanent memory structure.
4. The result would be a set of correction dreams which combined the elements of the earlier dreams with the new experience of the Thursday analytic hour. In the case at hand, we would expect Dream IA, from which representations of Father and his surrogates appear to have been deliberately excluded, to be dreamed over again with Father restored to his original place in the experiences which were matched to form the dreams. This would give us Dream IIA, in which Father's presence is connected with receptacle imagery associated with affectively charged libidinal activities.

Dream IIA: The Refrigerator Dream

M. A. spent the night immediately following the Thursday analytic hour in the sleep laboratory. When awakened near the end of each REM period, he reported three dreams in detail. Dream IIA was the first of these.

Manifest Content

> I was dreaming I was in the sleep lab, I believe, or I was one of a party of three, and I was a prisoner and the other two people were in charge of a refrigerator. I think I was one of three, and they were in

charge of a refrigerator which I had to move—part of the stuff which I had to move along belonged to my father—and I had to move that out of the refrigerator. And it was a big problem how it would go and where it was going—and against my will and against my timing, they took his things out. Then I guess they had me locked up somewhere and finally sort of forced me to cooperate, and I ended up on a three-man lift line—we were taking things, like Coca-Cola, out of the bottom shelf of the refrigerator and passing them up lickety-split and efficiently as possible into the other refrigerator, or into another receptacle. I was sort of working efficiently and putting in ice—there was not a bit of wasted motion—it was a beautiful operation in symmetry—and moves in the dream—I am not sure I can remember them. There were so many objects—I think there was an old hat of some sort, also objects of his clothes and my clothes—refrigerator and clothes—two other people, I think they were two brothers.

Further details of Dream IIA were added during the report of the dream to the analyst at the beginning of the Friday-morning hour:

F3 And then I found myself one of three people in some kind of a—I was a prisoner, sort of, and there was an icebox, and I had to move my father's things, you know, effects out of the icebox to make room for their stuff—but in reality it did not work that way.

F5 An icebox, a door open, there was three of us. One at the icebox door, one on a ladder, and one on top of the ladder putting stuff into another icebox. And I was not sure if I was one of those three at this point, but I was watching the way they worked, it was really a—I at first suggested that they work as some kind of water-bucket brigade. Everybody was putting things out of the box into the other box, but when they were lined up, I started handing things out of the icebox, and I handed them up to the next guy, and he handed it to the next guy and he shoved it in. It was really very efficient—I was marveling at the rhythm of the whole thing. I stepped back and another person took my place. And then when some person—when the guy down below who would stoop for a second, the second guy reached in and grabbed something and scurried up.

Present Component of the Latent Content

The day residues of Dream IIA include a very elaborate series of references to the transference situation. These references should be fully intelligible to the reader after our more detailed examination of the analytic hours. The analyst (and his double, the director of the laboratory, of whom M. A. was speaking just before falling asleep) is replacing Father as an adult male object of identification. M. A. is extremely ambivalent about this effect of the analysis, which has led to a reexperiencing of his loss of Father both in childhood fantasy and in recent actuality.

The connection between Father's death and the maternal references in the receptacle imagery of Dream IIA, however, did not originate during the Thursday hour. On the basis of the manifest content alone, in fact, we might infer only that the refrigerator dream (IIA) resulted directly from a superimposition during the dreaming state of the bathtub dream (IA), reported during the Thursday hour, and the interpretation of the paternal transference, which took place independently during the Thursday hour as the memory cycle model would predict.

But at this point we come upon direct evidence in M. A.'s associations that this connection was already on his mind when the bathtub dream was being constructed.

F7   And my father's possessions? Well, Mother, in fact, Tuesday, wanted me to look through some of his stuff to see whether I could wear it or keep it or what. There were ski boots and overshoes, and this and that. I have been doing that for the last two years—and it reminds me of that. So if there is anything left, I will give it away—for heaven's sake, the ski boots from the year two—they looked like hiking boots, not ski boots.

This experience, clearly represented in the manifest content of the refrigerator dream, actually took place on the dream day of the bathtub dream, Tuesday. It was considered important enough by the day-residue-selection mechanism to be preserved for two full days in order to be introduced into the permanent memory by the refrigerator dream.

The conversation on Tuesday has all the predicted characteristics of the emotionally significant original day residue which had been displaced from the bathtub dream. We can now surmise that the exclusion of Father from Dream IA was specifically related to Father's libidinal activities with Mother and to M. A.'s conflicting wishes to identify with him and to kill him. This hypothesis receives strong support from Dream IB, in which the absence of Father is much more clearly motivated. Dream IB contains no overt reference to Father or any surrogate male figure, in a context which otherwise has all the identifying features of the Oedipal triangle.

F9   Just to sidetrack—for some reason last night, I had a bad stomachache for a period of about two hours, and I am not sure what it was from. It was kind of interesting, though, why it should come on and why it suddenly went away. This was about eight-thirty to nine-thirty or ten o'clock. Now the date I had last night was named Jeanne—she is a skinny, sort of nondescript, awkward girl, a social worker from Cin-

cinnati, poorly dressed, not particularly personable, not too good-looking, just a waste-of-time sort of thing.

This early association (F9) followed *immediately after* the report of the refrigerator dream, and is undoubtedly the day residue which evoked the refrigerator imagery of childhood, discussed below. The connection between M. A.'s response to a woman and her adaptability to his fantasies of oral gratification is direct and clear. Later on we shall see that he imagines every woman to be "wasted" by the demands of his male rivals for her affection.

F47   I was thinking about food and family life. I was talking to this girl last night I brought. She visited some Italian family and they were feeding her and feeding her. We went to an Italian restaurant last night. She did not eat much. I ate quite a bit. The food was fair. I wouldn't push it particularly.

This reference (F47) to the same day residue *immediately precedes* the report of the childhood fantasy from which the receptacle imagery of Dreams IA and IIA was derived. It links the "boxes" of this fantasy with the "iceboxes" which represent them in the manifest content of the dream.

The Past Component of the Latent Content (Dream IIA)

F29–31

> PT: This icebox is higher up, you know—it is about six feet higher than the icebox we are taking the things out of.
> DR: What does that bring to mind?
> PT: A status stature—the higher you are, the higher you are, you know, and the higher you are physically, the higher you are status-wise. Worry about somebody else's icebox—some social plane—or something. I can see the icebox now—a big wide icebox. I don't know what else an icebox reminds me of. Where do I see iceboxes? There is an icebox in my home in Richmond at 236 Madison Street. It had a bad motor that was always humming at night. I used to get up to close the door to keep it quiet.

If "somebody else's icebox" is a representation of Mother (further confirmation will come in Dream IIB, where Mother is portrayed as "Miss Iceland, a beauty queen"), then the noises in the night are suggestive of parental sexual activity. This memory is dated by the house from about the same time as the memory of Alice "whisking by" in the nude, shortly after age twelve.

F47   I see a street corner curb, a washed street, red sidewalk, black street all wet. I could be in Ocean City. The only time I went to Ocean City

was—not the only time—but most of the times with my parents as a
young kid. I was looking, you know, seeing an Ocean City scene—the
Burgundy Hotel I stayed at, and then a floor scene and open box. The
open box turns into a smaller box, and suddenly the smaller box turns
into a big box of beetles, and they were slithering across the floor and
disappearing in the crevices—huge bugs. I started to laugh yesterday.
In all the dreams that I ever had I never laughed in a dream either. I
laugh sometimes but Jesus, images or dreams are usually somber.

This appears to be the memory of a fantasy or dream originally
experienced during the Oedipal period, perhaps at age three or four. It
is a crude representation of the "primal scene," parental sexual intercourse, through images derived from anal excretory functioning. We see
at once that this memory is the source of the activity represented in
Dream IIA. The transfer of Father's "effects" from lower to higher
refrigerator is a transformation of the anal impregnation fantasy represented in the childhood memory as the sudden change of a small,
empty box into a large box filled with beetles.

We now have a sufficiently complete set of elements for Dream IIA
to reconstruct the matching process during which it was constructed.
From the experience of the present, we have the conversation with
Mother, setting the overall theme: the patient's problem in identifying
with Father's strengths without acquiring all the vulnerabilities associated with his own Oedipal fantasies. The interaction of the Thursday
analytic hour has aroused M. A.'s hopes that the good and bad effects of
Father can be separated, but the new possibilities in relation to the
analyst are still fraught with conflict and ambivalence; hence the doubled
figure of the analyst in Dream IIA, whose efficiency is admired but whose
strength is still greatly feared. The report of the bathtub dream is part
of the same day residue, and, as we have seen, its presence facilitates the
choice of past memories for the matching.

From the past comes the image of the refrigerator, which, like Miss
Iceland, the beauty queen of Dream IIB, represents Mother in both her
enticing and rejecting aspects. This double image of Mother has been
superimposed on the anal-impregnation fantasy represented in the beetle
memory at the Burgundy Hotel.

This combination probably reflects an underlying common fantasy
dating from the earliest nodal points in the memory tree—a fantasy
which equates all pleasurable activity with the transfer of the contents
of one body into a cavity in another body. Seen in these terms, personal
interactions at the oral level involve the transfer of something good
inside Mother into the baby (*bottles* in Dream IIA). At the anal level,

something bad inside the baby is transferred into a cavity in Mother (*beetles* in the memory of the Burgundy Hotel). Intercourse is the transfer of something good inside the baby into a cavity in Mother (difficult to imagine). Death is the transfer of the whole body, instead of its contents, into a cavity in Mother (easy to imagine).

The day residue, compounded from the conversation with Mother on Tuesday, the report of Dream IA (the bathtub dream), the interaction of the Thursday analytic hour, and the unsatisfying dinner engagement on Thursday evening, was matched in Dream IIA (the refrigerator dream) with the image constructed from the combination of the childhood memories of the refrigerator and the anal impregnation fantasy at the Burgundy Hotel. The manifest content of the dream resulted from the superimposition of all of these elements.

The matching of Dream IIA was made easier by the presence in its day residue of the report of Dream IA. The anal-impregnation fantasy which formed the major past component of the refrigerator dream had already played a part in the construction of the bathtub dream.

We can now recognize the rooming house in Dream IA as the hotel in which the fantasy took place. The large and small bathrooms at the beginning and end of this dream are the "open box" which "turns into a smaller box" of the fantasy. The large bathtubs may represent either the next stage in the transformation of the boxes, this time into "a big box of beetles," or the crevices into which the beetles disappeared. The unmentioned toilets in the bathroom images would have provided the initial connecting link with the childhood memory.

The match between the boxes of the anal-impregnation fantasy at the hotel and the bathtubs and bathrooms of Judith's two houses was not completely successful, as the obscurity of the manifest dream indicates, but it is clear that such a match was attempted. What is missing from the bathtub dream is the idea of transferring the contents of one container into another—the idea central to the excluded element of the original day residue, the conversation with Mother about the removal of Father's belongings from her house.

This condensed version of the anal-impregnation fantasy, contained in the bathtub dream, was included in the Thursday residue which was to be matched during the dreaming of Thursday night with the existing contents of the permanent memory. The linking-up of the condensed version in the day residue with the original version in the permanent memory would have been a simple task for the matching mechanism.

It is now clear that in identifying the most significant elements in the present and past components of Dream IIA, the conversation with

Mother about removing Father's belongings and the anal-impregnation fantasy at the Burgundy Hotel, we have also identified the missing original elements of Dream IA. The conversation with Mother was excluded from the bathtub dream on Tuesday night by the censorship mechanism, and the memory of the anal-impregnation fantasy was incompletely matched with the substituted present component, the thought of Judith's bathrooms.

These original elements would have been matched with each other in the bathtub dream of Tuesday night if not for the intervention of the censor. By reassembling the identical elements with the aid of the dream report and the interpretations of the Thursday hour, the refrigerator dream corrected the deficit in the permanent memory which had resulted from the failure to successfully match these elements in the original Tuesday-night dream.

The correction dream puts the dreamer's current reality-oriented experience (in this case, the experience of the analytic hour) to work in the ongoing nightly process of expansion and reorganization of his permanent memory structure. In the sequence of Dreams IA and IIA, we have seen it circumvent a neurotic defensive operation: the censorship of the original day residue with its reference to the anxiety-laden subject of Father's death. We can assume with a high degree of confidence that prior to this episode in M. A.'s analysis, the censorship would have prevented the adaptive function of the memory cycle from successfully introducing the new information acquired in the analysis into the sector of the memory structure containing these very frightening early memories.

Let us consider what might have happened if the censorship mechanism had prevented the representation of the actual primal-scene experience at the Burgundy Hotel from being successfully introduced into the permanent memory at the time of the original childhood experience. Then a mismatch would have resulted and produced an anxiety dream—i.e., the beetle fantasy. The anxiety dream could have awakened M. A., become incorporated into a new day residue, evaded the dream censor, and finally have been introduced into the permanent memory *in place of* the original experience. This would then raise the interesting possibility that the past component of an adult dream may sometimes be a remembered anxiety dream of childhood.

The evidence that the beetle fantasy is actually a remembered dream is circumstantial but persuasive. First, there is the dreamlike quality of the imagery itself. There is M. A.'s remark immediately following the report of the fantasy in which he compares it with "all the dreams I ever

had" (F47). There is his statement a bit earlier (F31): "This is crazy—
I am having dreams just lying here."

Finally, there is the following series of associations early in the
Thursday hour. The second paragraph below, from T15, followed
directly on an association to the main theme of Dream IB, suggesting
that earlier dreams about the Burgundy Hotel were linked with this
dream as well as with IA.

T13   Let's bang away at this thing—maybe I can recall something. What
      rooming house means—I don't know except that I have had dreams
      about rooming houses before.

T15   Looking for girls—that is nothing unusual, and parties—that is nothing
      unusual. Why I am taking the film must be something else. Now . . .
      This might have been two or three dreams, and I got them all confused.
      This is probably right, because it is a funny thing—once I remember a
      dream and articulate it, I can't recall the bloody thing again. I can
      remember back—even back to dreams where I was at a beach with
      Ralph Farber, and the beach house, and driving along—my memory
      is not all that bad—it is just logged in at once.

Dreams about rooming houses and dreams about beaches and beach
houses suggest a series of recurrent dreams in which the experience in
the Burgundy Hotel at Ocean City was represented. The beetle "fantasy"
would have been the prototype for this series of dreams.

It is now possible to recognize the references to recurrent dreams in
each of the last two quotations as associations which identify elements
belonging to the past components of the latent contents of both Dreams
IA and IB. In the case of Dream IA, the bathtub dream, we have direct
evidence from the manifest content that the beetle memory was one of
its original past components.

Taking this line of reasoning one step further, we are led to the
hypothesis, subject to clinical confirmation, that every dream of the past
which is remembered in an analytic hour in association to a dream of
the previous night is either itself an element of the past component of
the recent dream or else contains within its own past component an
element of the past component of the recent dream.

In the bathtub dream–refrigerator dream sequence, the correction
dream directly incorporated the revived original day residue of the
index dream which had been deleted by the dream censor on Tuesday
night. This revived original day residue tended to overshadow the report
of the index dream in the new day residue of the correction dream. The
receptacle imagery of the bathtub dream was absorbed into the
refrigerator imagery of the correction dream during the process of super-

imposition. If we were unaware of the existence of the deleted original day residue, however, we would nevertheless have had little difficulty in recognizing the relationship between the two dreams.

In the case of Dreams IB and IIB, there will be no evidence of a deleted original day residue revived and incorporated into the correction dream. Dream IB supplies both the imagery and the action which form the day residue for the correction dream, IIB. Here the correction dream has the effect of clarifying and elaborating the index dream, which seems to have been much less damaged by the action of the dream censor than was Dream IA. This variant of the correction mechanism is closer to the theoretical model described in chapter 2, but it is clear that in both sequences the same adaptive purpose is being served.

Dream IB : The Photographer Dream

Manifest Content

T3   And then I put down married. What? Kate Davis instead of Ellen Thornwald.

T7   I decided something and I dropped her off because I made a mistake. I married one instead of the other. Now . . . a wife in here—I don't know what the hell she is doing in this dream, and I got a Fairfax and a local church—I was writing this in the morning and have not looked at it since then. And I go there or to an antique shop or a garden—I am not sure what—and I was single when I went there. This is quite a dream. I was making a film, and I was also looking for girls at parties where I was making the film, and I was single. I had to get married in a church or a garden or an antique shop. And Ellen looked much better in the dream then she looks in reality.

T15   And I was single. I am still single. I am making a film. I am always running around taking pictures of everybody, everybody's family, and this and that—I am the historian, the photographer.

Present Component of the Latent Content

T2–3 DR: This was Tuesday night?

        PT: Yes, not last night—it was Tuesday night. Tuesday night—where was I Tuesday night? I was in Richmond Tuesday night? Right—and I had just finished reading a couple of chapters of the book—*Reality Therapy*—if that means anything.

The status of this fragment as a day residue of Dream IB is confirmed later in the Thursday hour, when M. A. reports his fantasy that if he were undergoing "reality therapy" rather than psychoanalysis, his therapist would show him directly how to find the right woman (T55).

Past Component of Latent Content

No recognizable childhood memory contributing its imagery to Dream IB emerged during the Thursday hour. We are therefore unable to comment on the matching process as it took place in this dream. The Oedipal theme is obvious. The young women whose representations were suppressed in Dream IA are present here, but without sexual characteristics or individual personalities.

The image of M. A.'s father, or, indeed, any other adult male figure, has been excluded from both dreams. At the moment, we do not know at what stage in the construction of the dream this exclusion took place. The day residue, *Reality Therapy*, refers indirectly to the analyst in a paternal transference role, but this reference is not recognizable in the manifest content of Dream IB. M. A.'s labeling of himself as "the historian, the photographer," is a clear associative link, however, which suggests an attempt to identify with Father in childhood through a relationship which provided some gratification of a scoptophilic nature.

Missing Elements in Dream IB

The same basic considerations apply to Dream IB as to IA, although the manifest content of IB is more extensive in both time and space and more easily related to the current transference situation of the analysis.

1. As mentioned earlier, the considerable emotional significance of the day residue concerned with the reading of *Reality Therapy* was worked out in detail during the analytic hour. The search for the right woman was a constant preoccupation which appeared directly in the manifest content. We therefore know the source of one element in the present component. This is the analyst's nonparticipation in the patient's fantasied solution of the Oedipal conflict, in which Father indicates his compliance by selecting the perfect mate for M. A. The "unreal" analyst corresponds to the absent Father-surrogate in the dream. The obvious missing element of the present component is the one related to the women in his life at the moment, particularly to Judith, whom M. A. fears he will be forced to marry. The insignificant and interchangeable women who actually appear in the dream must have been substituted

for Judith in a contemporary context not yet known to us. Why the marriage will take place in "a church or a garden or an antique shop" is at this point in the sequence an unanswered question.

2. Specific experiences of the past which may have participated in the matching of Dream IB are missing. But we do have indications that these memories may be related to books M. A. has read, weddings he has attended, and photographs he has taken. All of these suggest a scoptophilic interest in his parents' marital relationship. It is possible that fantasy material from early in life concerning this relationship was presented to the matching mechanism but failed to be matched with the diffuse substituted day residues.

3. The complexity of this dream and the relative transparency of its present component suggest that Dream IB was less disrupted by the action of the dream censor than Dream IA, and that substitutions were made in a more piecemeal fashion.

4. One possibility of great interest, which will be explored further on, is that some of the elements missing from Dreams IA and IB may be common to the two dreams, despite the apparent lack of correspondence between their manifest contents.

Dream IIB: The King Ranch Dream

Manifest Content

I dreamed about a police officer named Phil—a school bus—dreamed about running a ranch and Miss Iceland—a beauty queen—and the rancher—his name was King, I guess. The King Ranch. And he married Miss Iceland, and I asked him how he met her, and he said his cousin fixed him up in Iceland. And about the police officer—I guess he was collecting furniture or something. Furniture? As I talk about this dream of a security member, mentioning furniture—I see an open casket, an image of an open casket.

F5   I was an owner of a ranch in Texas and my name was Mr. King—Robert King—King Ranch, and I married Miss Iceland, a beauty queen. This was a beautiful girl; this was a beauty queen. And then I stood back, and then I became a third person. I asked King how he happened to meet this beautiful beauty queen. He said he had a cousin who lived in Iceland, and he got fixed up. I said, hum, not bad.

This is the correction dream for Dream IB, the photographer dream, in which M. A. was unable to find the right woman and was compelled to marry someone who was literally unrecognizable to him. Father and the role he played in the patient's dilemma were excluded from the dream by the censorship mechanism. In Dream IIB, we see the same situation reworked with Father represented in three different roles. He is the superego figure (the policeman) who will punish the patient for his infractions against the incest taboo, the powerful phallic figure (Mr. King) with whom the patient would like to identify, and the supportive figure (the cousin) who provides the right woman for him.

Present Component of the Latent Content

As with Dream IIA—the other Thursday-night correction dream—three basic elements in the present component of this dream are easily identified. First, there is the report of Dream IB itself, with its theme of identity diffusion in the context of a choice of marital partners. Second, there is the original day residue of Dream IB—the fantasy evoked in the patient by his reading of *Reality Therapy* that the analyst would make the choice of a woman for him. This element was excluded from the manifest content of Dream IB by the censorship, but it is represented in the manifest content of the correction dream, IIB, by the cousin who lived in Iceland who "fixed him up." Third, there is the interaction of the analytic hour, which made possible the representation of Father in three quite distinct active roles, relative to each of which the patient imagined himself as a passive partner.

F11   Now this Icelandic beauty queen. I have seen her before. This is really a stunning girl, and Judith showed me a picture when she was married—an entirely different girl than she was now. She is very thin and sort of pale and emaciated-looking. When she got married she was a very round-faced—not plump, but an extremely blond, blond sort of a girl. If I saw her picture now, I mean, I still would say, "That is not you, absolutely not you." And there was some similarity between the beauty queen and what Judith used to look like. Maybe there is something there, I don't know—coming from Iceland—there has got to be a relationship there. Mr. King is another one of those characters like Howard Hughes, you know, that I admire—immense wealth—a lot of power—doesn't seem to—well, from what I know just a recluse, in a way. And he got married last in life I noted in the dream. I am sure he would appreciate me marrying a . . . again—whatever it is.

Although we do not know exactly when Judith showed M. A. her picture, we can tell from the context that M. A. identifies that time as the present. We do know that his ambivalence about marrying Judith is a current preoccupation. For these reasons, I think we would be justified in assuming that the comparison between Judith as she is and Judith as she was in the picture took place or was remembered consciously on Tuesday. Judith's wedding picture in the present component would then have been matched with the wedding pictures taken by M. A. in the past. F11 would then be the day residue missing from the present component of Dream IB. The two women in Dream IB, one of whom M. A. was compelled to marry, may represent Judith past and present, as well, ultimately, as Mother in childhood and Judith in the present.

The parapraxis "he got married last in life" suggests once again the fantasy that marriage is followed immediately by death. This would link the associations just quoted (F11) with the conversation with Mother on Tuesday and with the cemetery alluded to in Dream IB, the photographer dream, on Tuesday night. The image of "an open casket" which follows the marriage scene in the correction dream, IIB, makes this juxtaposition explicit for the first time.

Although the evidence here is not as strong as in the case of the receptacle dreams, it appears likely that the F11 associations, comparing Judith past and present, recall a conscious fantasy which took place originally on Tuesday and formed the major element of the present component of Dream IB. This element was altered by the substitution of two current female acquaintances—Kate Davis and Ellen Thornwald—for the images of the two Judiths. The correction dream, IIB, might then have recovered these deleted fragments and incorporated them into its own day residue along with the more complex view of Father which resulted from the interpretations of the Thursday analytic hour.

At this point, we can also deal with the unanswered question about the location of the forced wedding in Dream IB. In F7 we have had M. A.'s report of the conversation on Tuesday with his mother concerning the disposition of Father's remaining possessions. This is the clue to the meaning of "a church or a garden or an antique shop." We are now aware that the single entity which is related to all three of these images is a cemetery. It would appear that this hidden reference, despite its obscurity, was successfully matched in Dream IIB with the image of the casket, whose presence at the conclusion of that dream is otherwise completely unexplained. M. A. would be married where Father was buried—i.e., inside Mother. Removing Father's remains from Mother's house opened the way for the fantasied consummation of M. A.'s Oedipal wishes, with the same fatal consequences which befell Father.

Past Component of the Latent Content

F31–33

> PT: Here is a crazy image.
> DR: Yes?
> PT: I don't know. I just lost—about a book. Can you have two split-images at the same time? I see myself or somebody saying, "Do you hate me?" At least me saying, "Do you hate me?" A little boy standing there, and then I see the image of a book, and a pile of books, pocket books in front of a bookstore.

This childhood memory—perhaps also the memory of a childhood dream—must have been evoked for matching with the representation of the "Reality Therapy" fantasy during the preliminary scanning for Dream IB on Tuesday night. Further associations make it clear that it was parental hatred which the patient feared when he was the little boy in the "crazy image." This would correspond closely to the hatred he expected from the analyst for his disloyalty in reading about a form of therapy which promised better and faster results. The reading of books in childhood must also have signified disloyalty to his parents' mercantile way of life.

Although the book memory was probably deleted from Dream IB along with the experience of reading *Reality Therapy*, it does not appear in the manifest content of the correction dream, IIB, where it is represented indirectly by the cousin who "fixed up" Mr. King. The fact that the book memory emerged in M. A.'s associations to the Thursday dream does suggest, however, that the correction dream was instrumental in bringing it to conscious awareness.

F51

> A rug and a floor somewhere, and then a rug rolled up, and enters a man struggling to get out of the rug—struggling—you know he is wrapped up in his rug—that is how it looked lying on the floor. I know the rug—it is a cheap carpet, wool carpet of some sort. While I am talking about birds, etc., and traveling and analyzing this, I see this guy squirming out of the rug he is wrapped up in.

This memory, perhaps another remembered dream, appears to be related to the hidden cemetery image of Dream IB, the photographer dream. It suggests a man being buried alive, perhaps engulfed in the embrace of a powerful antagonist. In the associations which follow, the antagonist is identified as Mother, and a connection is made with the furniture collection of Dream IIB which had been matched with the antique shop of IB:

F55 PT: Rugs? Judith spending all her money on rugs, for one thing. I spend a lot of time on the rug in my apartment, handling my—gee, I am really creating rugs. Just made a white circle, a blue circle, and circle rug—brown rugs—like . . . three rings. Mother's white rugs—never walk on them, you know, get very upset about getting them dirty. Had a big oriental rug one time—we sold it to somebody in Richmond. In fact, it was the widow of Dr. Anderson who bought it. Why I remember that so distinctly? It is a funny thing—I sold a lot of things, and I never was interested in furniture then, but I remember the big to-do about it. It was huge, huge, it must have been 30 x 30 oriental rug—I thought anyway. Maybe it was 20 x 30, a big one. This was long before I even thought of furniture or anything.

Judith, Mother, and the doctor's widow are women who have been deprived of their men and are therefore likely to make impossible demands on the patient, whose childish inadequacy is represented by his exaggerated estimate of the size of the rug. (He had mentioned in the Thursday hour that the house was actually a fairly small one.)

The rug itself has a number of meanings. It is something which has outlived its usefulness and must be disposed of, like Father's remains. But it is also the maternal enclosure which caused Father's death. Walking on the rug with dirty feet is another version of intercourse with Mother represented in anal terms, as in the beetle fantasy. Yet M. A. mentions twice that his interest in the rug antedated his envy of Father's power, as represented by the furniture collection of the policeman in Dream IIB, and by the large and beautiful hand-rubbed executive desk of his fantasy earlier in the Friday hour (F15). The furniture, of course, also includes the open casket of Dream IIB, another deadly enclosure.

The rug memory is clearly one member of a cluster of images in the permanent memory relating to the imagined danger of engulfment at many developmental levels. Within this cluster, no distinction is made between oral, anal, and genital experiences of enclosure. The beetle fantasy, previously encountered, belongs to this cluster, too. In the matching process of Dream IIB, only the furniture image and the casket were able to survive from this complex of childhood memories, because of the paucity of corresponding imagery in the present component of that dream.

Other specific memories of childhood which may have contributed to the manifest content of the King Ranch dream are lacking. The figures of Mr. King and Miss Iceland would be typical parental representations for a child preoccupied by phallic narcissistic concerns during the Oedipal period. The quality of the actual imagery of the dream suggests to me that the immediate experiences which gave rise to it took place in adolescence and were introduced into the memory tree subordinate to nodes containing memories of the phallic/Oedipal period.

The King Ranch received national publicity when its racehorse, Assault, won the Triple Crown for three-year-olds. M. A. was then in his early teens. Assault was a small horse with a deformed foot, from whom little was expected. M. A. must have felt a close identification with this equine Oedipus. If so, we may have located the source of the missing past component which was matched with the report of Dream IB to form the correction dream, IIB. This identification would also explain the isolated references to horses scattered through M. A.'s associations.

It would be surprising indeed if every associative thread introduced during two rather eventful psychoanalytic hours could be woven into a complete explanatory fabric without the help of new associative material from later hours. We shall have to settle for an understanding of the past components of the latent contents of Dreams IB and IIB which is incomplete. In the background of these two dreams about marriage we have found repeated oblique references to the theme of death and burial. In Dreams IA and IIA, we have seen a vivid elaboration of the infantile spatial analogies between the receptacles within and without the body involved in the most intimate human experiences, including the powerful and puzzling experiences of love and death.

On the basis of our analysis of Dreams IB and IIB, we might expect to find that M. A.'s permanent memory structure also contains a convergence of imagery related to the public, social and ceremonial aspects of these most significant human events, dating, perhaps from the experience in close proximity during the Oedipal period of a wedding and a funeral involving members of his extended family.

A Note on the Mechanism of Superimposition

Is the mechanism of superimposition sufficient to account for the narrative complexity of a dream like the refrigerator dream (IIA)? Our data do not provide an answer to this interesting question, but they do leave open the possibility that the sequential arrangement of the superimposed images is determined by a higher-level integrative mechanism.

Greenberg and Pearlman, (1975b) following French and Fromm, have argued plausibly that dreams have an integrative function which goes beyond the matching process required by the memory cycle. The evolution of the central nervous system offers many examples in which a basic adaptive function like the matching process has become the foundation for a whole series of related higher-level functions.

Until more direct evidence of these higher-level integrative processes appears, however, I would prefer to assume that the matching process, together with the censorship, accounts for all the observable reatures of the manifest dream. Relatively simple mechanisms for arranging the dream elements in a sequence with narrative continuity are easily imaginable.

It is possible that the narrative sequence is itself a dream element derived from a memory representation. The superimposition of dream elements takes place in a virtual space-time of four dimensions. There is no obvious reason why images changing in time cannot be fitted together in a four-dimensional space as well as a space of two or three dimensions, using the corresponding four-dimensional Gestalt characteristics of the imagery.

If the narrative sequence were derived from only one of the memory representations, the superimposed three-dimensional images of the two components would appear in the dream with the original narrative sequence unchanged, giving the effect of a real "story" involving imaginary people and objects. In Dream IIA, I have the strong impression of a childhood memory in which M. A. watched his father at work in the factory with one of his employees, with the same mixed feelings of admiration and fear he later experienced while observing his analyst and Dr. R. at work.

If the narrative sequence in the dream is not derived from one or more of the experiences represented in the dream, it may be determined by a quasi-linguistic mechanism such as the one proposed by Edelson (1972). It is now a very simple matter to program a digital computer to produce grammatically correct sentences, given a set of nouns, verbs, adjectives, and so on to work with. The program need have no semantic capability whatever. Difficulties arise only if we ask the computer to determine the grammatical classes itself or if we insist that the sentences it produces be meaningful.

Some of the grammatically correct nonsense sentences created by such a program have a dreamlike quality, e.g., Chomsky's well-known example, "Colorless green ideas sleep furiously." It is possible to imagine a generative grammar of images which first assigns "grammatical" categories to images on the basis of their Gestalt characteristics (or even a primitive semantic segmentation) and then arranges them in sequences which have the subject-action-object ordering of grammatical sentences. The output of such a program would also give the appearance of real "stories" with imaginary characters in them.*

Neither of the alternatives outlined above would require an evaluation of the meaningfulness of the sequences it produces, in contrast to the higher-order integrative functions proposed by Greenberg and Pearlman. It seems to me that the dreaming state would not be burdened with problem-solving goals much easier to achieve with the conceptual tools available in waking consciousness. The matching process in dreams appears to be designed specifically to answer the requirements of the memory cycle for rapid lower-level processing of large quantities of information. Processing at a higher level of integration would impose very strict limits on the quantity of information that could be evaluated and the rapidity with which this small quantity could be handled.

I believe that Freud was correct in surmising that the cognitive mechanisms operant in dreaming are simpler and more primitive than those we are more familiar with in the waking state. But these primitive mechanisms have a critical adaptive function to perform: the linking of present and past experience through the memory cycle. In contrast with Freud's usage, "primitive" in this context does not imply disorder, aimlessness, or lack of determination.

---

* The ancient idea that the dream is a message has been undergoing a contemporary revival, stimulated by the recent achievements of transformational linguistics (Edelson 1972, Foulkes 1978). Foulkes, for example, conceptualizes the distortion of meaning by the dream censor as the transformational component of a generative grammar. This formula reverses the meaning-enhancing role of transformation rules in Chomskian linguistics. It also obscures Foulkes' own very interesting descriptive analysis of the mechanism of displacement, as well as the computational activity of the mechanism which initiates the construction of the dream.

CHAPTER 5

A New Foundation for the Theory of Dreams

The Data of the Sleep Laboratory

The original formulation of the memory-cycle model in Chapter 2 concerned itself with the adaptive function of dreaming which had been overlooked for so long by the traditional psychoanalytic theory of dreams. It made no attempt to specify how the dreamer's defenses might interfere with the carrying out of the information-processing function of the dream.

One result of this selective attention to the adaptive mechanisms of the matching process was a picture of the dream which was a little too good to be universally true. Although it still appears likely that the great majority of unremembered dreams have not been degraded by the censorship mechanism, it is clear that many—if not most—of the awakening dreams reported in analysis are of the pathological variety which led Freud to his discovery of the dream censor.

Thanks to the dream data collected in the sleep laboratory, we are now able to see precisely where in the process of dream construction the defensive operations of the censorship come into play. The contrast between M. A.'s originally reported *censored* dreams, IA and IB, and the

uncensored correction dreams, IIA and IIB, collected in the sleep laboratory, is striking.

In the censored index dreams, the final form of the manifest content
was the outcome of a struggle in which the defensive interference of the
dream censor had prevented the adaptive purpose for which the dream
was created from being achieved. In the correction dreams, much less
familiar to us, this outcome was reversed. The emotionally significant
material originally excluded by the censor was reincorporated into a new
set of dreams in which the adaptive function of dreaming was clearly
exemplified.

Together, these two sets of dreams give us a more balanced picture of
the process of dream construction, which now appears to us as an arena
in which primitive mechanisms of adaptation and defense may enter
into direct confrontation. In fact, these observations provide us with an
empirical foundation for a new psychoanalytic theory of dreams which
takes into account both the adaptive function of the memory cycle and
Freud's discovery of the defensive activity of the censorship mechanism.

The major points of this theory have been explained and illustrated
during our analysis of M. A.'s dreams and his associations to them. In
this chapter I will discuss a number of problems in the traditional psychoanalytic theory of dreams which appear to me to be resolved by the
memory-cycle model as amended here. Each of these issues spills over
into other areas of psychoanalytic theory, in some cases with what I would
expect to be very wide-ranging effects, but I will confine my comments
in this chapter to the process of dream construction.

The following topics will be considered:

1. Defense and adaptation
2. The mechanisms of substitution and superimposition
3. The concept of "latent content" in Freud's writings on dreams
4. Information and impulse in dream construction
5. Wish-fulfillment in dreams.

Defense and Adaptation

I will not attempt to trace the history of these many-valued terms in
psychoanalytic discourse. What is important here is the constantly recurrent tendency to collapse the distinction between the two. This

tradition began with Freud's characterization of the Ego as a derivative of the Id, which led him to think that all adaptive mechanisms—indeed, all structures in the psychic apparatus—originate as defenses against the overriding power of unconscious impulses.

More recent observations of developmental psychologists, both the followers of Piaget and child analysts, indicate that the ego has its own developmental line which can be clearly identified as early as the first week of life (Wolff, 1960, 1966). Defensive behavior cannot be recognized as such until much later. It has accordingly become customary, following Hartmann, to speak of both adaptive and defensive *aspects* of any given mental activity, relative to other lower- and higher-level activities which determine its intrapsychic context.

In a somewhat broader interpretation of the new developmental findings, all mental activity can be considered to be adaptive at the time it originates. Only the stereotyped repetition of the same activity in a context which calls for a novel response would then be considered "defensive." This formulation, when it is applied by the analyst in the clinical situation, often helps the patient acknowledge his responsibility for childhood wishes and fantasies without blaming or devaluing himself.

Greenberg and Pearlman (1975b) apply this broader approach to dreams. They consider the mechanism of dream construction to be adaptive in the sense that it integrates new information into the dreamer's overall view of the world, but defensive insofar as the result of the integration is consistent with previously held anachronistic patterns of thought and feeling. In Piaget's terms, the *accommodation* of the existing defensive structures to the new information is adaptive; the *assimilation* of the new information to the old patterns is defensive.

I have no quarrel with this view as long as it is clear that it refers to the *ultimate* disposition of the new information introduced into permanent storage by the memory cycle. However, our data indicate that in a given instance the process of dream construction may become the battleground between a primitive mechanism which is singularly adaptive and a primitive mechanism which is peculiarly defensive. The purpose of these mechanisms is unambiguous. One of them promotes the flow of information through the psychic apparatus, while the other retards it.

I would like to suggest that these mechanisms are not only primitive but prototypical, and that all higher-order mechanisms of adaptation or defense have the properties of promoting or retarding this flow of information. By this reading, any mental activity which creates a new connection between two elements of experience is adaptive. (Here we are allowing the term "element" to refer to units of any size.) After this adaptive step has been taken, a further choice between accommodation and assimilation can be made.

If the new element formed by the combination of the original elements is treated as something novel and unique, then the world-view of the subject must be accommodated to it. This second step is also an adaptive one. If, on the other hand, a decision is made to regard the new element as identical to some other previously existing element—most particularly, as identical to one of the original elements from which the new combination itself was formed—then the new element will have been assimilated to existing preconceptions. The second step in this case is defensive.

Rather than two such steps, we can imagine a whole series of steps in which the new element is combined with still other elements to form increasingly larger compositions. Each time a new composition is formed, it is tested again. If the decision at any given step is for accommodation, then the series continues and another new combination is formed. The series will normally end when an act of accommodation which does not involve the forming of new combinations requiring further evaluation occurs. It may be terminated prematurely at any step, however, if a decision is made to assimilate the newest element to previously existing elements.

In each case, the choice of accommodation leads to the creation of a new relationship, either with other experiential elements or within an expanded program for acting on the environment. The choice for assimilation leads to the substitution of an element which is less meaningful in context than the element being substituted for.

In the clinical situation, we frequently see an interpretation or clarification of the analyst's initiating a series of new connections in the development of the patient's thought and feelings. Most commonly, the series is broken off before it reaches the point at which the analyst had been aiming. The breaking-off of the series always involves the substitution of a preexisting element for the newest element formed in the series. Each of the completed steps in the series is an act of adaptation. Only the decision to break off the series is defensive. Once again, there is no ambiguity.

Greenberg and Pearlman appear to suggest a similar series of steps taking place unconsciously during the dreaming process itself. In my view, this is unlikely, though possible. The matching mechanism is designed to maximize its ability to make new connections as rapidly as

possible. It appears to be poorly suited for the repeated finely discrimina-
tive decision-making procedures required by the choices between accommodation and assimilation.

Nevertheless, even if such a series of integrative steps actually does
take place in dreaming, I would still be reluctant to refer to it as the
incorporation of a new experience into the dreamer's defenses, as
Greenberg and Pearlman do. The incorporation of new information into
larger elements can only be adaptive. While the decision to break off
the integrative series is certainly aimed at the preservation of the existing
defensive structure, any previously incorporated elements must always
be potentially available for further integrative steps if later experience
abrogates the decision to treat them defensively.

To sum up, the new dream data suggest clear and univalent definitions
of adaptive functioning as that which enhances the flow of information
through the psychic apparatus, and of defensive functioning as that
which retards the flow of information. The data also reveal simple but
efficient mechanisms which operate unambiguously within these definitions, the mechanisms of superimposition (adaptive) and substitution
(defensive).

I have gone beyond the data in suggesting that these mechanisms
may be prototypical of adaptive and defensive mechanisms in general.
In support of this hypothesis, I have offered an analysis of the more
complex act of cognitive and affective integration as a series of simpler
steps, each of which may be identified unambiguously as either adaptive
or defensive. For reasons of clarity and conceptual economy, it seems
reasonable to adopt this formulation as a working hypothesis in preference to the alternative of attributing both adaptive and defensive
qualities to every act of the psychic apparatus.

When seen in this light, adaptive and defensive mental activities
display a critical distinguishing feature. Adaptive activities are *bipolar*
and *symmetrical.* They involve the bringing together of *two* elements of
experience for comparison and evaluation, and, depending on the outcome
of these steps, for the formation of a new connection between them. An
adaptive activity creates a new *relationship* between two previously
existing elements, each of which is equally important to the overall
process.

By contrast, a defensive activity is *unipolar* and *asymmetrical.* It
intrudes on a *single* element of experience to minimize its significance
and deprive it of meaningful context. In the course of this action, a
second element is required to function as a substitute for the first, but
this element is chosen for its *lack* of significance in the area which

evokes the defensive response. The substituted element may have *any* of an enormous number of possible associative relationships to the original, as long as it lacks the attribute considered threatening by the defense mechanism.

The traditional psychoanalytic theory of dreams assumes that mental activities which participate in dream construction typically originate as unipolar and asymmetrical impulses which intrude themselves on passive elements in their surroundings. (Two such impulses may coincidentally converge on a single passive element, but never for a preexisting adaptive purpose.) This assumption reduces the process of dream construction to *defensive* activity. It denies the continuity and cumulativeness in dreaming which the memory-cycle model requires and which our data conclusively demonstrate.

We turn now to a more detailed discussion of the two simple mechanisms whose opposing aims have complicated our understanding of this process for so long.

Substitution and Superimposition

According to traditional theory, the mechanisms of displacement and condensation are both typical examples of nonrational primary-process mental activity. Our data indicate that these two mechanisms actually operate in opposition to one another in the process of dream construction. If we generalize this finding from dreams to unconscious mental activity *in toto*, as Freud did, what is the picture of primary-process activity which results?

We recall Freud's familiar image of the id as, "a chaos, a cauldron full of seething excitations . . . . Instinctual cathexes seeking discharge— that, in our view, is all there is in the Id." (1933, pp. 73–75) The activity taking place in this cauldron is, by definition, primary-process activity. Schur (1966b) suggests that this image was not meant by Freud to be descriptive of primary-process derivatives as they actually appear in the clinical situation. It is rather the concretization of an explanatory concept: the idea that all primary-process derivatives can ultimately be traced back to an instinctual impulse seeking discharge. In this view, which, according to Schur, cannot be demonstrated directly from clinical evidence, the *various primary-process mechanisms are all variations on the unitary theme of instinctual discharge.*

Schur points out that Freud's description of the primary process as it is observed in practice is in many ways antithetical to the cauldron image and the economic theory it represents. As it appeared in Freud's clinical writings, the primary process was first of all a primitive language or code, whose manifestations were meaningful intrapsychic communications, purposefully motivated and capable of being deciphered by a trained observer.

The clinical practice of psychoanalysis would be impossible if the primary process were not an information-conserving medium. Two of Freud's basic presuppositions are (1) that the analyst is capable of translating primary process material into everyday language, and (2) that the irrational but meaningful associative linkages which emerge from the patient's free associations and dreams have been stored intrapsychically in structures which have remained stable since childhood. In this case, the primary process is fulfilling an adaptive function concerned with the communication and storage of information.

To say this is not to deny that the activity of the psychic apparatus is ultimately concerned with the achievement of instinctual gratification. But the facts as observed in clinical practice suggest that, assuming an intact ego, instinctual impulses are always represented in a form which includes a structural link with adaptive processes which maintain a potential for realistic action leading to gratification. The fantasy of the Oedipal child or the adult neurotic that his impulse life is disconnected from his adaptive capabilities is just that, a fantasy. Without the adaptive infrastructure provided by the primary process, the interpretation of free associations and dreams would have no therapeutic value.

We would have to conclude that the primary process has at least two adaptive functions: the representation of instinctual impulses and the provision of a minimal structural context for them. In terms of their observable manifestations, however, these two functions cannot be separated. This is one area of mental activity, at least, in which instinctual and adaptive purposes coincide. We can refer to the structural aspect of primary-process organization as adaptive without excluding its instinctual role.

Can the primary process have yet another function, a function opposed to both the instinctual and adaptive purposes mentioned above—in other words, a defensive function? If this were so, in what form might it be observable? Thus far we have considered only a single observable function, although we have seen that both instinctual and adaptive purposes can be served by it simultaneously. In this sense, we have not yet departed from the traditional assumption that primary-process activity is convergent or unitary.

From evidence contained in the corpus of Freud's writings, Gill (1967) has argued that all of the various primary-process mechanisms are variations on the two basic but distinct mechanisms of displacement and condensation. Basic but distinct mechanisms are likely to be present only if they serve basic but distinguishable functions—perhaps even functions opposed to one another—as are the stimulating and inhibiting functions of the central nervous system.

The defensive employment of primary process activity to disguise unacceptable impulses is a basic tenet of psychoanalytic theory. There are two conflicting versions of this idea. Both are in accord with observation; yet the two have been very difficult to reconcile with each other.

In one version, the primary process is regarded as a code which is by nature so unlike ordinary rational thought that it is enough simply to *translate* any unacceptable impulse representation into primary-process language in order to render it unrecognizable. Here the primary process is seen as a *passive* instrument employed for defensive purposes by an agency belonging to the ego, such as the dream censor or dreamwork. (Note that this view denies that the primary process is the natural form of instinctual expression.)

According to the second version, the mechanisms of the primary process *actively* distort the ordinary meaning of the content on which they operate. At times Freud's writings show this distortion as incidental to the goal of immediate discharge of instinctual impulses. The meanings of things are, as it were, shouldered out of the way by the onrush of unsatisfied wishes. At other times, it seems very much as if the distortion of meanings is an end in itself, as if the primary process has its own vested interest in obscurity, independent of any external agency of the ego.

These ambiguities can be resolved if we recognize that the interior processes of the psychic apparatus are produced by opposing mechanisms whose purposes are, respectively, either adaptive or defensive. Confusion has existed in the past because the information structures employed internally by the adaptive mechanisms of the primary process are unfamiliar to us. The structures most suitable for efficient computation and storage internally are necessarily quite different from the structures most suitable for presenting the results of this interior processing to conscious inspection.

A simple analogy is the difference between the binary arithmetic employed internally by a digital computer and the decimal form in which it reports its output to the human operator. As the interior processes become more complicated, the differences between efficient internal and output structures increase. The composite image formed by the matching process in dreams is an example of an adaptive internal structure whose form is different from the forms normally employed in conscious problem-solving. Because the matching process makes use of the sensory-projection mechanisms, unlike most other internal processing, we are afforded an unusual opportunity to observe it directly.

The difference in form between adaptive internal-information structures and the output structures familiar in conscious life has led to two important errors in our understanding of these internal processes:

1. It has prevented us from seeing the adaptive function of internal processes which use information structured in nonoutput form; and
2. It has prevented us from seeing the difference between adaptive and defensive internal processes when the results of these processes are not presented to us in output form—that is, when they are presented to us as primary-process derivatives.

With these issues clarified, the following picture emerges: The internal operations of the psychic apparatus make use of information structures which are quite different from the structures employed by the output procedure which programs the results of internal processing for conscious awareness. When we observe these internal operations directly, without benefit of the output program, as we do in dreams and in the structure of free associations, we speak of the internal operations as primary-process activity.

Two qualitatively distinct varieties of internal operation are present: those which enhance the transmission and processing of information (the adaptive operations), and those which retard the transmission and processing of information (the defensive operations). These operations are set into motion respectively by adaptive and defensive agencies within the ego. The adaptive operations will tend to promote the gratification of instinctual impulses; the defensive operations, to retard this gratification. (The adaptive decision to delay gratification until a better opportunity arises must be carefully distinguished from the defensive decision to prevent gratification altogether.)

At the primary level of information processing, the level at which the basic internal structures are built and broken down, adaptive and defensive operations are performed by the mechanisms of condensation and displacement (with variants as described by Gill). Condensation builds new structure and enhances the transmission of information. Displacement breaks down structure and retards the transmission of information.

It is here that the evidence of M. A.'s dreams is critical. First, the data they provide permit us to give a characterization of the mechanisms of condensation and displacement sufficiently detailed to make their distinct and opposing functions entirely clear.

Second, the data include a natural experiment in which identical dream elements were brought together for matching in two different dreams which took place two nights apart. In the first dream (the bathtub dream, IA), a successful matching was prevented by the action of the dream censor through the mechanism of displacement or substitution. In the second dream (the refrigerator dream, IIA), the dream censor did not interfere, and the matching was successfully completed. In the index dream, the mechanism of displacement dominated the process of dream formation and minimized the adaptive outcome of the matching process. In the correction dream, the mechanism of displacement was inactive, and the adaptive function of the mechanism of condensation was fully demonstrated in the matching process.

Our discussion begins with new and more descriptive names for the two mechanisms. In the memory-cycle model, the process traditionally called *condensation* is the process of *superimposition*. Our new data indicate that the process referred to by Freud as *displacement* is a process of *substitution*. The new terms give a simpler and more accurate picture of the actual cognitive operations involved. These operations are not self-motivated processes which occur spontaneously and unpredictably in the flux of primary-process activity. They are mechanical procedures introduced purposively to enhance or retard the processing of new information by the memory cycle, as also with other nonconscious adaptive processes.

Moreover, the terms "substitution" and "superimposition" stress the antithetical nature of the two purposes being served. Confusion exists because each operation is concerned with a degree of similarity between two representations of experience. Let us consider the case of substitution first, since its defensive function is already familiar in the traditional theory.

Here an *already existing* relationship of similarity is exploited for defensive purposes because of its *irrelevance* to the ongoing information process in which a perceived threat has arisen. The substituted item is selected because, although it is associated in some way with the item substituted for, the nature of its similarity is unrelated to the characteristics which give the original item its affective and cognitive significance.

The act of substitution *subtracts* the significant aspects of the original item. The substitute is similar in a way that, from the adaptive point of view, represents the *least* common denominator of shared meaning. For this reason, a given instance of substitution may be based on any of a variety of possible associative links.

The connection between an original representation of experience and the item substituted for it can be any which will suffice for a link in the associative memory tree. The range of criteria for relatedness is extremely large. It includes cognitive resemblance in each of the sensory modalities, both singly and in arbitrary combinations; resemblance in the quality and intensity of affect associated with the experience; similarities in Gestalt and spatial configuration; relationship based on chronological contiguity; resemblances between the words associated with the experience, both vocal and semantic, and between other symbolic meanings assigned to them at any time in the past history of the subject.

Substitution may consist of the replacement of part by whole or whole by part. One value of a given quality or attribute may be replaced by its opposite. Two items unrelated to each other directly but each subordinated to a third item, or "tertium comparationis," may be exchanged. It simply does not matter what relationship the substituted item has with the item substituted for, so long as that relationship excludes the quality found to be alarming by the censorship mechanism.

But some form of relationship must exist. The act of substitution relies on items of experience already in the associative neighborhood of the original item to be excluded. A minimum degree of relatedness is necessary for the continued functioning of the memory cycle. The substitution mechanism is designed to retard the processing of information under threatening circumstances, but not to bring it to a complete standstill.

It must be emphasized that the minimum of shared meaning between the two items being exchanged in the act of substitution already exists in the associative organization of the short- and long-term memory structures. A relationship established prior to the substitution is being exploited for purposes of defensive evasion. In the superimposition of experiential representations during the matching stage of the memory cycle—i.e., dreaming—new relationships are being created *for the first time*.

Freud's minimizing of the significance of the day residue led him to obscure the preexisting connection between the substituted day residue and the deleted original. For example, in writing on *displacement* (1900, p. 305), he said:

> The dream is, as it were, differently centered from the dream thoughts—its content has different elements as its central point. Thus in the dream of the botanical monograph, for instance, the central point of the dream content was obviously the element "botanical"; whereas the dream thoughts were concerned

with the complications and conflicts arising between colleagues from their professional obligations, and further with the charge that I was in the habit of sacrificing to much for the sake of my hobbies. The element "botanical" had no place whatever in the core of the dream thoughts, unless it was loosely connected with it by an antithesis—the fact that botany never had a place among my favorite studies.

From the context in which the dream was reported and discussed, however, it is clear that the *cyclamen*—the plant which was the subject of the monograph in the dream—was closely associated in Freud's memory structure with *cocaine.* At the time Freud was in intense conflict between the emotional demands of his research on cocaine and his new discoveries in psychoanalysis. Cocaine represented his "botanical" interests, which were less suited to his talents and temperament than the "zoological" subject matter of human sexuality.

Freud had studied botany in school in order to please his teachers, rather than himself. His research on cocaine was pursued with a similar hope of impressing the members of the scientific establishment but was diverting him from a full commitment to his vocation as the creator of psychoanalysis. The element "botanical" was directly available to the dream censor as a substitute for the highly charged subject of his cocaine research, with its ambivalent associated wish to attract the admiration of paternal authorities. The substituted image could not have been closer to the central point of the dream thoughts without altogether losing the character of a disguise.

In contrast to substitution, superimposition is an *additive* process. The composite image which results from the act of superimposition is both new in itself and new in its result: the establishment of a connection in the permanent memory between representations of present and past experiences. In fact, comparison by superimposition appears to be the primary creative act of the psychic apparatus: the act which lays out the structural foundations for the massive pyramid of conceptual thought.

In referring to the concept of condensation, Schur (1966b, p. 82) says:

It applied not only to the dream work but also, in one of its principal aspects, to that amazing process by which some, if not most, memory traces are stored in the "mental apparatus." The process might be compared to that of producing an "ultra-microfilm" which simultaneously would record its material in a certain code that defied all laws of Aristotelian logic, but would nonetheless follow certain "rules" so that it could be deciphered by Freud with the aid of clues furnished by free association, a study of neurotic symptoms, dreams, parapraxes and jokes. Fisher and his co-workers (1954, 1957; Fisher and Paul, 1959) have shown convincingly that percepts are turned into memory traces and stored in the mental apparatus in accordance with similar rules.

Although Schur does not say so explicitly, it is clear that the "percepts" he refers to include perceptions of internal need as well as external reality. As I have suggested, the task of establishing and recording how and in what manner these two classes of perceptions can be related is fundamental to the very existence of the psychic apparatus.

In his description of the process of condensation in the *Interpretations of Dreams* (SE 4, pp. 279ff., 1900), however, Freud pictures it as a *subtractive* process which serves to eliminate the representations of unacceptable impulses from the manifest content of dreams. The elimination is said to take place when two images or image complexes are superimposed. The portions of each image which are similar reinforce each other in the resulting composite image which stands out from the neutral background. The portions which are dissimilar obscure one another, fade into the background, and become unrecognizable.

Dream IA, the bathtub dream, shares some important features with the fragmentary dreams frequently reported by analytic patients in which gaps and lacunae of various sorts appear. Can we show that the fragmentary quality of Dream IA was caused by the mechanism of displacement or substitution and not by a *subtractive* process of condensation? We can, aided by the natural experiment provided by our data. We have two dreams in which the same experiential components (present and past) were initially positioned by the memory cycle to be matched with each other. In the index dream, IA, the match was prevented from taking place by the interference of the dream censor. In the correction dream, IIA, the censorship mechanism was inactive, and the matching was completed successfully.

It has been demonstrated that in the index dream, IA, the interference of the censor was in all respects outside the process of superimposition, and that the mechanism of superimposition opposed the censorship throughout. In Dream IIA, where the censorship was inactive, the *additive* effects of the mechanism of superimposition were abundantly realized.

In order to see what is at stake here, we must first bring out the various assumptions embedded in the traditional view of condensation. The subtractive model pictures the mechanism as follows: It begins the story when the censorship mechanism is faced with an image complex which contains the representation of an unacceptable impulse. The censor seeks out another image complex whose meaning or reference overlaps the first one, but *does not include* the representation of the unacceptable impulse. The two image complexes are superimposed. The similar portions of the two complexes coincide and reinforce each other, and thus are retained in the composite. The unmatched portions of the two complexes, *including the unacceptable representation,* are eliminated from the final composite image complex, although the affective charges of the eliminated portions remain attached to it. The censor is satisfied because the composite now lacks the representation of the unacceptable impulse. At the same time, the composite image is thought to have an increased chance of achieving consciousness or hallucinatory gratification, since it is presumed to carry an increased charge of psychic energy.

However, if the superimposition which took place in Dream IA had been brought about by the dream censor in order to eliminate the representation of unacceptable impulses, then the manifest content of this dream would have constituted a completely successful result from the censor's point of view. It would have made no sense at all for the censorship to initiate another act of superimposition involving the same two images or experiential representations, as we saw happening in the construction of the correction dream, IIA. The composite image in the manifest content of Dream IA contains no recognizable references to the instinctual material represented in either the original day residue, M. A.'s conversation with his mother on Tuesday, or the original past component, the childhood memory of the Burgundy Hotel. Yet these two image complexes were rematched, this time successfully, in the correction dream IIA. We can only conclude that it was not the censorship which initiated the act of superimposition in Dream IA, but the adaptive mechanism whose purpose was to be defeated by the censor in that dream. The renewed superimposition of the identical elements in Dream IIA was an attempt by the adaptive mechanism to undo the damage caused by the censor in the index dream.

If the dream censor did not disrupt Dream IA through the act of superimposition, then how did it do so? Our data show clearly that the major disturbance in the construction of the bathtub dream was the substitution of the bathtub residue for the original day residue. We have seen that in all probability the substitution took place after the selection for matching with the original day residue of the childhood memory at the Burgundy Hotel. The result was an unsuccessful matching between the bathtub residue and the hotel memory, simultaneous with a successful match between the bathtub residue and the later childhood memory of Alice "whisking by in the nude."

The composite image which resulted from the successful matching of the substitute day residue *was also unacceptable* to the censor. In this case it was the double image of a libidinally invested young woman, Judith/Alice, which was eliminated from the dream by the censorship mechanism. We have already seen that this act of elimination is incompatible with the subtractive model of condensation. According to that model, it should have been the *unsuccessfully* matched portions of the overlapping images which dropped out of the dream contents. In reality, the *successfully* matched, mutually reinforced, double image of the women was eliminated from the dream, and the poorly matched receptacle imagery derived from the houses, bathrooms, and bathtubs which originally formed the background for the attractive women was substituted in the final form of the dream for the imagery of the female body.

Here we see the mechanism of superimposition trying to make the best of the bad situation presented to it when the first substitution had deleted the original day residue. This effort had two results: the relative success with the matching of the young women, and the relative failure with the matching of the receptacle imagery. The censorship once again acted to defeat the *successful* superimposition by substituting the obscure imagery resulting from the failed match.

In Dream IB, we have another instance in which an initial substitution for the same original day residue led to an unsuccessful match with a memory of the past. The unsuccessful match was represented in the dream by the idea: "I had to get married in a church, or a garden or an antique shop." This extremely obscure image was *retained* in the manifest content of Dream IB and then rematched in the correction dream, IIB, with the furniture collection of the policeman and the open casket.

The evidence is therefore conclusive that *unsuccessfully* matched portions of the superimposed images may be retained by the censor precisely because they are *unsuccessful,* and that mutually reinforced composite images may be eliminated when they are found to be threatening. In each case, the mechanism of superimposition itself acted only to make new connections between the present and past components of the dream. It persisted in this aim despite every obstacle presented to it by the censorship mechanism in the form of substitutions which *minimize* the basis for a successful matching. In Dream IA, the censorship has the final word, and the manifest dream is devoid of elements with a recognizable instinctual denotation.

With the correction dream data in hand, however, we now understand that the disruption of the matching process in a particular dream is not the final word on the *disposition* of a significant new experience, such as M. A.'s Tuesday conversation with his mother. If the objections of the censor to the excluded material are worked through, as they were during the Thursday analytic hour, then the adaptive mechanisms of the memory cycle are fully capable of reviving the original day residue and successfully matching it with the representations of childhood experience through a new act of superimposition.

The new act of superimposition in the correction dream is not simply an iteration of something which might have taken place in the index dream. In accordance with the requirements of the memory-cycle model, it combines the missing elements of the index dream with the new waking experience which has intervened since the index dream took place. This expansion in the present component of the correction dream leads to a corresponding expansion in the selection from the permanent memory which will be matched with it.

In Dream IIA and M. A.'s associations to it during the Friday-morning hour, we saw a proliferation of composite images linking the present and the past, together with many (though by no means all) of their individual component experiences. This abundance of imagery appeared when the mechanism of superimposition was permitted to function without interference from the defensive substitutions of the dream censor. The fading and fragmenting of imagery which Freud associated with the mechanism of condensation is not in evidence here.

We must now take up another aspect of the function of condensation in the traditional theory of dream construction. With the elimination of unmatched imagery during the process of condensation, Freud thought he saw the opportunity to explain the emergence into consciousness of repressed libidinal impulses. This would be accomplished by the accumulation of the affective charges of all the elements whose cognitive representations were excluded from the mutually reinforced composite image which results from the act of superimposition. The accumulated energy attached to the composite image would then be sufficient to propel it through the barriers of repression into consciousness.

This formulation was motivated, at least in part, by Freud's attempt to find an impetus for dream formation entirely within the contents of the dream itself, without the postulation of an unknown adaptive function which might provide an external cause for the construction of dreams.

We now have firsthand knowledge of an adaptive function carried on during the process of dreaming. We have seen the primary mechanism of this adaptive function, comparison by superimposition, working at all times in opposition to the dream censor. The impetus for the dream arises from the higher-level adaptive purpose for which the experiential material represented in the dream forms the lower-level subject matter.

The success or failure of a given instinctual impulse to achieve representation in a dream is clearly a matter which is decided by the defensive operations of the dream censor itself. We have seen that these operations are capable of aborting a dream (IA) whose very high priority from the adaptive point of view is indicated by the effort of the mechanisms of the memory cycle to reconstitute it two days later (IIA). Moreover, our natural experiment demonstrates that these defensive operations *eliminate* affective charge as well as representational content from the disrupted dream.

The differences between Dreams IA and IIA illustrate this point in detail. Dream IA, aborted by the defensive substitution for the principal Tuesday residue, was a lifeless image reported without feeling. In retrospect, it is clear that much of the affect expressed in the remainder of the Tuesday hour had originally been part of the experiential material which was excluded from Dream IA by the censor. During the analytic session, this affect was successfully dissociated from the imagery of the excluded experience, which remained inaccessible throughout the hour. (The affect was related during the Thursday hour to M. A.'s relationship with his father, but not to the incident on Tuesday involving Father's belongings.) In the correction dream (IIA) on Thursday night, the affect and the imagery were reunited and represented together without the interference of the censor.

Given this sequence, there could hardly be any justification for saying that an accumulation of affect attached to the manifest content of Dream IA had provided it with any sort of impetus. Where we saw an affective charge breaking through into consciousness during the analytic hour, and this affective charge had been deliberately excluded from the dream. Far from being carried into consciousness by the "vehicle" of dream formation, the wishful impulses associated with this affective charge achieved consciousness apart from the dream and in spite of every effort of the dream censor to prevent them from doing so.

In the case of Dream IIA, where the censor did not interfere with the mechanism of superimposition, we saw a proliferating complex of superimposed images represented together with the conflicting affects which had accompanied the original experiencing of these images. What was common to the two dreams was the *adaptively determined impetus* to match by superimposition the principal Tuesday residue and the identical affectively charged memory of early childhood. What was variable between the two dreams was the presence or absence of the affect appropriate to these experiences, in accordance with the success or failure of the matching procedure as determined by the disruptive activity of the dream censor.

Freud's view of condensation as a subtractive process specified that the affective charge originally attached to the material excluded from the dream, what he would have called the "latent content," was transferred in the process of dream formation to the mutually reinforced composite images which were retained to become the "manifest content" of the resulting dream. In Dream IA, we see no evidence of this transferred charge in the dream itself. It was excluded from the dream along with the excluded content. In Dream IIA, where the content which had been excluded from Dream IA was incorporated into the manifest content, we find the associated affects incorporated along with it. According to our data, then, there is no point in the process of dream construction at which affective pressure is built up through a *separation* of representational content and its associated affect.

The picture presented by our data is one in which distinct mechanisms of substitution and superimposition perform distinct defensive and adaptive functions in the process of dream construction. The tendency to confuse these mechanisms and to subordinate the adaptive function to the defensive is easily understandable when we consider the incompleteness of the dream data with which psychoanalysts have worked in the past. In the sections which follow, we will consider some of the theoretical problems caused by this confusion, and the resolution of these problems by the memory-cycle model.

The Concept of "Latent Content" in Freud's Writings on Dreams

In the last section, our attention was drawn once again to the different usages of the term "latent content" in traditional psychoanalytic theory and in the memory-cycle model. The traditional theory would consider as "latent content" whatever experiential material had been excluded from the manifest dream by displacement, condensation, or any other primary process mechanism, and it would stipulate that some material is excluded in this way from *every* dream.

According to the memory-cycle model, the term "latent content" refers to the representations of experience from both present and past which are superimposed in the matching process and consequently viewed by the dreamer as distorted. This theoretical model requires that every dream contain a component of the latent content derived from present experience and another derived from the experience of the past. As we have just seen, the exclusion of experiential material by substitution, as exemplified in Dream IA but not Dream IIA, would be a variable factor in dream construction.

One advantage conferred by the memory-cycle model is that it specifies clear, stable, and unambiguous relationships between the impetus which sets the construction of the dream in motion and the experiential contents, which supply the raw materials for the construction process. The impetus arises from the adaptive mechanisms of the memory cycle itself, which have the task of matching new experience with the accumulated knowledge of the past. The latent contents are those experiences of present and past whose matching fulfills this adaptive purpose.

Variability enters into the memory-cycle model only with regard to the two major factors dependent on the individual experience of the dreamer. First, there is the local organization of his permanent memory structure, which determines the availability of specific items for matching, and the nature of the experiences *associated* with these items .(Freud's "latent contents"). Second, there is the system of defensive criteria which determines the nature and quantity of experiential material to be excluded from the adaptive process which normally strives to maintain effective communication between the present and the past.

In the traditional theory, the situation is quite different. In Freud's writings, the relationship between the impetus for the dream and the "latent contents" fluctuates continuously, despite what appears to be a general impression to the contrary. This fluctuation results from Freud's attempt to derive the impetus directly from the latent contents. The attempt was defeated by conflicting evidence which pictures the latent contents at one moment in the dreamer's present experience, at another moment in the experience of childhood. Because of his assumption that intrapsychic events are driven by unipolar and asymmetrical forces, Freud felt obligated to locate the impetus *either* in the present *or* in the past *exclusively*. His model called for a single psychic agency to impose its will on another, or for two such agencies to engage in a conflict of wills. It could not allow for a *single* mental act which deliberately and purposively brings together experiential materials from widely separated areas in the psychic apparatus.

We have seen that the unipolar model provides a reasonably accurate picture of the unilateral activity of the dream censor in its attempt to disrupt the memory cycle. This is one reason why the dream censor played a predominating role in Freud's theory of dream construction. (The primary reason, I believe, was the practical importance in the clinical situation of casting the patient's defensive activity in the strongest possible light. In this, as in many other instances, Freud's psychological theory was designed to reflect the practical issues of psychoanalytic treatment. See chapter 7 herein.)

Freud's observations of the process of dreaming were extremely difficult to reconcile with the unipolar theory. They provide a good deal of evidence that both the present and past experience of the dreamer are essential components of every dream, and that the task of locating the impetus for the dream in one or the other component is a hopeless one. The evidence is often obscured by Freud's manner of reporting it. At any given time and place in his writing, it appears that one or the other component is the more important one, but never both at once. It is only when the observations reported over many years are drawn together that the broader picture emerges. In this section and the next we shall try to reconstruct this broader picture and to show how it repeatedly turns our attention in the direction of the memory-cycle model.

In the earliest chapters of *The Interpretation of Dreams*, Freud's concept of the latent or hidden content of the dream was derived directly from his clinical experience with patients. It included whatever repressed material emerged from the patient's associations to the dream during analysis. Freud conceptualized this repressed material as "latent dream thoughts"; that is, primarily as structured in cognitive terms. Affects were considered to be associated with specific thoughts and not separable from them.

The thoughts in question were those which had arisen on the dream day or in the immediate past. For example, a latent dream thought might be one which revealed "a second source of the dream . . . in another experience of the same day" (1900, IV:174).

But it was during just this time that Freud was making his great discoveries about the determining role of childhood experience in emotional development. In chapter V of *The Interpretation of Dreams*, we find him suggesting for the first time that the hidden meaning of the dream is derived from the distant past:

Stated in general terms, this would imply that every dream was linked in its manifest content with recent experiences and in its latent content with the most ancient experiences. (1900, IV:218)

As a result of these discoveries, a number of changes had taken place in Freud's thinking. The mechanism which distorts and disguises the content of the dream became distinct from the mechanism of repression in general. The term "latent content" was consequently to be reserved only for the specific element of the dream which had aroused the censoring activity of the dreamwork. This element was an experience of childhood which must have been included in the content of every dream.

According to this formulation, current thoughts associated with the manifest content of a dream might be hidden, in the sense that they had been repressed, but since they had not been hidden specifically *by the dreamwork* they could not be considered to be the latent contents *of the dream.*

Although the components from which the dream was constructed were still considered at this time to be experiences, there were now two distinct classes of experiences involved. One was the class of childhood experiences, which alone were thought to provide the impetus for the construction of the dream. The other was the class of current experiences which contained the day residues. It was clearly the childhood experience that provided the impetus which would alarm the censorship and which would therefore have to be concealed.

Freud then had to explain how the childhood experience could be disguised without diminishing its ability to provide the impetus for the dream. He thought this could be accomplished by making the affective charge contributed by the childhood experience detachable from the cognitive contents of the experience. In the process of condensation the affective charge of the childhood experience could then be added to the cognitive content of the day residue (chapter VII):

Pursuing this conception, we may further describe the dream as the substitute for the infantile scene modified by transference to recent material. (1900, V:546)

The manifest dream formed in this way would contain the cognitive elements of the recent experience together with the affective charge detached from the experience of childhood. The latent content of such a dream would then consist of the cognitive elements of the childhood experience which had been excluded from the dream, rather than the childhood experience as a whole, as earlier in chapter V.

A problem which arises in *The Interpretation of Dreams*, mentioned there by Freud (p. 546) and emphasized recently by Jones (1965), is the apparent difficulty in identifying the precise childhood experience which was thought to supply the impetus for the formation of the dream, even after analysis of the dreamer's associations.

The difficulty of identifying the past experience which contributed to the dream led Freud's thinking in a new direction. This was to minimize the significance of the actual experiences of childhood by giving a greater degree of independence to the impulses he now associated with them.

By the time Freud wrote "A Metapsychological Supplement to the Theory of Dreams" (1915), the component of the dream derived from childhood was no longer an *experience* as such, but rather an unconscious instinctual *impulse*. Such an impulse would exist in the child's mind prior to any specific experience which embodied it. It could manifest itself in a variety of different experiential situations, all of which would have an equivalent psychodynamic significance. Which of these experiential situations might or might not have contributed to the dream would be of little importance.

Proceeding under this assumption. Freud could no longer consider the latent content of the dream to be derived from the distant past. The actual experiences of childhood were no longer essential constituents of the dream. The unconscious instinctual impulses were not to be thought of as having a cognitive shape of their own, but as surges of mobile energy which could attach themselves to the experiential content of the day residues.

The latent content would therefore have to reside once again in the component of the dream derived from present experience, the day residues. It would no longer supply the impetus for the construction of the dream.

In analysis we make the acquaintance of these "days residues" in the shape of latent dream thoughts; and, both by reason of their nature and of the whole situation, we must regard them as preconscious ideas, as belonging to the system *Pcs.* (1915, XIV: 224)

The deemphasis of the experience of the past in Freud's 1915 model of dreaming was in accord with his feeling at the time that he had overestimated the importance of the actual experiences of childhood (as opposed to the fantasies generated in childhood by unconscious instinctual forces) in the pathogenesis of the psychoneuroses.

By 1933, when Freud wrote *The New Introductory Lectures on Psychoanalysis*, the significance of childhood sexual experiences had been restored to a more prominent position in dreaming. Coincidentally, the difficulty in observing them had diminished considerably.

Now these first sexual experiences of a child are linked to painful impressions of anxiety, prohibition, disappointment and punishment. We can understand their having been repressed; but, that being so, we cannot understand how it is that they have such free access to dream-life, that they provide the pattern for so many dream-phantasies and that dreams are filled with reproductions of these scenes from childhood and with allusions to them. It must be admitted that their unpleasurable character and the dream-work's wish-fulfilling purpose seem far from mutually compatible. But it may be that in this case we are magnifying the difficulty. After all, these same infantile experiences have attached to them all the imperishable, unfulfilled instinctual wishes which throughout life provide the energy for the construction of dreams, and to which we may no doubt credit the possibility, in their mighty uprush, of forcing to the surface, along with the rest, the material of distressing events. (1933, pp. 28–29)

The relationship between these powerful experiences of childhood and the latent content of the dream was not spelled out in this later work. It appears that the latent content as it is described in the *Lectures* could include components both from the present life of the patient, the day residues, and from the germinal experiences of the past. But the experiential is still considered to be incidental to the instinctual here. There is no attempt to explore the reasons why either one or both should appear in a given dream, Freud apparently being satisfied that the relative strength of the impulses involved could explain all the observed phenomena.

The migration of the "latent contents" back and forth and back again between the present and past components of the dream structure has attracted little notice in the psychoanalytic literature. This may be due to any of several factors, among them:

1. The difficulty in reconstructing both the past and present components of the composite image of a given manifest dream, especially when most dream reports are fragmentary, associations are incomplete and correction dreams generally unreported. This observational problem might lead to the supposition that in his various theoretical writings Freud was actually describing different varieties of the dream.

2. A tacit understanding among analysts that experiences of both the present and the past contribute to all dreams. Freud's theoretical revisions would then be construed as changes in emphasis rather than in substance.

One of the difficulties facing any commentator on Freud's work is that contradictory theoretical formulations arise from different observations each of which is quite valid in itself. The commentator who shows a preference for one theoretical formulation over the other is often thought to be ignoring or denying the validity of the observations which led to the formulation he is rejecting.

In this case, we can affirm almost all of Freud's *observations* with full confidence. The latent contents can be derived from either current or past experience. In fact, they must always include the representations of experiences both present and past, even when one or the other of these is not clearly apparent at the moment.

We may discover powerful affects associated with either the present or the past component of the latent contents. As Freud was finally aware, however, we cannot identify the impetus for the construction of the dream with the affects associated with either of these categories of experience. In this respect, the assignment of the impetus to an "unconscious instinctual impulse of childhood" was clearly a step in the right direction, for it freed the impetus from its assumed but unobservable dependence on the migratory latent contents.

Similar difficulties arise when we try to identify a specific childhood impulse as the motivating factor in every dream, however. In addition, problems arise when we attempt to locate the point of impact of this impulse on the materials of the dream during the process of dream construction.

Once again, an examination of Freud's writings will be helpful. We shall be especially interested this time in tracing his struggle with the difficulties just mentioned, and in a closely related theme, his effort to deal with issues concerning the transfer and processing of information in explanatory terms which reduce all mental activity to colliding and coalescing impulses.

Information and Impulse in Dream Construction

Freud's theoretical explanation for the genesis of dreams does not appear to allow for the purposive transfer of new information from waking experience into the deeper structures of the psychic apparatus. Although he recognized that the day residue is not *necessarily* an innocuous bit of the previous day's experience, Freud maintained that the importance in reality of the experience incorporated into the day residue has no bearing on its usefulness as a vehicle for bringing the repressed infantile wish into consciousness.

But clinical experience directs our attention to the *information content* of dreams, and in "The Handling of Dream Interpretation in Psychoanalysis" Freud noted that this information may have a pattern:

We have found from fine examples of fully analyzed dreams that several successive scenes of one dream may have the same content, which may find expression in them with increasing clarity; and we have learnt, too, that several dreams occurring in the same night need be nothing more than attempts, expressed in various forms, to represent one meaning. In general, we may rest assured that every wishful impulse which creates a dream today will reappear in other dreams as long as it has not been understood and withdrawn from the domination of the unconscious. It often happens, therefore, that the best way to complete the interpretation of a dream is to leave it and to devote one's attention to a new dream, which may contain the same material in a possibly more accessible form." (1911, XII:94)

The idea of the correction dream is here in germinal form, but the flow of information is described as going all in one direction, from past to present. This would appear to suggest something that Freud could not have intended; namely, that the meaning of the analyst's interpretation is not conveyed to the mechanism responsible for the construction of the dream. If this were so, how could the sequence of impulses emerging from the unconscious be influenced by the progression of the analysis?

The same question is implicit in Freud's observation that it is when an impulse has been understood that it can be withdrawn from the control of the unconscious. How is the information that the impulse has been understood conveyed to the control mechanism which must release it?

In the final paragraph of his 1911 paper on dreams, Freud mentions the most obvious exception to his rule that the influence of waking experience on the content of the dream is fortuitous:

In conclusion, I will mention a particular type of dream which, in the nature of the case, occurs only in the course of psycho-analytic treatment, and may bewilder or mislead beginners. These are the corroborative dreams which, as it were, "tag along behind"; they are easily accessible to analysis, and their translation merely presents what the treatment has inferred during the last few days from the material of the daily associations. When this happens. it looks as though the patient has been amiable enough to bring us in dream-form exactly what we had been "suggesting" to him immediately before. The more experienced analyst will no doubt have some difficulty in attributing any such amiability to the patient; he accepts such dreams as hoped-for confirmations, and recognizes that they are only observed under certain conditions brought about by the influence of the treatment. The great majority of dreams forge ahead of the analysis; so that, after substraction of everything in them which is already known and understood, there still remains a more or less clear hint at something which has hitherto been hidden. (1911, XII:96)

A dream which exactly reproduces what the analyst has been suggesting is not a dream which employs a convenient bit of day residue material as the vehicle for a repressed wish. It is a dream which attributes significance to the day residue in and of itself. We are left wondering why the dream which consolidates what has just happened in the analysis must be placed in a different category from the dream which forges ahead of it. Why should dreams not be able to do both at once?

In "A Metapsychological Supplement to the Theory of Dreams" (1915), Freud gave the day residues a more independent status in the construction of the dream:

Observation shows that dreams are instigated by residues from the previous day—thought-cathexes which have not submitted to the general withdrawal of cathexes, but have retained in spite of it a certain amount of libidinal or other interest. . . . If, then, certain day's residues have retained their cathexis, we hesitate to suppose that they have acquired at night so much energy as to compel notice on the part of consciousness; we should be more inclined to suppose that the cathexis they have retained is far weaker than that which they possessed during the day. Here analysis saves us further speculation, for it shows that these day's residues must receive a reinforcement which has its source in unconscious instinctual impulses if they are to figure as constructors of dreams. (1915, XIV:224)

The retention of cathexis by the day residue is phenomenologically equivalent to the selection of the day residue for permanent storage during Stage II of the memory cycle. In this essay of Freud's, for the first time, the impetus for the dream was seen to be coming from *both* the present (the day residue) and the past (the unconscious instinctual impulse). But the direction in the flow of energy was still the same for both impulses; they appeared to meet each other accidentally along a pathway leading to discharge in consciousness which both happened to be traveling at the same time. The possibility that the derivatives of present and past experience are deliberately brought together for the purpose of a mutual interchange was never raised.

Without the concept of a purposeful interchange of information, Freud was led to expect that in every dream one or the other impulse, past or present would necessarily predominate. In "Remarks on the Theory and Practice of Dream Interpretation" (1923b), he says:

It is possible to distinguish between dreams *from above* and dreams *from below*, provided the distinction is not made too sharply. Dreams from below are those which are provoked by the strength of an unconscious (repressed) wish which has found a means of being represented in some of the day's residues. They may be regarded as inroads of the repressed into waking life. Dreams from above correspond to thoughts or intentions of the day before which have contrived during the night to obtain reinforcement from repressed material that is debarred from the ego. (1923b, XIX:111)

We are now in a position to see that the distinction between dreams from above and dreams from below is an artifact. Every dream is both a dream from above and a dream from below, just as the planet Venus is both the morning star and the evening star, although at a given moment it appears to the observer to be either one or the other.

Freud's program for reducing mental activity to a flow of energy from a state of higher potential to a state of lower potential makes it difficult to conceptualize any sort of purposefully collaborative or communicative intrapsychic process (Pribram and Gill, 1976). The joining of forces in the dream must accordingly be described as a choice between "inroads of the repressed on waking life" and "Thoughts or intentions of the day before which have contrived . . . to obtain reinforcement from repressed material." The imagery suggests that these actions are both forced and unnatural.

It was this picture of the inner world which deflected Freud from the full recognition of a process which draws together, with an independent and equally distributed impetus, the derivatives of present and past experience.

We may ask whether it was inevitable that Freud should have seen the forces operating in the construction of the dream and in the unconscious generally as blind and unremittingly competitive. Such a theoretical position seems to contradict his usual emphasis on the contribution of the unconscious to all creative and integrative experience, from myth to art to the practice of psychoanalysis itself.

A possible alternative appears in his vision of Eros, the life instinct. Here Freud permitted himself to imagine a power at large in the universe which expresses itself through the binding together of things separate and distinct; a binding together which nevertheless preserved the identities of its separate objects. Many have supposed that Freud's death instinct was meant to be a psychological correlative of the physical law which describes the constant increase of entropy in a closed system. If that is so, then the life instinct as Freud conceived it would have had as its objective the reduction of entropy and the increase of organization (i.e., information) in those biological systems able to control the interactions across their boundaries with the outer world.

Here Freud's vision would have been prophetic. Today we would define an organism as a system which actively accumulates information against the entropic drift of its surroundings. In Freud's time, however, it was difficult to translate the principle of Eros into a deterministic system such as Freud conceived the psychic apparatus to be. Moreover, the mechanism of superimposition in dreams, which epitomizes the information-accumulating character of the human organism, may appear to destroy the identities of the objects it binds together. This will be especially so if the observer has access only to the composite image of the dream, but not to the past and present components of the latent content.

This apparent loss of information in the dream is dispelled when we understand the function of the dream in the computations of the memory cycle. The composite image of the dream is a means toward the end of connecting the coded representation of a new experience with the coded representations of past experiences closely related to it in the permanent memory. These representations remain intact while their duplicate sensory reconstructions are superimposed in the dream. When the dream has served its purpose in confirming a connection, its "distorted" imagery is discarded—i.e., excluded from memory—and the original representations are linked together permanently.

Only when the composite image of the dream produces an unexpected or alarming result is the dreamer alerted to take note of the dream and incorporate it into his waking life; to transfer it, in effect, from the category of intermediate computation to the category of raw data about his internal state of mind. It is this transfer which makes the occurrence of the correction dream possible.

We can surmise that for Freud there were also strategic reasons for keeping Eros at a level of abstraction removed from the day to day workings of the psychic aparatus. Freud saw himself—and rightly so—as the adversary of sentimental hypocrisy and human narcissism in general. He warned us again and again that we can decide our own destinies only insofar as we acknowledge and overcome the anonymous biological forces within us. Making a place for Eros in everyday life might have seemed to him a retreat from his discovery that the great enemy we face is within ourselves.

The balance he tried to achieve in his later philosophical speculations is a balance sorely needed in the explanatory concepts of psychoanalytic theory. The conflict he saw between the "principles" of Eros and Thanatos is reflected in the contemporary concepts of information and entropy. (We must not make the mistake of identifying Freud's "principles" with individual wishes or impulses.) We have seen this conflict enacted at the microcosmic level in the opposition during dream formation between the information-enhancing mechanism of superimposition and the information-retarding mechanism of substitution. We can expect to find a similar situation wherever adaptive and defensive operations act in opposition to one another.

The limitations of the unipolar model are especially conspicuous when we try to understand the therapeutic effect of the two-party interaction between patient and analyst while using a vocabulary restricted to internal forces acting blindly and unilaterally. Changes leading to an improvement in the patient must be conceptualized in the traditional language as unilateral intrapsychic events; the process through which the analyst's interpretations interact with the patient's internal state remains essentially mysterious.

The unipolar model cannot account for a situation in which two systems, each quite different from the other and each acting under the direction of a higher-order impetus, can direct their individual behavior so that it converges on a mutually satisfying goal. Freud recognized that at what he called the "genital" level of psychosexual development this kind of interaction becomes possible, and he understood quite clearly that in a successful analysis this level is somehow achieved.

The term "genital" directs our attention to interpersonal events in which differences are reconciled for the sake of mutual satisfaction. It does not explain how it is possible that such goals are achieved. We know from abundant experience that the discharge of tension in the genital organs, though characteristic of successful adult human relationships, is neither necessary nor sufficient to produce them.

Since Freud's death, this gap between theory and practice has been filled, in part, by the development of the psychoanalytic theory of object relations. This theory, to which a great many analysts have contributed, recognizes that, from the beginning of development, intrapsychic events are shaped by the mutual interaction of ego and object. From this point of view, the genital level is the culmination of a sequence of increasingly reciprocal stages of mutuality. Changes in the patient during analysis can then be seen as a function of changes taking place in the analytic relationship in parallel with the transformations of normal development.

In object-relations theory, the mutually interacting systems are people, and the field of their interaction is interpersonal. Nevertheless, the intrapsychic events which result from this interaction continue to be conceptualized in Freud's earlier language appropriate to a unipolar, noninteractional model. Information processing theory, and the memory-cycle model generated by it, provide an alternative intrapsychic model more consistent with object-relations theory itself. The memory cycle as a whole, and the matching process in dreams, most vividly, are examples of *intrapsychic* systems mutually interacting in order to establish a set of meanings common to both the meanings attaching to the composite images of the dream and other instances of comparison by super-imposition.

We may then wish to regard the operation of the memory cycle, which we know to be more active at birth than later on in life, as the intrapsychic *Anlage* or model for the more slowly developing reciprocities of the ego/object field. It would follow from this that as the ego matures it seeks closer and closer approximations of the intrapsychic matching process in the arena of interpersonal relations.

If we take this idea seriously, we find that it casts an entirely new light on the issues of genital sexuality, sexual curiosity, and the significance of the primal-scene experience. To the developing child, the sexual mating of his parents will become symbolic not only of their power and privilege in the usual sense, but also of their ability to fully realize the interpersonal analogue of the intrapsychic matching process.

The child's failure to grasp what is happening between his parents, although it may be maintained defensively in order to reduce Oedipal guilt, as in the case of M. A. and other patients with psychoneurotic conflicts, would have a profoundly negative effect on that part of his self-image concerned with the realization of successful intrapsychic functioning in interpersonal terms.

The revision during analysis of infantile distortions of primal-scene fantasies and memories is often accompanied, as with M. A. in our example, by an intense feeling of relief. For M. A. this feeling had a number of meanings, prominent among them the idea that in order to get along with his father, he would not have to submit himself to emasculation and fecal contamination as he seemed to imagine his mother had done.

But the uncovering of the primal-scene experience behind the fantasy of a sadistic parental antagonism often brings with it, first, an exultation which seems to go far beyond a mere feeling of relief; and second, an imagery which evokes the splendors of landscape and palace common to the distant paradises of fairy tale and mystical revelation. The possibility of parental harmony brings to life a vision of harmony in the natural world which can only be a projection of the child's sense of a reciprocity in his own inner nature.

Some of this feeling appears to be present in M. A., and perhaps the "bird . . . in Norway, in Oslo, Norway—some city by the ocean" is the fragment of such an imaginary landscape. Perhaps we should have been more than a little suspicious when M. A. immediately told the analyst that this image signified nothing more than a wish to escape from the grim realities of an engulfing relationship with his mother.

It is instructive to see how effectively Freud dealt with the doubts of a similarly obsessive patient about the efficacy of dream interpretation:

At this point I recall a discussion which I was led into with a patient whose exceptionally ambivalent attitude was expressed in the most intense compulsive doubt. He did not dispute my interpretations of his dreams and was very much struck by their agreement with the hypotheses which I put forward. But he asked whether these corroborative dreams might not be an expression of his compliance towards me. I pointed out that the dreams had also brought up a quantity of details of which I could have had no suspicion and that his behaviour in the treatment apart from this had not been precisely characterized by compliance. Whereupon he switched over to another theory and asked whether his narcissistic wish to be cured might not have caused him to produce these dreams, since, after all, I had held out to him a prospect of recovery if he were able to accept my constructions. I could only reply that I had not yet come across any such mechanism of dream-formation. But a decision was reached by another road. He recollected some dreams which he had had before starting analysis and indeed before he had known anything about it; and the analysis of these dreams, which were free from all suspicion of suggestion, led to the same interpretations as the later ones. (1923b, XIX: 116)

Here, as in many passages in his *Remarks on the Theory and Practice of Dream Interpretations* (1923b), Freud comes close to recognizing the information-processing function of dreams. He has abandoned the argument that in a corroborative dream the patient is merely reproducing the analyst's interpretation, for, as he now observes, the corroborative dream always brings up a quantity of details unknown to the analyst. The correction dream is a corroborative dream in which the analyst's interpretation is guided to this quantity of unknown details by the presence in the day residue of a previously reported dream, a dream which had itself been constructed from historical materials located in the same sector of the permanent memory as those now emerging for the first time.

In the case of M. A.'s bathtub and refrigerator dreams we can specify this location in the memory structure as a set of branches containing affectively charged receptacle imagery, all of which are subordinated to (or radiate from) the node containing the fantasy-memory-dream of the primal-scene experience at the Burgundy Hotel. Not only did the analyst have no suspicion of the newly emergent details, but during the hour in which he interpreted the dream index, he was unaware either of the original day residue or of the historical antecedent which were to emerge as associations to the correction dream. In fact, he did not possess a theoretical model which might even have suggested the existence of a specific childhood memory (as opposed to a generalized libidinal impulse) which was part of the latent contents of the first dream in the sequence.

In the next paragraph of his 1923 paper, Freud says:

It may well be that dreams during psycho-analysis succeed in bringing to light what is repressed to a greater extent than dreams outside that situation. But it cannot be proved, since the two situations are not comparable; the employment of dreams in analysis is something very remote from their original purpose. On the other hand, it cannot be doubted that within an analysis far more of the repressed is brought to light in connection with dreams than by any other method. In order to account for this, there must be some motive power, some unconscious force, which is better able to lend support to the purposes of analysis during the state of sleep than at other times. (1923, XIX:117)

We can no longer agree that the use of dreams in analysis is remote from their original purpose. The analytic process enhances and accelerates the information-processing function of dreams by exploiting the feedback opportunity presented by the awakening dream. But the latter half of his statement is fully in keeping with our new understanding of the special biological role of the memory cycle, if for the word "force" we substitute "mechanism" or "process."

Freud goes on to say:

What is here in question cannot well be any factor other than the patient's compliance towards the analyst which is derived from his parental complex—in other words, the positive portion of what we call the transference; and in fact, in many dreams which recall what has been forgotten and repressed, it is impossible to discover any other unconscious wish to which the motive force for the formation of the dream can be attributed. So that if anyone wishes to maintain that most of the dreams that can be made use of in analysis are obliging dreams and owe their origin to suggestion, nothing can be said against that opinion from the point of view of analytic theory. (1923, XIX:117)

This passage suddenly throws into doubt one of the basic assumptions of Freud's theory of dreams. In his immediately previous writings, the unconscious wish which provides the impetus for the formation of the dream is the finite manifestation of an instinctual impulse, a charge of psychic energy which acts in close analogy to a physical action at a specific time and place. There is at least one such impulse for each dream and this impulse is discharged by the formation of the dream. We are not prepared to see a general predisposition or state of mind assume the role of a specific impulse in the model he has presented to us.

Moreover, a repressed infantile wish ordinarily asserts itself in the dream, according to Freud, by *reproducing an event of the past which has given pleasure to the dreamer.* In this case, it appears that an unconscious wish derived from his parental complex can be expressed in the dream *by the creation of a new event whose aim is to give pleasure in the future to someone other than the dreamer.*

I suspect that this is Freud's way of saying that the experience recalled in a dream, "what has been forgotten and repressed," may not be associated with any instinctual impulse which stands out above the ordinary background of psychobiological activity. Put slightly differently, this would mean that the impetus for the dream comes from elsewhere than the instinctual impulses associated with its contents. A theory of dreams which recognized their conflict-free adaptive function would have eliminated some of the logical difficulties apparent here.

Freud's reference to the prior role of the patient's parents in the production of dreams during analysis is very much to the point, however, although for a reason quite different from the one he gives. Parents are in reality the original "interpreters" of dreams. The repeatedly reassuring presence of his mother or her surrogate after the experience of an awakening dream is a crucial element in any infant's learning to distinguish between his inner and outer worlds. The introduction of this comforting experience, through the matching process of the correction dream which follows, acts to stabilize the contents of the memory structure at a time when its relative poverty of information may lead to a much higher frequency of mismatching than later in life.

The child just learning to talk brings his awakening dreams to his parent both for reassurance and to take advantage of their ability to translate his strange experience into words. By the time he reaches the Oedipal period, the child has become impatient with a literal paraphrasing of the dream and appears to be seeking something resembling the beginnings of psychological insight. The parent's failure to supply what is needed at this point may have a serious effect on the later accessibility to the child of his early memories and of fantasy material in general.

With dream interpretation, as in so many other ways, the analyst begins where the parents have left off. The primary motive for the patient to report the dreams *he already has had* is not to please the analyst by producing the dreams for him, but to join him in an ego-enhancing interaction which recalls a series of pleasurable and developmentally critical experiences early in life.

Other kinds of "exceptional dreams" are provided by Freud with their exceptional explanations. To solve the problem of the terrifying dreams of the traumatic neuroses, Freud invoked a *repetition compulsion* which he considered somehow to be more basic than the wish-fulfillment function operative in other dreams. What we actually observe in these cases is an attempt to avoid a repetition in reality of the terrifying past experience by repetitively matching its representation in the memory with contemporary events which resemble it even remotely. This results in a series of awakening dreams which serve as a warning to the dreamer. This explanation would also account for punishment dreams, for which Freud must postulate, again contrary to his usual position, that the critical agency of the ego "has been temporarily re-established even during the sleeping state."

The recurrent traumatic dream is unusual because an abnormally wide range of new experiences are selected for matching with a single traumatic past event. In other respects, the traumatic dream, like the punishment dream, is similar to the more common recurrent anxiety dream, which is of special interest to us here.

The recurrent anxiety dream is an indication that the censorship has prevented the matching mechanism of the memory cycle from producing a successful correction dream, which would normally introduce new linkages between the traumatic past event and related but less threatening experiences which would, in turn, have been successfully matched with the new day residue.

Recurrent anxiety dreams are not exact repetitions. The imagery of a new day residue is always included in the composite formed by the matching process. But the new day residue is not the significant current experience originally selected for the matching. It is a substitute introduced by the censorship. For this reason it tends to be overshadowed by the vividness of the traumatic past experience with which it is eventually matched, or by the representation of earlier dreams in which that experience had been incorporated.

If M. A.'s anxiety about his father's death had not been reduced during the working through process of the Thursday hour, the Thursday night dreams would not have had the characteristics of the correction dream we actually observed. In other sequences recorded by the original investigators, the outcome of the struggle between the adaptive and defensive mechanisms was not as decisively favorable as in the case we have analyzed here.

The correction dream for a recurrent series of anxiety dreams can often be recognized during analytic treatment. For example, two of my patients (male and female) had had recurrent examination dreams dating back to early adolescence. In each case there was a strange classroom, filled with unfamiliar competitors who were busily engaged in taking the examination. The dreamer felt totally unprepared and extremely frightened about the impending failure.

During the analysis the examination dreams appeared again, but this time included an erotized parental surrogate of the opposite sex who provided support and guidance which enabled the dreamer to pass his test. The work of the analysis had alleviated the dreamer's anxiety about the same-sexed parent's retaliation for an Oedipal fantasy in which the love of the opposite-sexed parent would make it unnecessary for the child to endure the effort and delay of growing up. The dream censorship had been acting to prevent the matching of new experience relating to this fantasy, and had, in the process, prevented the representation of the fantasy from being updated by later experience in which achievement was accepted and encouraged by the parent whose retaliation was feared.

The series of ad hoc solutions proposed by Freud to deal with "exceptional" cases eventually concludes by denying many, if not most of the basic assumptions built into his original theory of dreams. However, none of these problem cases are "exceptional" for the memory cycle model. They require no modification of the information-processing function of dreams as we now understand it or of the mechanisms through which it operates.

Freud's final postscript to *The Interpretation of Dreams,* written in 1925, is concerned primarily with technical problems of interpretation. It raises one issue of importance to our discussion, however. On the subject of "immoral" dreams he says:

But others of them—and, it must be admitted, the majority—really mean what they say and have undergone no distortion from the censorship. They are an expression of immoral, incestuous and perverse impulses or of murderous and sadistic lusts. The dreamer reacts to many of these dreams by waking up in a fright, in which case the situation is no longer obscure to us. The censorship has neglected its task, this has been noticed too late, and the generation of anxiety is a substitute for the distortion that has been omitted. In still other instances of such dreams, even that expression of affect is absent. The objectionable matter is carried along by the height of the sexual excitement that has been reached during sleep, or it is viewed with the same tolerance with which even a waking person can regard a fit of rage, an angry mood or the indulgence in cruel phantasies. (1925, XIX:132)

We must remember that throughout his writings on dreams, Freud has regarded the censorship as an essential component of the dream-work, responsible in large measure for the form taken by the manifest content. We cannot reconcile Freud's usual view with the idea that the censorship can occasionally "neglect its task." Moreover, the dreams

Freud alludes to, in which the representation of powerful impulses is accompanied by an absence of the usual cognitive "distortion," caused in reality by the matching process, simply do not exist. In the dreams he refers to here, it is only the mechanism of displacement or substitution which is absent.

The exclusion of M. A.'s father from his Tuesday-night dreams provides a clear and concrete example of the censorship working through the mechanism of substitution. An emotionally charged element in the day residue was deleted from the incipient dream. When this happened in Dream IA, another element in the day residue, previously connected to the deleted element—i.e., Judith's bathtubs—was automatically moved into the place of the deleted element in the matching process. This mechanism of substitution can account in full for the role played by the censorship in the construction of dreams. Unlike the obligatory "distortion" caused by the mechanism of comparison by superimposition in the matching process—i.e., what Freud called "condensation"—the work of the censor may or may not be present in any given dream.

The censorship in Dream IA altered the construction of the dream by interrupting the operation of the independent mechanism of the memory cycle, which would have produced another dream, similar to Dream IIA, the correction dream, if there had been no such interference.

There are many points in the memory cycle which may be vulnerable to a variety of defensive substitutions. But the distortion of cognitive elements in the manifest content of the dream can be fully accounted for even when they are absent. For our purposes here this is the important point.

The need for defense arises when wishful thinking threatens to falsify the perception of reality. The employment of defense mechanisms varies greatly from person to person; the mechanism which produces dreams is remarkably consistent. Although defense mechanisms may be modified extensively by the therapeutic process, there is no corresponding change in the form or structure of the dreams which accompany such modifications.

Freud says, "On the mechanism of dream-formation itself, on the dream-work in the strict sense of the word, one never exercises any influence: of that one may be quite sure" (1923b, XIX:114). He can only be speaking here of the dreamwork minus the censorship mechanism, which was dramatically influenced during the Thursday hour in our example. What remains can be nothing else but the memory cycle.

My emphasis on the independence of the memory cycle is not intended to minimize the importance of the mechanisms of defense in psychopathology or character formation. But an exclusive interest in these mechanisms not only obscures our perception of the information-processing substrate of the psychic apparatus, it also deprives us of a vantage point from which to study the defense mechanisms themselves.

Defense mechanisms obstruct the orderly flow of information through the psychic apparatus, just as resistance hinders the flow of information between patient and analyst. Consider once again the dream censorship. Freud suggested that when an unacceptable item is deleted from a dream, the censorship must undertake a wide-ranging search for a substitute that will be different enough from the original item to be nonthreatening, yet similiar enough to fit into the psychological context left open by the deletion. In pursuit of this theme Freud often attributed to everyman while asleep an ingenuity which is comparable in waking life only to his own unique powers of imaginative synthesis.

This attribution becomes superfluous once we have grasped the notion that the substitute item has not been fished uncannily out of an ocean of affects and images, but is in reality an adjacent item in a train of associations en route from one processing locus in the psychic apparatus to another. The work involved in forging the associative link between the deleted item and its substitute is not an extraordinary measure undertaken in order to conceal the original item. It is a routine operation designed to facilitate storage, which automatically provides a new (and necessarily related) item to fill the empty place in the sensory projection mechanisms when an unacceptable item is prevented from entering into the matching procedure.

For a theoretical system whose ultimate terms are impulses devoid of information content, any meaningful event must appear to be either accidental or supernatural. Identical particles charged with energy, in any of its various forms, must eventually reach a state of equilibrium comparable to a perfect gas in random Brownian motion. Only a mechanism able to recognize similarities and differences can begin to assemble the particles into larger structures.

At the lowest levels of material organization (atoms and simple molecules), it is possible for distinguishable properties of the particles themselves to carry all the information necessary to form new combinations. But as soon as we reach the level of self-reproducing nucleic acid chains, the situation changes radically. Smaller units are now added to larger preexisting units, according to a condition of desirability determined by the information content of the larger unit as a whole. Each nucleotide base is added only after it can be matched to a template structure provided for the purpose by the enormous nucleic acid molecule.

From the very beginning, life requires choice, and choice requires structures capable of tracing the information content of each of their constituent parts. We have seen that the structure of the associative memory tree is a rather loose one by the usual standards of rational discourse, but that it serves its function of storing a huge amount of information with a minimum number of connecting links very effectively. Every new item entered into it must first be related to the whole of its present contents. This is the task of the memory cycle and the process of dreaming, a task no impulse-based mechanism could begin to perform on its own.

Wish-Fulfillment in Dreams

If the impetus for the construction of the dream comes not from the contents of the dream but from the adaptive purpose of matching present and past experience, then what role, if any, remains for the fulfillment of unconscious wishes?

Let us begin by asking what constitutes an "unconscious wish" or "wish-impulse." We have inherited the notion that wishes are atomic entities, each an indivisible source of mental activity. But even the most casual observation will show that there are at least three distinct components to every wish: a cognitive image of the event wished for, an affective signal indicating the desirability of the event, and a program of action aimed at bringing the desired event into being. (See also Schur, 1966b, passim.)

When a wish is actively at work during waking consciousness, we are subjectively aware of each of these distinct components. Although this awareness may be simultaneous, it may also be experienced as a sequence which takes time to develop, or which may be interrupted by the intervention of defensive operations or other distractions. In neurotic illness, we continually see the components of a single wish separated from each other and often recombined with the components of other wishes to form substitute or compromise wish-formations.

Neurotic patterns are often based on a selective inattention to one or more of the components of wishes in general. The obsessive patient often appears to have conscious access only to the cognitive component of his wishes, the hysteric to the affective component, and the patient with a behavioral disorder only to the action component.

If the components of a wish can be activated independently and selectively, then they must also be capable of existing independently in inactive or unconscious form, the form suitable for storage in short- and long-term memory structures. What might this form take? It must be something which in itself lacks the properties of arousal and incitement which accompany the wish when it is active, yet capable of eliciting these subjective states on very short notice. The stored version must be, in effect, a program or set of instructions for reproducing the subjective experience of wishing.

The wish-program must contain the three components we have already mentioned: a program for reproducing the sensory and cognitive aspects of the experience, a program for setting the limbic and autonomic nervous systems to the appropriate affective readings, and a program for patterning the motions of the skeletal muscle system in pursuit of the desired goal. Each of these major component programs will include within themselves a great many detailed subprograms.

The decision to introduce the representation of a new experience into the permanent memory is based in large measure on its relevance to the fulfillment of the subject's wishes. Here we must distinguish between the affective component of the wish, which is the biologically given feeling of pleasure or unpleasure, and the cognitive and action-oriented components, which can be acquired only through learning. Of the two learned components, the storing of representations of events which give satisfaction must be the primary one.

During the "intake" phase of development described by Erikson (1950), which covers the first twelve months or so of life, precedence is given to the process of psychological incorporation: that is, the identification of desirable events. At this stage, the child can ordinarily rely on other people to provide the means for achieving the desired and avoiding the undesired outcomes. Only during the second and third years of life does he begin in earnest to explore the possibilities for autonomous action. The psychoanalyst is continually made aware that the image of a desirable event may be present throughout life without an effective program of action to achieve it. The fantasied images of adult competence which originate in the Oedipal period take many years to acquire appropriate action programs, even when circumstances are completely favorable.

The first step in the development of a wish-program must therefore be essentially a two-component program which associates the instructions for reproducing the cognitive-sensory representation of an event with the feeling state which accompanied the actual experience of the event. (There must also be a simple, nonspecific action component for signaling to others that something needs to be done.)

At the beginning of life, then, after a brief experience of pleasure and pain, this two-component program will be capable of reproducing a combined cognitive-affective image of an earlier experience. Since the affective component of this combined image indicates whether it is desirable to repeat the original experience or to avoid a repetition of it, the image becomes, in effect, the *statement* of a wish with respect to new experiences which may resemble the original one.

A *wish-statement* is not a *wish-fulfillment*. The fulfillment of the wish requires, in addition to the statement of the wish, a program of action which will create an actual event capable of providing the gratification of current biological and emotional needs. At the same time, the behavioral signs of distress which accompany the wish-statement may bring about an actual fulfillment of the wish without further effort by the infant, so that the wish-statement under ideal circumstances of maternal responsiveness may be subjectively equivalent to a wish-fulfillment.

I hope it is sufficiently clear that by the term "statement of a wish" I do not mean a verbal description of it, but a *representation* which is subjectively similar to the actual desired event. This is the kind of "statement" made by a successful work of art: not a statement *about* something desirable, but a statement *of* the desire itself.

The representations of current and past experiences which are superimposed in the dream are wish-statements in the sense just defined. Freud recognized that for the infant it may be difficult to distinguish between the wish-statement and the actual fulfillment of the wish, and that the affective component of the wish-statement may temporarily screen out the current biological signal of an unfulfilled need. His theory of wish-fulfillment in dreams is based in part on the idea that this infantile error is deliberately propagated during sleep in order to ward off the stressful effects of needs which cannot be actively attended to.

Our data indicate clearly that as far as the genesis of the dream is concerned, this infantile self-deception cannot have a causative role. The adaptive function of dreaming, which is essential to the creation of an organized long-term memory structure, cannot have originated incidentally to a perceptual error of infancy, nor can each individual instance of dreaming which carries out this essential function have done so.

However, there is one important respect in which the mechanism of dreaming is vulnerable to confusion between the wish-statement and the actual fulfillment of a wish. This has to do with the double nature of affects, which in waking life function both as sources of information about the internal state of the organism and as initiators of action to modify that internal state. In evolutionary history, it is certain that the second function preceded the first, yet in the process of dreaming the information-carrying function is the one that takes precedence.

We know that the information-carrying function of affects tends to be reduced whenever their action-initiating function comes into play. (This is one of the fundamental observations on which psychoanalytic treatment is based.) This means that for integrative activities beyond the level of the reflex arc the phylogenetically earlier action-program must be inhibited. *The wish-statement alone must be given precedence over the complete wish-impulse of which it normally forms a component part.* It is very likely that without this evolutionary reversal the formation of the long-term memory itself would have been impossible. Those who are condemned to repeat cannot remember.

It is of great interest, therefore, that for the matching process of the memory cycle the opposition between wish-statement and wish-impulse as a whole is in one important area absolutely critical. Wish-statements can be compared rapidly and efficiently through the process of super-imposition; wish-impulses cannot be compared in this way at all. The superimposition of images takes place in the virtual space within the psychic apparatus which is created and controlled by the sensory projection mechanisms. The action initiated by a complete wish-impulse takes place outside the psychic apparatus, in the real world where only one thing can happen at a given moment in time.

Here the necessity to distinguish between wish-statement and wish-impulse is imperative, and the difficulty in doing so created by the sequence of evolutionary development becomes a serious problem. We would expect the creation of the long-term memory by the operation of the memory cycle to be a precondition for the development of higher-level intellectual capabilities. The essential simplicity of the mechanisms of superimposition and substitution, as we have observed them in the dream, support this expectation, as does the evidence that lower mammals, including the marsupials, already display all the physiological concomitants of dreaming.

Is there a correspondingly simple mechanism for isolating the wish-statement from the complete wish-impulse during the process of dream construction? There is such a mechanism, and it is a very crude one. Instead of distinguishing the wish-statement from the wish-impulse on the basis of psychological differences—i.e., by separating the components of the wish-impulse program—the wish-impulse as a whole is converted into a de facto wish-statement by the removal of any possibility for voluntary physical action during the dream. The entire skeletal muscle system is disconnected from the affects which ordinarily set its various members into motion.

This suspension of skeletal-muscle activity cannot be explained by the assumption that the executive apparatus of the ego is inactive during sleep, since the suspension does not occur during the many hours of nondreaming sleep every night. Sleepwalking and talking, for example, take place in the nondreaming stages of sleep.

The dreaming state is then a primitive natural precursor of developmentally more advanced states of mind in which the subject consciously and voluntarily promotes the display of affect and simultaneously inhibits the action which would normally follow. The adaptive goal in these states of mind is the achievement of self-knowledge through an examination of feelings ordinarily beyond the range of casual introspection. It is this goal which distinguishes the Greek theater from Dionysiac revels, and psychoanalysis from abreactive versions of psychotherapy.

In dreams, a similar goal is achieved through purely *mechanical* means, and the *psychological* distinction between wish-statement and wish-impulse remains ambiguous. For the adaptive purpose of the memory cycle, this ambiguity is not an obstacle. The matching process can be successfully carried out provided only that no action takes place to disrupt the exclusive use of the sensory projection mechanisms for that purpose.

The psychological ambiguity of the dream has two significant effects on the subjective experience of the dreamer. First, the experience of the affects reproduced in the dream has psychological consequences similar to those which accompanied the original experience of those affects: e.g., they produce a feeling of gratification which temporarily reduces the desire for action. Second, these reconstructed affects and the images associated with them are responded to by the mechanisms of defense as if they were actual experiences in the real world. Each of these effects played an important role in the development of Freud's theory of dreams. As we see them here, they are incidental effects of the adaptive functioning of the memory cycle, however, not sources for the impetus which creates the dream.

Moreover, it is unlikely that the reexperiencing of remembered affects is the only source of the gratification produced by the experience of dreaming. To the extent that the adaptive purpose of the dream is actually realized—that is, that a successful match is completed—the dream will provide the pleasure of achievement, even when the affects reproduced in the superimposed wish-statements are negative. In the case of Dream IIA, M. A. appeared to be already experiencing a degree of this ego gratification at the time he reported the dream to his analyst. But it is also clear that this form of gratification was enhanced during the hour by the working through of the meaning of the dream, independently of the pleasure provided by the derepression of previously warded-off impulses.

In the clinical situation, the identification of the patient's warded-off wishful impulses remains a matter of primary concern. In the case of M. A., we have seen how this identification was aided by recovery of the specific experiences whose representations were selected for matching in the dreams reported at the beginning of the Thursday hour.

In actual practice, the analyst seldom has the opportunity to analyze a dream reported by a patient in such depth. He makes do with approximate identifications based on his knowledge of human development generally and of the patient's history and associative patterns. In a successful analysis, the patient is able to respond to these approximations with new associative material which brings him closer to the goal of understanding the juxtaposition of impulse and defense which makes up his neurosis.

I do not suggest a modification of this successful procedure, adapted as it is to the limitations of the analyst's time and short-term memory capacity, in any significant way. I do suggest that the analyst direct his attention, as far as it is possible to do so without interrupting the patient's associative flow, to the actual experiences (i.e., the "latent contents" as defined here) which have contributed to the manifest content of the reported dream, and which are often directly accessible to the patient's recall. The impulses warded off in the formation of the dream are more readily available once these memories have been recognized and understood.

On the theoretical level, however, important changes are necessary. We must begin by realizing that the analyst's success in using the patient's dreams to identify his warded-off impulses does not require, in principle or in practice, that these warded-off impulses be responsible for the existence of his dreams.

We have seen that the deflection of unacceptable impulses by the dream censor is likely to be responsible for the vagueness and incompleteness of a remembered dream. But we have also seen that in such a case the censor is acting against the adaptive mechanism which brought the dream into existence.

A New Foundation for the Theory of Dreams

Our successful search for the correction dream has rewarded us with an unanticipated dividend; a view of the original dream as it might have been, had not the interference of the censor emptied it of its deeper meaning. In addition, our search has revealed to us that the deeper meaning in question is a relationship unconsciously constructed by the memory cycle, which links together the dreamer's current life situation and the formative experiences of his earliest childhood.

One of the most important events in the history of psychoanalysis was Freud's realization that the derepression of warded-off impulses has only a minor therapeutic effectiveness when these impulses cannot be re-integrated with the patient's mental life as a whole through the synthetic activity of the ego. We now have evidence that this synthetic activity plays a critical role at even the most basic level of mental functioning, the level at which the memory cycle operates.

In the early stages of vertebrate evolution, the complete wish-program, with its cognitive, affective and conative components, emerged as the basic unit of mental life. This unit, called into play on an all-or-none basis by inner and outer events, could be treated by the psychic apparatus as a single entity, without separation into its components.

As soon as it became necessary to interpose a new level of internal processing between the stimulus and the response, however, the unitary wish became an adaptive liability. The suppression of voluntary muscular activity during dreaming was one of the earliest attempts to circumvent the difficulties caused by the tendency to immediate action built into the older system. The wish-statement, consisting of the cognitive and affective components of the wish, had to be distinguished from the complete wish-program.

At first, as we have seen, the separation of wish-statement from complete wish-impulse was purely functional. The action mechanism of the entire organism was inhibited, while the wish-program itself remained psychologically intact. The much more economical procedure familiar to us in waking consciousness, an inhibition *limited to the action component* of the individual wish-program, must have evolved much later.

In the course of these changes, a contrast or opposition developed between the wish-statement and the complete wish-impulse. The wish-statement is the essential ingredient of the intellectual activity which splits the reflex arc and delays or abolishes the action originally intended to complete it. As in the process of dream construction, the activity which makes possible the accumulation and effective utilization of the information acquired through actual experience in the real world is the isolation and comparison of wish-statements.

Piaget's developmental data indicate that this sequence is followed in the maturation of the child's waking capacity for problem-solving activity. Only after the complete sensorimotor unit of behavior has reached a relatively high level of complexity, toward the end of the second year, does it become possible for the child to isolate sensory images in order to manipulate them intrapsychically in simulated or trial actions (Holt, 1967). This is the stage at which the wish-statement is separated from the complete wish-program in waking consciousness. (It is not the point at which mental imagery *originates*, as some interpreters of Piaget's findings seem to believe.) The psychological separation in waking life must occur much later in the child's development than the mechanical separation in the dreaming state.

Perhaps the most useful way of stating the contrast between wish-statement and wish-impulse is to say that fundamental activity of the *psychic apparatus* is the comparison of wish-statements, while the fundamental activity of the *organism as a whole* is the realization or gratification of wish-impulses. Neurotic defense mechanisms have in common their tendency to treat the psychic apparatus as if it were the whole organism, and the wish-statements contained in the psychic apparatus as if they were complete wish-programs in the course of active fulfillment. The ubiquity of this error suggests that defensive activity originated before the evolution of the wish-statement as an independent psychological unit had been completed.

We have seen that in dreaming the wish-statement is distinguished from the wish-impulse at the organismic level but not at the psychological level, and that the dream censor appears to be responding to the intrapsychic events without taking into account the organismic context (immobilization) in which these events take place. The memory cycle is surely typical of the primordial ego as a whole in the tentativeness with which it approaches the necessity for differentiating thought and feeling from action. We can therefore recognize that the defense mechanisms are both primitive and ancient, yet without attributing to them a decisive role in the formation of adaptive psychic structure. It is much more likely that defenses interfere with the specific adaptive mechanisms which select and activate the available wish-impulse programs than that they directly inhibit the impulses themselves.

The data of free association suggest that defense mechanisms respond to wish-statements as if they were complete wish-impulses not only in dreams, but in general. This would suggest that the defense mechanism acts by disrupting the internal processing which might ordinarily lead to a decision to activate the complete wish-impulse, rather than by disrupting the activation itself. In the case of dreaming, we have observed the defensive operations of the dream censor interrupting a processing sequence which *under no circumstances* could have resulted in the immediate or even short-term activation of a wish-program. In spite of this limitation, the censorship mechanism in M. A.'s Tuesday-night index dreams appears to have been functioning very close to its maximum level of efficiency.

What is important to us here is that dreams are necessarily expressive of wishes in the normal carrying-out of their adaptive function. Our data provide no evidence for the existence of "impulses" which do not include cognitive and affective as well as conative elements. This finding is consistent with the work of Gill (1963) and Schur (1966), who have shown that in Freud's clinical writings no actual impulse originating in the past is ever identified without reference to its cognitive component.

Our data do provide a partial explanation for the widespread belief that isolated action-programs or affect-and-action-program combinations form an unconscious background to the usual conscious awareness of wish-statements. Since defense mechanisms respond to wish-statements as if they were complete wish-impulses, it would be understandable for the immature ego to subjectively interpret the activity of its own defenses as evidence that dangerous impulses were operating actively but outside its awareness and control.

This subjective impression would be produced if, as seems to be the case, the action components of those wish-impulses ordinarily undergoing internal processing were selectively inhibited by the adaptive mechanisms of the ego. There is no logical necessity for the psychoanalyst to agree with the neurotic patient that these inhibited action components have in some way been disconnected from their cognitive contexts and transferred to another agency of the psychic apparatus.

The traditional psychoanalytic theory assumes that these "separated" action components are identical to the original contents of the psychic apparatus, a set of blind and naked impulses from which all other elements of thought and feeling are said to be derived. There is a kernel of truth in this assertion: that the wish-statement is derived from the complete wish-impulse by inhibition of the action component. But here an isolated action component (or a combination of action and affect components) has been substituted by the traditional theory for the complete cognitive-affective-conative unit from which the wish-statement has been derived.

Desire is not a biological given. The signals of discomfort we receive from our viscera do not inform us of the appropriate means for satisfying them, which is something we must discover through our interactions with the outside world. It is the ego which makes these discoveries and which establishes the category of desire by anticipating the repetition of successful efforts to relieve the biologically given discomfort. Central to the possibility of desire is the *image* of the event desired.

Dreaming plays an essential role in this primary synthetic activity of the ego. The memory cycle helps to establish the overall context of cumulative experience in which newly arising biological needs can find appropriate expression. It is in the carrying out of this long-term adaptive goal that dreaming makes its principal contribution to the fulfillment of wishes. The modicum of "hallucinatory" gratifications experienced while the dream is in progress is of importance primarily when it is misinterpreted by the dream censor as an actual event in the real world.

To summarize, the memory cycle and the dreaming state are essential links in the complex adaptive process through which the gratification of biological needs is achieved in a context of relative safety and security. Dreams therefore play a major role in the reality of adaptive wish-fulfillment. The mechanisms of defense, including the dream censor, come into play when the normal adaptive processes cannot be trusted to avoid excessive risk. This situation might come about through the immaturity of the adaptive mechanisms early in life, because of adverse experience, or both.

The defense mechanisms in general, perhaps following the evolutionary example of the dream censor, operate by treating intrapsychic wish-statements as if they were actual attempts by the organism to achieve gratification in the real world. By interfering with the adaptive processing of these wish-statements, the defenses prevent the activation of the action components associated with them.

The use of the sensory projection mechanisms in dreaming, and the nonpsychological procedure for inhibiting action while the dream is taking place, maximize the potentiality for confusion between the wish-statement and the complete wish-impulse in the dream. Psychoanalytic theory became entangled in this confusion when it adopted an oversimplified model in which defenses act directly against impulses, without consideration of the adaptive mechanisms necessary for the activation of these impulses. For this reason, it fails to account for the complex relationship between wishes and dreams required by our data.

CHAPTER 6

The Psychic Apparatus

The Problem of the Id

A theory of dreams leads inevitably to a theoretical model of the psychic apparatus as a whole. This is so because dreaming is the only psychic process that makes systematic use of the sensory projection mechanisms in order to fulfill its adaptive function, without simultaneously transforming its contents through an output program into the logical and grammatical narrative structures familiar to waking thought.

The absence of output programming in dreams gives us an opportunity to observe the psychic apparatus at work at an organizational level that is much nearer to the more general structures appropriate for internal processing than is the conscious problem-solving activity of which we are more usually aware. What we can now learn from these observations is that nonconscious information processing is organized in its own way for adaptive purposes that are complementary to those approached through different methods in waking consciousness.

In this chapter I will develop some of the implications of the new theory of dreams for a model of the psychic apparatus that takes into account both the interactive, information-processing aspects of adaptive functioning and the intrusive, defense-oriented operations emphasized in traditional psychoanalytic theory. Once again my point of departure will be the theoretical model developed by Freud: a model which, for all its flaws, attempts to comprehend the full range of human experience in terms of motivational trends which operate on a scale comparable to the human lifespan.

Many others have been over this ground before. Some appear to believe that the essential truth of the Freudian model has been established beyond doubt, others that Freud's views have long since been irretrievably discredited. My belief is that many of the questions raised by Freud's approach to the psychic apparatus are still very much alive, even though Freud's answers to these questions may often be incomplete or outdated. It is with the hope that some new light may be shed on these issues that I proceed.

It is not my intention to present a comprehensive alternative to Freudian metapsychology here, but rather to deal with a set of critical problems which appear to me to stand in the way of the substantive improvements which need to be made, if psychoanalytic theory is to become accessible to the scientific world in general.

In order to understand the complex relationship between dreaming and wish-fulfillment, we have had to distinguish three separate stages in the development of that elusive entity usually referred to as an *impulse*. We shall discover in this section that by anatomizing the impulse in this way we have made it possible to resolve one of the most vexing problems of psychoanalytic theory, the problem of the Id.

The three stages in the development of an impulse are:

1. The biologically given affective signal of distress or discomfort. There is a question as to how much information this signal contains about its source. It may, without the necessity for further interpretation, indicate the *location* in the body at which the distress or discomfort originated. What seems certain from infant observation and the study of eating disorders in adults (Bruch, 1961, 1962) is that the affective signal does not initially include any information about the *kind of activity* which might eliminate the physiological source of the distress. This information must be acquired through experience. The distress signal itself is an organismic activity, one which acts across the usual boundary between the physiological and psychological aspects of experience.

2. The intrapsychic wish-program. This is a mental construct which links together a representation of the affective signal, an image of the desired event which is likely to relieve the discomfort indicated by the signal, and a plan of action to bring about this desired event. The affective signal itself exists in the immediate present. It may lead to direct reflexive action without the intervening formation of a wish-program. In the more usual case, however, the action is postponed and the affective

signal is incorporated into a wish-program. The wish-program is then evaluated by comparison with other wish-programs and a decision is made whether it is to be activated. If the decision is made not to activate the wish-program in the immediate or short term, it must be stored, and a further decision must eventually be made in Stage II of the memory cycle concerning the desirability of permanent storage and possible activation far in the future. The construction, evaluation, and disposition of wish-programs are purely intrapsychic activities, and the wish-program may exist indefinitely in the virtual time created by the psychic apparatus.

3. The activated action component of the wish-program. If the decision is made to activate the wish-program, the plan of action which it incorporates is put into effect. Like the affective signal, activation is an organismic activity which crosses the boundary between mind and body. It exists in real time and is much more difficult to modify or control than was the wish-program in its purely intrapsychic state.

Psychoanalytic theory has paid little attention to the stages of impulse development for an important *practical* reason. The mechanisms of defense in the neurotic patient respond to affective signals and to intrapsychic wish-programs as if they were both identical with the final activated form of the impulse. When defense mechanisms are successfully circumvented in the course of psychoanalytic treatment, we find that *currently experienced* affective signals and wish-programs *reconstructed from memory* are simultaneously derepressed. It was natural for the traditional theory to assume that these two impulse-forms were sequestered together within the psychic apparatus prior to their joint emergence into consciousness.

As long as we think of the *Id* simply as the class of all mental contents which are rendered inaccessible to consciousness by the defense mechanisms, we are on solid observational ground. If we try to go further, however, and elevate the Id into a *structure* within the psychic apparatus, trouble follows immediately.

The difficulty arises from the structural incompatibility of affective signals which reflect the current state of the physiological substratum of the organism *and exist for a limited duration in real time*, on the one hand, and purely intrapsychic wish-programs which *exist indefinitely in the virtual time of the psychic apparatus*, on the other. How can one conceive of a structure which could "contain" both of these?

Within the psychoanalytic literature, the statement of this problem has taken on a particular form. (See, for example, Applegarth, 1973). One asks whether the Id is *structured* or *unstructured*. Freud clearly preferred to think of it as unstructured, despite the paradoxical implications. For him the Id was "a chaos, a cauldron full of seething excitations . . . it has no organization, produces no collective will, but only a striving to bring about the satisfaction of instinctual needs." (1933, p. 73) In this image, the walls of the cauldron represent the mechanisms of defense, which separate the "contents" of the Id from the rest of the psychic apparatus. Yet, within the same paragraph, Freud tells us of "impressions which have sunk into the Id by repression"; that is, memories of experiences in which forbidden impulses had been expressed.

These experiences must be highly structured. How can they be contained unaltered within the chaos of the Id, to be recovered intact years or decades later? Freud gave no direct answer to this question.

Among those investigators who have struggled with this issue in recent years, a consensus appears to have developed that the Id is in reality not a chaos without organization, but rather a structure which is organized in a very primitive way. For example, Holt (1967) suggests that the primitive cognitive structures of infants, which Piaget has demonstrated to be coherent and systematic in their own terms, can mistakenly appear to be entirely lacking in structure when compared with examples of rational adult thinking. He appears to believe that the "seething cauldron" metaphor grew out of an observational error based on adultomorphic preconceptions. Gill (1963) and Schur (1966) agree that observation fails to confirm the existence of an unstructured Id. However, they suggest that the "seething cauldron" image was never meant to be a description of observed phenomena, but rather a statement at another level of scientific discourse, metapsychological or theoretical.

The concepts of the associative memory tree and the memory cycle help to explain why the record of impulses experienced in the past must be structured. To the extent that the "contents" of the Id include such a record, the Id, too, must be structured. When they conclude that the Id is structured in its entirety, however, the more recent writers appear to be attributing the structure of remembered impulses to the *currently experienced affective signals* which are traditionally included among the contents of the Id. This is the *reverse* of Freud's procedure, which was to transfer the structurelessness of immediate affects to the repressed memories said to be contained in or by the Id.

Freud's meaning will be clearer if we examine his famous description of the Id more closely. The "cauldron full of seething excitations" is a reference to affective signals which have not yet been incorporated into wish-programs. "A striving to bring about the satisfaction of instinctual needs" is not the same thing at all, but a reference to action components already activated, released finally from intrapsychic control. The chaotic sense he ascribes to the Id as a whole is a property of the organismic stages of impulse development before and after intrapsychic processing and evaluation have modified and modulated the biological substratum.

Freud's critics are correct in denying organismic status to repressed memories, which by their nature can only be intrapsychic constructs. But they misrepresent Freud's conception of the Id if they restrict it to the purely intrapsychic structure characteristic of the permanent memory. What is the solution?

We notice, first of all, that the argument concerning the nature of the Id is isomorphic to the dilemma faced by Freud when he traced the impetus for the dream alternately to the present and past components of the latent content, while excluding the possibility that both components were essential to dream construction. In this case, we have a larger entity, the Id, and two of its constituents, affective signals experienced in the present and wish-programs reconstructed from the past. It is claimed that the larger entity has the overall characteristics first of one, then of the other of these constituents, but the evidence suggests that each of them plays an essential role in determining the nature of the larger entity. Once again, the obstacle which prevents the problem from being solved is the assumption that one or the other constituent must be the dominant factor.

The problem of the latent content was solved through the realization that dream construction is not a process in which one constituent element imposes its will on the other, but in which both elements are coordinated by a higher-level structure with the purpose of comparing the information content in each of them. Can the same formula be applied to the problem of the Id? The answer is not only that it can, but that it must.

The mechanisms of defense draw a curtain over the developmental history of the individual impulse. By treating all stages of this development as equally threatening, they draw our attention away from the transformations which bring about this adaptively necessary development. Without these transformations, the organism would be limited to making reflexive responses to immediate stimuli, with no possibility of learning from experience.

For higher-level adaptive purposes it is necessary to give the unstructured affective signal an experiential context within which the pursuit of gratification can be undertaken in a practical way. To do this, the signal and the circumstances in which it arises must be compared with wish-programs which have incorporated closely similar signals experienced in the past. The processes through which this comparison is made are in general less familiar to us than the procedure of comparison by superimposition as we see it in dreams. For the most part, it takes place outside consciousness, apparently without the use of the sensory projection mechanisms. When these more primitive procedures fail to operate smoothly, however, we find that more deliberate techniques for locating matching experiences from the past are brought into play.

These techniques involve a replay or simulation of past experiences in which a similar affective signal was followed by a successful program of action to achieve gratification. Occasionally the replay becomes conscious and organized, as in daydreams and reveries. More often it is a kind of stream of consciousness, though not quite conscious, which frequently accompanies the problem-solving activity of waking thought. The dream-like states which often occur during the entry into sleep are prolongations of this stream of semiconscious replay beyond the cessation of more organized problem-solving activity.

Elements of current experience are worked into the replay from the past in order to test the degree to which they fit these previously established patterns. How this procedure is related to comparison by superimposition is still a question. In daydreaming, the use of the output program creates a narrative which is more naturalistic and subtle than the interweaving we see in the superimpositions of the nocturnal dream. In the more usual case, when the replay is not fully conscious, the mechanism of condensation or superimposition is frequently, if not generally, employed. Freud's early work on puns and parapraxes (1901) brought this layer of everyday information processing to our attention.

Whatever mechanisms are involved, the new affective signal must be compared with existing wish-programs which incorporate similar affective signals. This comparison determines whether the currently experienced situation provides the opportunity for a gratifying event, and, if so, what program of action is likely to bring about such an event. If the current situation is ripe for immediate gratification, a successful wish-program of the past may possibly be activated directly, without the formation of a new wish-program.

Otherwise, a new wish-program must be constructed which includes the currently experienced affective signal, a sensory representation of the current situation, and the action components of successful wish-programs of the past which might be applicable to the current situation. If the affective signal is sufficiently intense, new problem-solving activity will be initiated to modify the new wish-program so that immediate action of some sort may be taken. The final form of the modified wish-program, together with a record of the results of its activation, will then be transferred to the short-term memory. If the intensity is low, and other ongoing programs are given priority, the new wish-program will be stored in the short-term memory without activation.

This sequence of events gives a more detailed account of the activity during Stage I of the memory cycle than we have attempted previously. It is obvious, however, that this description is itself only the very sketchiest outline of an enormously complex process. The point to be made here is that all of this complex activity must have taken place before what we ordinarily call "an impulse" takes on the form in which it can be recorded permanently.

We cannot specify as yet the precise sequences and mechanisms involved in this massive processing effort, but we know enough about the adaptive requirements of the situation to establish a very powerful generalization. The basic procedure, applied repeatedly and in a variety of ways, which converts reflex automatism to intelligent biological activity, is *the comparison of the relatively unstructured experience of the present moment to the more highly structured experience of the past.*

This generalization applies across all three steps outlined above in the development of the wish-program. New affective signals are compared with those wish-programs of the past which incorporate closely similar affective signals. Newly constructed wish-programs are compared intrapsychically (as wish-statements) with wish-programs whose adaptive value is attested by their retention in memory. When wish-programs are activated in the present, the feedback information generated by the new activity is compared with expectations based on past experience.

We are now prepared for an adaptive definition of the Id. The Id is the class of intrapsychic activities in which wish-programs derived from current or recent experience are displayed together with wish-programs derived from the past for the purpose of comparison and evaluation. In the case of wish-programs derived from current or very recent experience, we include the *component programs* of the complete wish-program at various stages of assembly. In this phase, the already complete wish-programs of the past act as templates which model the construction of the newer programs.

It is the necessity for the display of the elements of past and present in the process of comparison which makes them accessible to observation. For this reason, we would expect the "contents" of the Id always to be double, always to include both unstructured and structured elements. In the case of impulse formation, the unstructured elements include the unprocessed affective signal and the not-yet-organized flux of sensory data which must be severely reduced to form a representation of current experience. In the dreaming state, the representations of recent experience have already been assembled into wish-programs, but their relationship to other wish-programs is still highly unstructured when compared with the organization of the permanent memory.

It would be misleading to think either of the unstructured elements of present experience or of the structured memories of the past, before they have been brought together for comparison, as the "contents" of the Id. The sources from which these representations are supplied to the comparative mechanisms of the Id are entirely different and structurally incompatible. The affective signals which initiate the process of impulse formation are generated organismically in real time, in relative isolation from one another. The memories of the past with which they are to be compared are intrapsychic programs permanently stored in a fixed and very complex structured relationship to a very large body of other programs. From the information-processing point of view, it is enormously difficult to bring these disparate elements together, and the comparative mechanisms of the Id, including the process of dreaming, must be given very high priority in the allocation of processing capabilities.

The problem of the Id, with which we began this section, has a rational solution. The nature of the Id is determined neither by the source which supplies it with currently experienced affective signals nor the source which supplies it with structured memories. The nature of the Id is a reflection of its adaptive function in bringing these formally dissimilar elements together, for comparison and evaluation.

The adaptive definition of Id activity provides a theoretical basis for the clinical definition. Currently experienced affective signals are de-repressed in the course of psychoanalytic treatment *together* with memories of events in which similar signals were experienced, because the Id activity of comparison and evaluation is an essential part of the decision-making process which allows them to enter consciousness.

The fragmentary evidence we now have available suggests that comparison by superimposition (condensation) is the typical, though not necessarily the exclusive, adaptive procedure employed during Id activity. In our dream data, we have observed the high degree of vulnerability of this procedure to substitutive disruption (displacement) by the defensive operations of the dream censor. This vulnerability is very likely to extend to other types of Id activity as well. Accordingly, we can expect to find that if there is a particular area of adaptive functioning which is most likely to be obscured and distorted by the mechanisms of defense, that area is the one which Freud designated as the Id.

Under ordinary circumstances, Id activity is not conscious, yet is capable to a degree of being made conscious when special difficulties arise which require new problem-solving efforts. Freud referred to this level of activity as the system Preconscious. When the mechanisms of defense prevent material associated with forbidden wish-programs from achieving consciousness even under these special circumstances, this material becomes part of the dynamic Unconscious.

Freud assumed that "impulses" have a mobility of their own within the psychic apparatus, and that defense mechanisms operate by interfering directly with the self-activated movements of these impulses. It is this assumption which dictates at the theoretical level that the Id be a "chaos without organization." Once we have understood that defense mechanisms interfere with the adaptive processing of wish-programs, rather than with the movements of impulses, the Id can take its natural place in the hierarchy of adaptive information-processing structures.

The *subjective* impression of disorder which generally accompanies Id activity has three sources. For us as for Freud, the most abundant and accessible sampling of Id activity is the data of remembered dreams. Here the sense of disorder arises directly from the procedure of comparison by superimposition, the fundamental adaptive function of dreaming. Added to this is the frequent disruption of the adaptive mechanisms by defensive substitutions. As we have noted, these disruptions are much more likely to occur during dreams which are remembered and reported than during more typical uncensored dreams.

Although it is purely an intrapsychic process, dreaming is sufficiently typical of Id activity to provide an adequate model for all of the primary processes in which elements of new and relatively unstructured experience are compared with structured wish-programs assembled and recorded in the past. However, the subjective sense of disorder during Id activity has one other source which is external to the dream. This is the effect produced by organismic activity on the self-observing mechanisms of the psychic apparatus.

If we think of mental activity as occupying the space created when the afferent and efferent limbs of the reflex arc are split apart, then we see that sensory input and motor output represent the absolute limits of direct intrapsychic control over events. Within the psychic apparatus itself, all actions are trial actions, subject to revision or reversal as ongoing evaluative procedures determine. At the sensory and motor interfaces between the psychic apparatus and the organism as a whole, however, actions have a finality about them which can only seem arbitrary and unmotivated to an information-processing mechanism designed to have maximum control over a domain consisting almost entirely of mental representations.

When the psychic apparatus is crippled internally by its own defense mechanisms, the inherent strangeness of these limiting organismic events may be experienced as a terrifying independence from intrapsychic influence and control. Freud's description of the Id as "a chaos . . . without organization" corresponds very closely to a view of organismic reflex activity as seen by a psychic apparatus which has lost the consciousness of its own mediating adaptive influence. Freud's overall view of the Id, as developed throughout his writings, was essentially a picture of the intrapsychic process of dreaming, onto which he superimposed the subjective experience of mental activity at the borderlines of mind and body.

The *intuitive* success of this superimposition of Freud's is one of a great many historical examples of the creative process at work in the Unconscious. Koestler (1964) suggests that the act of creation is an act of "bisociation," a bringing together of two ideas or images from areas of experience which had never before seemed connected or related. This is clearly the work of that primitive but not yet overspecialized portion of the adaptive ego which we have until now been calling the Id.

The Archaic Adaptive Ego

In resolving the problem of the Id, we have encountered an equally serious problem in the traditional psychoanalytic concept of the "ego." There are two clear and distinct meanings of this term which must be separated. The first of these, which we have been using throughout this discussion, designates as *the ego* the system of adaptive structures within the psychic apparatus which functions to advance the interests of the individual organism of which it forms a part. This is the adaptive definition of the ego.

When we consider the Id as the set of adaptive processes whose function it is to bring together elements of current and past experience for comparison and evaluation, the Id we refer to is clearly a portion of the adaptive ego. In fact, it appears quite likely that the Id in this sense constitutes the original or archaic adaptive ego. Having understood this, we need have no difficulty in assenting to Freud's often repeated claim that the ego evolves from the Id.

The second distinct meaning of the term "ego," which I shall refer to with capitalization as *the Ego*, is the region of the mind and its contents which is ordinarily accessible to consciousness and identified by the subject as an essential part of himself. This Ego is the counterpart of the Id as the Id is defined by the repressive powers of the mechanisms of defense. This is the defense-determined definition of the Ego. In this sense of the terms, the Ego and the Id must be created *simultaneously* by the boundaries set up between them through the operation of the defense mechanisms.

Many difficulties for psychoanalytic theory have arisen from attempts to combine the adaptive ego and the defense-determined Ego into a single concept. The basic error has been to regard the presence of structure, a feature of the adaptive ego, as equivalent to or coextensive with accessibility to consciousness, the defining characteristic of the defense-determined Ego. But no such simple relationship exists.

Freud's major effort to describe the psychic apparatus as a whole, usually referred to as the *structural* model, suffers from this confusion. The Ego of the structural theory is first of all a development of the Preconscious in the topographic theory. It includes everything in the psychic apparatus which is ordinarly accessible to consciousness. Opposed to it is the Id, the inheritor of the system Unconscious. The structured elements of the old Unconscious have now been transferred to the new Ego, however, emptying the Id of all internal structure. The new Ego therefore contains everything in the psychic apparatus which is accessible to consciousness *and* everything in the psychic apparatus which is structured. It attempts to be an adaptive ego as well as a defense-determined Ego.

The acknowledgment of an unconscious portion of the ego would seem to be an important breakthrough, but Freud did not take full advantage of the conceptual possibilities opened by it. For the most part, he restricted his interest in the unconscious ego to the mechanisms of defense, never giving unconscious adaptive structures a significant role in his theory. This restriction allowed him to maintain his earlier view that the only explanation for inaccessibility to consciousness was the presence of warded-off impulses, on the assumption that if the defense mechanisms were conscious, they would reveal the presence of the impulses being defended against.

This explanation for inaccessibility would not have ruled out the assignment of repressed memories to the *unconscious ego,* however, since the mechanisms of defense had already been accommodated there. Yet Freud felt compelled to locate repressed memories in the Id, thus undoing the elaborate effort of the structural theory to destructuralize the contents of the Id. The motive for this gross departure from the logic of the structural theory is clear. Freud knew from clinical observation that unstructured, currently experienced affects underwent derepression in analysis *simultaneously* with the structured memories of similar experiences in the past. In his own theoretical language, this observation could be translated only by a statement that the two phenomena were "contained" in the same intrapsychic structure.

These internal contradictions can be eliminated if we approach the relationship between structure and consciousness without unnecessary preconceptions. Our identification of the Id with the archaic adaptive ego suggests a new model for the psychic apparatus as a whole which is both simpler and closer to observation.

In this new model, we reserve the term *structure* to the various components of the adaptive ego. These *structures* are biologically given and develop through a relatively constant maturational sequence (subject, of course, to the necessary feedback from an average expectable environment). From the psychoanalytic point of view, the most interesting and important major component of the adaptive ego is the archaic adaptive ego mentioned above.

This structure includes the series of mechanisms which evaluates and assimilates new affective experience by comparing it with the body of information stored in memory throughout the past life of the organism. These mechanisms are designed for rapid processing of large amounts of information, as exemplified by the mechanism of comparison by superimposition in dreaming, rather than for the reflective problem-solving typical of the mature adaptive ego.

The rapidity of processing and the lack of reflection at this primitive level of ego functioning leave the organism vulnerable to serious dangers in the evaluation of new experience. An emergency system for interrupting the flow of information when these dangers threaten is needed. This system must also act quickly and without reflection. It must deflect the flow of information without stopping it since continuity in the associative flow is critical to the operation of the adaptive mechanisms. This emergency system comprises the mechanisms of defense, of which the substitutive activity of the dream censor may be taken as typical.

The antagonism between the adaptive mechanisms of the archaic ego and the mechanisms of defense is an intimate one. There are many critical points in the sequence of decisions which follows from the registration of a physiological signal of discomfort or stress. The perceptual elements of the defense mechanisms must be in position to monitor these decisions continuously, for the level of danger attaching to a given wish-program must be subject to sudden alterations as it makes contact first with one and then with another related wish-program which has been recovered from storage in order to be compared with it. We cannot reasonably picture the defense mechanisms observing the processing of wish-programs from across the gulf which is said to separate the Ego and the Id in Freud's structural model.

The most striking characteristic of the archaic adaptive ego is that it is involuntary. Decisions are made by the application of various generalized procedures to particular cases. In the case of the adaptive mechanisms, these procedures are sufficiently flexible to permit some degree of growth and creative innovation, but they are quite different from the problem-solving methods of conscious thought. In the archaic ego, decisions are computed rather than willed, automatic rather than thought through.

There is, in fact, no obvious need for the activity of the archaic ego to be fully conscious and for the most part it is not. The exceptions to this generalization appear to arise only when the scale of comparison is large enough to require sensory reconstruction. As suggested earlier in relation to dreaming, this is the most efficient method for comparing information derived from a variety of sensory modalities, especially when complex affective states are at issue. If we consider sensory reconstruction for the evaluation of wish-programs to be a state of consciousness, then it is very likely to have been the original or primary state of consciousness. Primary consciousness would then have evolved as the final stage in the evolution of the archaic ego.

The crucial step in this development would have been the point at which the sensory projection mechanisms were withdrawn from direct contact with the external world and first became available for reproductive rather than merely receptive activity. Such reproductive activity would have acquired adaptive value to the extent that it could bring the record of relevant past experience into the arena of current events.

The reproduction of a past event must initially have involved the reproduction of an action indissolubly linked with affect and sensory imagery. The fact that the entire skeletal muscle system is incapacitated in the dreaming state indicates both the importance and the difficulty of separating the imagery and information content of a reproduced memory from the action program associated with it. Unless and until this separation was made, there could be no possibility of *comparing* the present and the past without *confusing* them.

The crudity of the means by which the separation between imagery and action is achieved in dreaming suggests that the mechanism of dream construction may have been the first instance in which the separation was made in a systematic way. The uses of the sensory projection mechanisms for receptive contact with the outside world and for reproductive comparison of internal imagery would then have developed in isolation from each other during the waking and sleeping states. In the next momentous evolutionary development, these two isolated functions of the sensory projection mechanisms would have been combined. It would then have been possible to maintain the imagery of present and past in the sensory projection mechanisms during waking consciousness, while at the same time performing the actions appropriate only to *the present*.

The voluntary aspects of conscious thought, the sense of "making up one's mind" or "making a conscious choice," would have followed. Only at this later stage of evolution would consciousness have been shaped and organized by the narrative, grammatical, and logical conventions of the output program which now dominates our awareness, and which Freud referred to as the *secondary process*.

Most of what happens in the archaic ego is meant to be automatic and unconscious, but is presumably capable of becoming conscious whenever the problem at hand becomes too large or complex for the simpler processing methods. It is not entirely clear whether the mechanisms of defense operate at the lower, more automated levels of information processing, or only at the higher levels within the archaic ego where sensory reconstruction takes place, as in the dreaming stage of the memory cycle. The argument from expediency suggests that the mechanisms of defense should have access to all levels, but our data includes only situations in which sensory reconstruction has occurred. The "unconscious fantasy" of which we see so much evidence in psychoanalysis may really be *unconscious*. It is my impression, however, that "unconscious fantasy" is experiential material which has reached the level of sensory reconstruction but has been prevented in one way or another from being transformed by the output program into reflective thought.

The important point here is that the mechanisms of defense operate within the archaic ego. Higher-level conscious thought, when it is applied to a particular problem situation, alters and improves on the work of the defenses as well as on the work of the more primitive adaptive mechanisms. This is not surprising, since the defense mechanisms themselves evolved as an emergency system for monitoring adaptive processes which already were functioning either below the level of consciousness entirely or else at the primary conscious level of sensory reconstruction.

It would be natural, then, that the material excluded from consciousness by the defense mechanisms is structured in the form appropriate to processing by the more primitive adaptive mechanisms of the archaic ego. It follows from this that beyond the boundaries of the conscious Ego, which have been set up by the mechanisms of defense, we should find a largely unconscious archaic ego with its content of wish-programs.

I have suggested that we reserve the term "structure" to the adaptive ego and its various components. I would like to propose now that we refer to the divisions of the psychic apparatus established by the mechanisms of defense as "superstructures." Here we follow Freud's usage with regard to the *Superego,* which in its clearest meaning is another portion of the adaptive ego rendered inaccessible to consciousness by the mechanisms of defense. But we go further than Freud to include the defense-determined Ego and Id as superstructures along with the Superego.

We indicate the relationship between structure and superstructure by saying that a given superstructure *covers* certain components of the various adaptive structures. For example, the superstructure Id *covers* a portion of the archaic adaptive ego, as it has appeared in our discussion thus far, and its content, the wish-programs currently undergoing processing. The superstructure Ego *covers* the sophisticated problem-solving equipment of the mature adaptive ego, and the rational conscious thought which takes place within it.

But new questions arise immediately. Does the *Superego* cover a component of the adaptive ego which is different in structure from the archaic ego described above, which is covered in turn by the Id? Or do the Superego and the Id merely cover different regions of the archaic ego? Or different contents within the same structure? Does it make sense to include both structures and their contents in the superstructures?

A good case can be made for removing the *mechanisms* (as opposed to the contents) of the archaic adaptive ego from the superstructure Id. It is not entirely clear that these mechanisms are excluded from consciousness for dynamic reasons; i.e., because the mechanisms of defense consider conscious knowledge of them to be dangerous. The example of dreaming suggests that there may be a generalized prohibition against the remembering of intermediate computational results, results which are not intended to be representations of real events, outer or inner. Most of the activity of the archaic ego falls into this category.

If we accept this argument, we may wish to restrict the superstructure Id to the contents of the archaic ego, the wish-programs currently undergoing processing. This choice would lead us to a conception of the Id not very different from Freud's structural model, although wish-programs are neither unstructured nor self-activating, as Freudian impulses are said to be. To be consistent, however, we would have to apply the same procedure to the superstructure Ego, restricting that term to the contents of ordinary waking consciousness. We would then have a set of super-structures which cover the contents of the psychic apparatus rather than contents and structures together. In this case, the superstructure Ego would have no relationship at all to the structural components of the adaptive ego, and would once again resemble the system *Preconscious* of Freud's topographic model.

It is, in fact, quite unclear what it means to say that the structures of the adaptive ego are accessible to consciousness, except insofar as we speak of the structure as being covered by the Ego when its contents are accessible. To what extent, for example, are the functions attributed to the "conflict-free ego sphere" by Hartmann (1939), such as perception and motility, accessible to consciousness? One is certainly aware of the results produced by these activities, but hardly of the intermediate steps leading to these results.

These considerations apply when the development of the adaptive ego has proceeded normally at least until the Oedipal period. In that case, the defenses are responsible for the greater or lesser accessibility to consciousness of various components of the functionally intact archaic ego. When the defenses play a major part in the earlier history of the psychic apparatus, however, they may interfere with the growth of the adaptive ego, as well as determining the allocation of its components to the superstructures.

This is because the defenses operate by disrupting the information links which connect the various elements of the adaptive ego involved in the processing of a given wish-program. We would expect the defenses to become increasingly discriminating in their disruptiveness as the capabilities of the adaptive ego increase during the maturational process. At the earliest stages of development, it is likely that a relatively large region of the archaic ego would have to be disturbed in order to prevent a given wish-program from being activated. In a repetitive traumatic situation during the first year of life, the overall integrity of the archaic adaptive ego may be permanently compromised.

As the infant grows older and his defenses grow more discriminating, the danger of permanent damage to his adaptive ego decreases progressively. A critical point comes when the defenses are able to isolate the threatening wish-program from its surroundings in the archaic ego. Only when this point is reached can the dangerous wish-program be rendered inaccessible to consciousness *without hindrance* to the capacity of the adaptive ego to deal effectively with other wish-programs.

The patient whose major difficulties arise during the Oedipal period, after the critical point has been passed, is the familiar neurotic whose functioning adaptive ego permits him to take full advantage of the psychoanalytic process. It is only in such a patient that the defense-determined boundary between the psychic superstructures (Ego and Id) corresponds even roughly to the functional limits of the adaptive ego. And it is only in such a patient that the excluded wish-program has the subjective contours of an isolated and alien "impulse."

Memory and the Ego

When we come to the problem of memory, the questions are multiplied once again. The evidence of free association (Palombo, 1973) indicates that the barriers to accessibility of a given memory representation are localized around the particular nodal point in the memory tree which contains it. Access to a highly charged memory which has been forcibly repressed is achieved in analysis through repeated approaches to this nodal point via a great many associative branches. Analytic experience also indicates that such highly charged memory representations are frequently clustered in relatively compact regions of the tree structure, so that the recovery of one such memory often initiates a train of highly charged associations (Palombo, 1976). We would have to say that the superstructure Id which covers these inaccessible memories is not necessarily connected or continuous in its topology. This would mean that the permanent memory is filled with islands, both large and small, each of which has the property of inaccessibility attributed in the past to the Id as a whole. Some of these islands would be much more "Id-like" than others.

The permanent memory structure itself is a component of the archaic adaptive ego. Because it is specialized for inclusiveness of content rather than rapidity of access it is unsuitable for the connected thought processes of the mature adaptive ego. The mature ego requires memory structures which are much more highly organized, so that they can supply frequently used memory items almost instantly. These structures comprise what I have called the *working memory*. Among the features of the working memory which maximize the accessibility of its contents are *reversibility* of associations and *classification* by content. Reversibility means that all associated items are both superordinate and subordinate to one another, so that each may be reached directly from the other. *Classification* means a hierarchical system of classes which makes it possible to locate all individual items which share a given common property, as well as all classifiable properties attributed to a given individual item.

Because of the complexity of its organization, the working memory must be limited in size to a small fraction of the contents of the premanent memory. This limitation requires that the contents of the *working memory* be allowed to change over the course of time. An item which is frequently recalled for use in the early years of life may drop out of the working memory later on, after it has been rendered obsolete or irrelevant by newer experience. This is the common fate of most formal learning, unless it is incorporated into the occupational routines of adult life.

It takes only a simple stacking model to illustrate how this might be done. The stack of useful memory items in the working memory is limited to a certain number. Whenever a new item is added to the top of the stack, the item at the bottom is removed. Whenever an item already in the stack is used, it is advanced to the top of the stack. This system would provide that the least useful items be eliminated, but not until a considerable period of time has elapsed from their original insertion into the stack. The actual system employed by the working memory would have to be much more complex in structure; the principle need not be.

Items dropped from the working memory would still be preserved in the permanent memory, available for those new or special situations which go beyond the capacity of the currently constituted working memory. Recourse to the permanent memory entails acceptance of the extra time and effort required to search it. As we know from our work as psychoanalysts, the cost may be very great, especially since it is difficult to estimate the chances of ultimate success even after the goal has almost been reached. The routine daily search of the permanent memory in dreaming, when the recovered wish-statements are potentially available to waking consciousness, often provides a valuable shortcut to the information being sought.

The working memory appears to be more vulnerable physiologically than the permanent memory. An elderly colleague has told me that in working with psychoanalytic patients he finds his memory for routine details of the patient's life to be somewhat diminished, but that he has no difficulty remembering the nonroutine associative jumps which appear during the patient's free associations. This suggests that it may not be recent memory as a whole which is interfered with when brain function is minimally impaired, but only the memory of those experiences which are ordinarily handled by the routine mechanisms of the working memory, while the mechanisms of the memory cycle, as well as the permanent memory structure itself, remain relatively intact.

Can we identify the precursors of the working memory among the mechanisms of the archaic ego? The principle of reproducing a certain limited portion of the information stored in the permanent memory for a special purpose would seem to be a very general one, not necessarily requiring the refinements of secondary process thought. In fact, the mechanisms of defense must employ limited memory structures meeting this description. In order to recognize a supposed threat, the defense mechanisms must have available to them a stereotyped listing of wish-program components considered to be dangerous. This listing must have been compiled in the course of earlier experience.

As we have seen in our study, the dream censor is able to make use of the pool of day residues in the short-term memory as a source of nonthreatening components for substitution. For defense mechanisms operating during waking consciousness, this procedure may not be possible, and a stereotyped list of substitute items may be necessary. Colby (1973) has provided a striking demonstration of the effectiveness of a defensive system operating with what would appear to be a very small number of items.

Colby has shown that an automaton (a computer program) can respond to a psychiatric interviewer in a manner which is indistinguishable to a panel of trained psychiatrists from that of a paranoid patient. At first glance, this experiment seems peculiarly simpleminded; after all, defenses protect a vulnerable living organism from a multiplicity of events which it imagines to be threatening to its psychological integrity and perhaps to its very existence.

On reflection, however, we perceive that this complexity applies to the *origin* of defenses rather than to their manner of operation. The point of a defense mechanism is that it is a *mechanism*, an automatism which interrupts the flow of new information before it reaches the deeper structures where the threat would be felt and possibly acted upon. For this purpose, a small set of stereotyped substitute items is perfectly adequate, as Colby's experiment convincingly demonstrates.

The memory lists employed by the mechanisms of defense lack one very important feature of the adaptive working memory. This is the procedure for automatic updating and revision. We can attribute this deficit to the emergency function of the defense mechanisms as well as to the lack of sophistication of the archaic ego. But it is clear that the archaic ego as a whole is "timeless" in a sense closely related to Freud's description of the properties of the Id. The archaic ego operates by establishing what seems at the moment to be the best *possible* solution to a given adaptive problem. If this solution is successful, it is adopted for all similar situations which may arise in the future, regardless of changing circumstances.

For the human organism, there is a built-in guarantee of changing circumstances which is lacking in lower animals. This is the enormous increase in problem-solving capabilities which accompanies maturation. For the human infant in isolation from other people, almost every event imaginable would be threatening to life or bodily comfort, and all but a very tiny proportion of these threatening events could be managed without difficulty later in life. The archaic ego is unable to anticipate this series of momentous changes. Hence we have the crucial importance of parental buffering, which delays the necessity for serious confrontation with the external world until the archaic ego has been superceded by an adaptive ego which can assign *different* meanings and values to *similar* events occurring at different stages in the life cycle.

The natural immutability of the defense mechanisms makes them difficult to deal with in psychoanalytic treatment. We know that eventually their influence over the mental life of the patient is markedly reduced, but we do not really know how this change is accomplished. The most attractive hypothesis—and the simplest—is that the defenses do not change at all, but rather that new information-carrying structures are assembled which serve to bypass or bridge them. It would follow that under sufficient stress these circumferential structures might break down, giving the defenses an opportunity to reassert themselves, which would not be the case if they had been worn away by a process of therapeutic attrition.

This picture accords well with clinical observation and supports our characterization of the defense mechanisms as primitive emergency structures of the archaic ego. However, the dramatic inactivation of the dream censor between M. A.'s Tuesday- and Thursday-night dreams about his father suggests that something else is involved in addition to the building of new structure. This would have to be a change in the censor's criteria for intervention, which would imply an alteration of its memory lists. Here it would be helpful to have further data from later in the analysis, which might tell us whether the change we observed was permanent or subject to a continuing need for reworking and reinforcement.

However these changes are brought about, it appears that the defense mechanisms are more resistant to modification through experience than any other purely intrapsychic structures we know of. The permanent memory provides an interesting contrast, since it is continually updated by the memory cycle. The memory cycle may be the principal structure of the archaic ego specifically adapted to the processing of *new* experience beyond the requirement of current needs. Conceivably, it may be the only such structure.

The working memory of the mature adaptive ego incorporates the major capabilities both of the memory cycle and of the defense mechanisms. It combines the capacity for constant revision of the memory cycle with the functions of simplification and automation which originated with the defense mechanisms. The working memory must have evolved through a convergence of these properties at a higher level of integration.

Structure and Superstructure

Our understanding of the information structures employed by the adaptive ego is still rudimentary. As I have suggested, separation of the question of structure from the question of accessibility to consciousness should serve to simplify the task of elucidation which lies ahead of us.

The distinction between these two properties of the psychic apparatus is a very important one. Let me illustrate what is involved with an analogy from the recent history of an older observational science.

Since the seventeenth century, telescopic observations of the planet Mars have revealed a pattern of bright orange-yellow markings interspersed with areas that appear to be a dark greenish-gray. As telescopes improved, the pattern became more distinct. A few very faint variations within each of the two major zones have occasionally been glimpsed, but almost every claim that finer structure had been observed (for example, the famous "canals") was proven unreliable. The attention of astronomers was drawn primarily to the borders between the light and dark areas, which could be seen to shift over time. Some of these shifts were cyclical, depending on the season of the Martian year. Others appeared to be random, though they were sometimes correlated with the appearance and subsidence of planetwide dust storms. It was generally assumed that these light and dark areas were manifestations of large-scale topographic differences in the surface of Mars, and that the changes in their boundaries indicated important alterations in the topography, perhaps even the presence of a seasonal pattern of vegetation.

When the first interplanetary probes were being planned for close-up photography of Mars, it was expected that the relationship between the differences in color and brightness observed from the earth would be correlated with the geographical structure of the planet as revealed by the detailed photographs. These probes, especially Mariner 9, which took photographs from Mars orbit for nearly a year (in 1971–72), have revealed an enormous amount of detailed information about impact craters, lava flows, gigantic volcanoes, and many other geological formations.

The relationship between these newly identified geologic structures and the previously observed markings is neither simple nor obvious. There are no geologic structures which appear exclusively in either the light or dark regions, and the boundaries between these regions do not coincide with changes in the topography. The detailed photographs show many rather small, dark patches, which appear to be areas of bare rock swept free by the Martian wind of overlying layers of bright dust, but these small, dark areas are associated with many different kinds of geological formation. Our best guess at the moment is that the dark regions observed from earth contain a larger number of these small, dark areas than the brighter regions, and that with earth-based resolution, these small areas appear to coalesce. The revised Martian cartography is described by Hartmann and Raper in *The New Mars: The Discoveries of Mariner 9* (1974):

The Martian map forming the front endpaper is an example of one of the best representations of the surface of Mars shortly before the Mariner 9 mission. It shows the dark and light markings due to regions of different albedo, or reflectivity. These regions have long been visible from Earth. The classical names given by 19th- and 20th-century astronomers are shown on the map. The map shows no geological structure because none could be detected from Earth.

The Martian map forming the rear endpaper is the product of the Mariner 9 mission and shows the abundant, varied geologic structures of the planet, including craters, volcanoes and river-like channels. Selected examples illustrate the names assigned to these structures in 1973 by the International Astronomical Union. These names do not replace the classical names, but refer to *structures* instead of albedo features indicated on earlier maps.

We are now in a similar situation with regard to our map of the psychic apparatus, although not quite so far advanced. From our clinical perspective, we observe what appear to be large-scale regions of the mind which are either accessible to consciousness (bright) or inaccessible (dark). We see hints of finer structure, but our attention is constantly drawn back to the larger picture of the patient's life situation determined by the boundaries of the superstructures, which is the object of our immediate therapeutic concern. We have assumed until now that the larger regions of clarity and obscurity represent the large-scale underlying structures of the psychic topography.

An observational instrument of higher resolving power, such as that provided by the method of Greenberg and Pearlman (1975a), gives us a rather different picture. In the dreaming state, which appears to be a dark region when observed from the usual clinical distance, we have seen the adaptive structures of the memory cycle clearly illuminated. There are local areas of obscurity, the work of the dream censor, but we have found it possible in one case at least to uncover the underlying structure temporarily obscured by this defensive activity.

For many reasons already elucidated, we can expect to find a higher density of these localized obscurities interspersed among the experiential materials undergoing processing in the archaic adaptive ego. For some (but not necessarily all) clinical purposes, it is sufficient to characterize the archaic ego in its entirety as a dark area, the Id. But we must be aware of the limitations imposed on our deeper understanding of the psychic apparatus when we adopt this point of view. In particular, we are prevented from observing the detailed interplay between adaptive and defensive structures which is responsible for the therapeutic benefits of psychoanalysis, as well as for the creative contributions of the archaic ego to human culture generally.

The archaic adaptive ego is an area of special vulnerability to the obscuring activity of the defense mechanisms. But to know the details of this obscuration for the individual patient, we must know how the experiential wind was blowing during each of the important stages of his development.

CHAPTER 7

Theory and Practice in Psychoanalysis

Growth and Change

The inadequacy of traditional psychoanalytic theory to explain the therapeutic effect of psychoanalytic treatment is not a problem for psychoanalysts alone. Analytic theory is the public face of psychoanalysis. Scientists in other disciplines have no other means of access to the important discoveries about the nature of the mind which have developed from observation of the interactive process of psychoanalytic treatment.

The notion that psychoanalytic practice is entailed by or derived from the traditional theoretical structure as a whole is destructive in two ways. It permits the practicing analyst to assume that the truth of the theory is demonstrated by the improvements he sees in the lives of his patients. This is perhaps the lesser evil, since the humanitarian goals of the analytic practitioner may be achieved nonetheless. But it also serves to convince the nonanalyst that psychoanalytic practice is a hodgepodge of heuristics without a reliable scientific basis, and that therefore nothing of lasting value can be learned from it.

This concluding chapter will try to show that the discrepancy between psychoanalytic theory and practice is not a cause for excessive alarm. It is, in fact, a normal development, both in the context of scientific history generally and in the evolution of psychoanalysis as a clinical discipline. To close the gap between theory and practice, it is not necessary to begin over again with a new and different theory, but rather to enlarge the conceptual framework of the older theory in the manner I have tried to illustrate here. In doing so, I believe it is possible to set the stage for a general psychology which can more fully exploit the remarkable contributions of Freud and his many successors in psychoanalysis, without at the same time adopting Freud's notion that normal psychology is a subdivision of psychopathology.

The patient entering psychoanalytic treatment imagines that the changes he is about to undergo will deprive him of a highly valued and essential part of himself. Something vital within him will be dissected, cut away, removed for good. Both his horizons and his self-image will be compressed and diminished. (Hence the ubiquitous slang term for the analyst.)

We recognize the familiar castration fantasy. But there is another meaning hidden behind this one, a meaning for which the all-too-real fear of castration serves as a desperate metaphor. This is the patient's inability to believe that the changes within him which result from growth and new experience can ever add up to anything, can ever be cumulative. Every event that alters the course of his life must therefore be either the loss of a piece of himself or the intrusion of something alien and unwanted. In either case, the self is invaded and reduced.

This fantasy reflects a state of mind in which communication between the archaic adaptive ego and the mature adaptive ego has been severely constricted by the mechanisms of defense. When this happens, the adaptive methods developed by the mature ego remain dissociated from the adaptive ends formulated earlier in life by the archaic ego. All questions of ultimate value receive answers appropriate to the timeless automatisms of the archaic ego. The self-as-it-is is the best possible self; all change is disequilibrium; only those efforts are useful which aim at making the future identical with the past.

Freud frequently referred to these archaic ego functions under the rubric of the *repetition compulsion*. Much of what I have been saying here was anticipated by Freud, in fact, in the passage from *Beyond the Pleasure Principle* (1920) quoted in chapter 1:

It is impossible to classify as wish-fulfillments the dreams we have been discussing which occur in traumatic neuroses, or the dreams during psychoanalyses which bring to memory the psychical traumas of childhood. They arise, rather, in obedience to the compulsion to repeat, though it is true that in analysis that compulsion is supported by the wish (which is encouraged by "suggestion") to conjure up what has been forgotten and repressed. Thus it would seem that the function of dreams, which consists in setting aside any motives that might interrupt sleep, by fulfilling the wishes of the disturbing impulses, is not their *original* function. It would not be possible for them to perform that function until the whole of mental life had accepted the dominance of the pleasure principle. If there is a "beyond the pleasure principle," it is only consistent to grant that there was also a time *before* the purpose of dreams was the fulfillment of wishes. This would imply no denial of their later function. (Pp. 32–33)

Left to itself, the archaic ego is narcissistic, pessimistic, and authoritarian. Fortunately, when things go well, it is not left to itself. The sense of growth and new opportunity is provided from outside by healthy parents. As the child develops, the archaic ego is increasingly brought under the supervision of a mature adaptive ego modeled after those of parents and other successful adults. The mature ego develops gradually, but a quantum leap occurs during the transition from the Oedipal period to latency.

The mature ego is a work ego. But work takes time and effort, and must be reserved for problem-solving in new situations beyond the scope of programs already in storage. Routine activities must be left to the automatisms of the archaic ego. The mature ego is called into play only *after* the archaic ego has failed to provide a satisfactory response to a new stimulus. When the lines of communication between the mature ego and the archaic ego are constricted by the defenses, the result is therefore to release the archaic ego from the supervision of the mature ego, but not to inhibit the activity or influence of the archaic ego itself. From the long-term adaptive view of the mature ego, this outcome is paradoxical. But for the defense mechanisms, living as they do in a futureless world of immediate dangers, the archaic adaptive ego is tried and true. It is for this reason that repression *increases* the influence on behavior of that which is repressed.

There is reason to think that change in social institutions is subject to similar psychological resistance, perhaps even to an exaggerated degree when compared with the human individual. An institution is for many purposes defined by its automatisms, and these automatisms, unlike those of the individual archaic ego, require a constant expenditure of effort to maintain. Moreover, the supervisory role taken by the mature ego in the individual is generally assigned in institutions to older people who are more concerned with integrating and redefining the experience of the past than with preparation for a future which is difficult to foresee.

A special form of resistance to change arises when an institution is successful in performing the practical task for which it was organized. For this benefit, most of its members will be justifiably grateful, and it will seem quite natural to them to adopt the system of beliefs associated with the practical benefit, even when the belief system goes far beyond what is observable and relevant to the actual task at hand.

This point is a truism when applied to the political and religious institutions of the historical past, as Freud and many others in the modern world have shown. It is now becoming apparent that it holds even for the informal institutions within the scientific community whose manifest intention is to promote the advance of human understanding (Kuhn, 1962). When it is believed that a particular theory explains a practical procedure which has proven itself to be useful, then the theory acquires an immunity to criticism which may last for centuries.

For example, it is often forgotten that astronomy began as a practical science. The ability to predict the changing of the seasons, the calendar, travel at sea, at night, and away from familiar landmarks, all depend on a knowledge of the cyclic movements of the heavens. For all of these purposes, the geocentric point of view was not only adequate, but conceptually by far the most economical. Aristotle and Ptolemy systematized what was common knowledge to all practical men of the ancient world. (Hoyle, 1962, de Santillana and von Dechend, 1969).

Anomalies in the motions of the planets became an issue as the systematization advanced. The heliocentric theory of Aristarchus was known but rejected. In order to save the phenomena of the everyday world, Ptolemy developed a highly sophisticated mathematical description of the visible cosmos. For practical purposes, its failures were minute and inconsequential. It was not seriously challenged until Neoplatonic aestheticism achieved an equal footing with pragmatics as an intellectual motivation during the Renaissance (Kuhn, 1957).

The history of the Ptolemaic system carries a lesson for all of science, which often goes unheeded. A theory may "explain" a set of observations which has immense practical importance, and do so with a high degree of mathematical elegance (Copernicus's mathematics were no better than Ptolemy's), and yet be totally inapplicable to a view of the same phenomena from a different and more comprehensive vantage point. The pattern of natural events organized and represented in the Ptolemaic system was real. When Copernicus wrote, the most accurate measurements available could not demonstrate the inferiority of the Ptolemaic theory to his own. Tycho made better observations, in the hope of refuting Copernicus. Not until more than sixty years after the death of Copernicus, when Kepler used Tycho's new data to discover that the orbit of Mars is elliptical, was the greater comprehensiveness of the heliocentric theory established.

Truth in science is relative to point of view. Point of view is determined by practical considerations, by cultural conditions, by the stature of prevailing authorities. Irrational loyalties and narcissistic identifications prolong the life-spans of outmoded ideas, but these ideas cannot have survived without a history of useful service. The patterns in nature discovered by Aristotle and Newton were admired because they were authentic. The magnitude of their achievement was not diminished in the least when the range of events they described was extended by others and the universality of their generalizations limited by the discovery of still-larger patterns.

Psychoanalytic Technique

Like other sciences, psychoanalysis began with the search for a practical method to improve the conditions of human life. It is a difficult method, requiring much time and effort from the patient and a high degree of skill from the practitioner. Under favorable conditions it is an extraordinarily successful method. (True, it has not reached everyone who needs it. But neither has the wheel or the alphabet. The limited availability of psychoanalytic treatment is a social problem over which psychoanalysts unfortunately have little control.)

From the beginning Freud's interest in individual human beings dictated the direction of his theoretical development. In the suffering of his neurotic patients he saw the human mind turning against its own desires and evading wherever possible the harsh demands of the outer world. He learned through many frustrating trials that hope for a lasting recovery depended on the patient's taking personal responsibility for everything within himself which he had previously treated as alien, imposed, and beyond his control. Psychoanalytic theory was designed to serve the analyst's strategy in bringing about this shift in the patient's perception of himself.

The analyst's therapeutic strategy must be implemented with tact, timing and respect for the patient's efforts to resolve his difficulties prior to entering treatment. It is easy to be moralistic about the patient's self-deceptions, which often deceive others as well, and this must be avoided. But the long-term therapeutic benefits of analysis come only when the patient realizes that he is actively shaping the present and future after an image of the past created and maintained by the automatisms of his archaic ego. Unhappiness is not psychopathology. To paraphrase Freud, psychopathology is the internal condition of the patient which leads him to make things even worse for himself than they otherwise might be.

What kind of theory would best support a treatment strategy whose aim is to reveal to the patient what he has purposefully but unconsciously concealed from himself? Freud's answer, which survived a number of historical changes, was a theory which concentrates its attention on the boundaries between the defense-determined Ego and Id, and which assumes the adequate functioning of an adaptive ego at all developmental levels—in short, a theory of conflict among the psychic superstructures.

If the matter had rested there, a number of problems would have been avoided. The patient in analysis experiences the boundary between his Ego and Id as a barrier. The unconscious decision-making procedure which determines when a wish-program undergoing processing in the archaic ego is to be transferred to the mature ego for higher-level problem solving is perceived as a conflict of forces across that barrier. Assuming that the adaptive ego is intact and functioning effectively when it is free of defensive interference, we can focus our therapeutic interest on those contents of the psychic apparatus which have been distorted by the defense mechanisms into a form which is subjectively experienced as noninteractional, noninformational and maladaptive. With the right kind of patient, psychoanalytic treatment can be and has been successfully accomplished by strict adherence to this strategy.

Under favorable circumstances, the analyst can help the patient's mature ego expand its awareness of warded-off wish-programs through his knowing which wish-programs are most likely to have been repressed and which conscious fantasy material is likely to be associated with these censored wishes. He brings the wish-programs to the patient's attention, and, sooner or later, the patient's adaptive ego will incorporate and integrate them.

This simple model is valuable because it crystallizes the therapeutic rule that when the analyst does for the patient what the patient can do for himself, he defeats the ultimate aim of the analytic method and postpones the patient's achievement of autonomy and independence. If the model were sufficient as a description of how analysis is actually done, as many analysts believe it to be, then it would be superfluous for the analyst to understand how the adaptive ego functions—perhaps even dangerous.

What we find with most of our patients, however, is that the developmental level of the adaptive ego at the time a wish-program is assembled and stored has a marked influence both on the form taken by the wish-program and on the conditions under which it will become accessible during analysis. For the analyst to recognize the presence or influence of a wish-program which is as yet outside the patient's conscious awareness, it is often necessary for him to know how the immature ego would have simplified, transformed, or misunderstood the reality with which it had been grappling during the patient's early childhood.

The need for the analyst to know how the immature ego functions posed a dilemma for Freud. His commitment to the therapeutic goals of psychoanalysis came before everything else. It appeared that these goals would be most clearly understood if the analyst confined his interpretations to the contents of the patient's Id, the one area of the patient's mental life where there seemed to be no question of the analyst's usurping the functions of the patient's adaptive ego. The dilemma could be circumvented, in part at least, by identifying the mature adaptive ego with the defense-determined Ego and the archaic adaptive ego with the Id.

Now the analyst could go about his business of investigating the primitive aspects of the patient's mental life without infringing the patient's autonomy in the sphere of mature and conflict-free ego functions. Freud was able to develop a theory in which the archaic ego could be understood, up to a point, without upsetting the delicate balance of the therapeutic relationship. For the time in which he was working, when the distinction between psychoanalysis and directive psychotherapy was still difficult for many of his students to grasp, Freud made the most reasonable choice.

The necessity for the analyst to interpret only the Id disappeared as psychoanalysts became more confident of their method, however. Hartmann (1939) made the adaptive ego a respectable subject for psychoanalytic investigation. It became apparent that the contributions of adaptive ego and Id to a given production of the patient were often difficult to separate. Anna Freud, Hartmann, and others showed that interpretation of the distortions introduced by the immature adaptive ego facilitated the emergence of forbidden infantile wishes. Psychoanalytic technique became more subtle, and, in important details, more sophisticated.

Hartmann and his colleagues were responsible for major theoretical advances in the area of ego development. Erikson's emphasis on the epigenetic sequence of interactions between the maturing adaptive ego and its facilitating environment has been especially significant and suggestive. Nevertheless, psychoanalytic ego psychology did not address itself with enthusiasm to the relationship between the structure ego and the superstructure Id. Although the Id had relinquished its monopoly over the technique of interpretation, on the theoretical level it has retained its former domination over the archaic adaptive ego.

The Psychoanalytic Theory of Motivation

The reason for this hesitation must be traced to the theory of motivation which grew out of Freud's conception of the Id. This theory originated in the clinical finding that the transfer of wish-programs across the repression barrier between the superstructures Ego and Id is frequently accompanied by subjective feelings of compulsion or force, often of forces in conflict, as we noted earlier. Freud made the plausible assumption that these subjective feelings are an inherent property of the wish-programs, rather than a function of the interaction between the wish-programs and the transfer mechanism which determines whether or not they become conscious. The intensity of the subjective feeling would then be a measure of the inherent strength of the "impulse" represented by the wish-program, a quantity which Freud reified in the concept of *psychic energy.*

Behavior was to be motivated by the subjective sensation of compulsion or force. One feels a desire to do something and, *ceteris paribus,* one does it. The feeling of desire is taken as evidence that a significant quantity of psychic energy is present. But a serious difficulty arises here. The *absence* of the subjective feeling of compulsion is *not* to be taken as evidence that a significant quantity of psychic energy is absent. If the behavior is present without the subjective feeling of force, then the behavior itself is to be considered evidence that the psychic energy is present and determining the behavior. The subjective feeling has been repressed by the mechanisms of defense, but the psychic energy, which was introduced into the argument initially as the quantitative measure of the subjective feeling, is now considered to survive the abolition of the subjective feeling and to have exactly the same behavioral consequences as the feeling itself.

The idea of "psychic energy" as a shadow form of subjective compulsion is useful in clinical practice, where the analyst is continually concerned with the feelings the patient has excluded from consciousness for defensive reasons. "Psychic energy" functions as a place-marker to indicate the absence of an expectable expression of affect. If we take our theorizing seriously, however, we find this shadow taking on a considerable substance. By the time of Rapaport's explication of the basic Freudian model of motivation (1960), we find the concept of psychic energy sinking through the depths of the psychic apparatus and disappearing into the physiological substrate below.

According to Rapaport, mental activity begins in the mind of the infant only when direct action has been frustrated (P. 26ff.). When an action is successfully completed, it is said to be accompanied neither by thought nor feeling. Rapaport's model for direct action appears to be the spinal reflex, which does not, in fact, involve the psychic apparatus. But Rapaport insists that when the psychic apparatus is *bypassed* by a successful action, the result is the discharge of a quantity of *psychic* energy. Moreover, if the action is frustrated and the impetus for it is diverted into the psychic apparatus, the quantity of *psychic* energy with which the mental representation of the desired action is charged will be *lower* than the quantity possessed by the original *nonmental* action state.

Freud and Rapaport have collapsed three levels of motivation into the single concept of psychic energy. The uppermost of these levels is the subjective feeling of compulsion. The lowermost level is the signal of a physiological imbalance which is received by the psychic apparatus from the organism. The psychic energy concept was meant to bring about an identity between these phenomena by bridging the unknown territory of unconscious information processing which lies between them. From the clinical point of view, this maneuver is extremely useful, since it follows the lead of the defense mechanisms, which treat all three levels as equivalent. In reality, however, the decisive stage in the motivational process comes at the intermediate level, which we can now recognize as the *archaic adaptive ego*.

The actual source of the motivation can only be a mechanism which evaluates the probable outcome for a newly constructed wish-program by matching it with similar wish-programs whose consequences when activated in the past are known. The subjective feeling which accompanies the decisions of this evaluative mechanism has a signal function which serves to alert the supervisory action of the mature adaptive ego when the activation of the wish-program in question involves an element of risk or the possibility of unanticipated difficulties. The mechanism which makes the original evaluation belongs to the archaic adaptive ego, but the recruitment of the mature adaptive ego opens the way for possible revokation or revision of the original decision.

When the mechanisms of defense abolish the subjective feeling which ordinarily accompanies a risky decision by the archaic ego, the result is not to weaken or modify the conditions for motivated action, but merely to eliminate the possibility that this action will be reviewed and reconsidered by the mature adaptive ego. This is what we observe routinely with analytic patients who are in a phase of resistance to analysis.

Feelings enter the motivational evaluation in two ways. First, the feelings of the moment determine the experiential context of the current state of need. They provide the starting point for the assembly of new wish-programs designed to reduce the indicated mismatch between the actual and the optimal. Second, the feelings recorded as feedback from the activation of similar wish-programs in the past form the basis for determining the desirability of reactivating similar wish-programs in the present. In both cases, the affect is useful for the information it supplies about conditions in the inner and outer worlds.

The current affective signal indicates that the occasion is opportune for evaluative activity; it does not supply the impetus for that activity. Every experience permanently stored in the memory structure includes an indication of the affects associated with that experience; the storage of an actual quantity of "psychic energy" with each such experience would not only be unnecessary but technically impossible. The subjective feeling of force or compulsion which accompanies the activation of the wish-program finally selected by the evaluation mechanism is an after-effect of the decision; it plays no part whatever in the original evaluation.

The idea that the adaptive structures of the ego originate *de novo* from the frustration of instinctual impulses is based on another false analogy with the clinical situation. The symptoms of the neurotic patient. represent a *regression* from a higher level of adaptation to a lower. Adaptive structures at the higher level, which have already passed through a relatively normal maturational sequence, are excluded by the defense mechanisms from participation in the search for gratification. As a result, more primitive libidinal goals, less threatening to the defenses, are substituted for the appropriate ones.

In order to bring the neglected areas of gratification to the attention of the patient, the analyst must abstain from gratifying the substituted primitive wishes. This will give the patient an opportunity to realize that the gratification of the primitive wishes is not essential to his well-being, and that other, more effective alternatives are open to him. The search for gratification may then be resumed at a higher developmental level, making use of the adaptive structures previously excluded from participation.

The frustration of the more primitive wishes by the analyst therefore leads to the restoration of higher-level adaptive structures to more appropriate pleasure-seeking activity. From this sequence, we infer that in the therapeutic setting frustration directs the patient back onto the developmental track from which he had been diverted by his defenses. It is a short (and unfortunate) step from this clinical observation to the idea that frustration directs the unstructured infantile ego onto the developmental track in the first place.

But this step is theoretically unjustified and unsupported by observation. The events being identified are in reality quite different. In the clinical setting we are concerned with the *restored* use of *already existing* structures which have been made inaccessible for the solution of certain problems by the action of the defenses. This is an entirely different matter from the development of new structure as observed in the infant. Here the opportunity for undistracted experimentation and the freedom to repeat unsuccessful attempts at mastery are essential. The normal infant willingly gives up a gratifying routine once it has been mastered if his maturational status permits him to advance to a more challenging level of accomplishment.

Normal children do not learn to crawl, walk, talk, or feed themselves through a grudging concession to reality. They seize the opportunity to do something new as soon as they are physically able, no matter how frustrating the new experience of learning may be when compared with continued dependence on a happily compliant mother.

The Language of Psychoanalysis

Freud's theory of motivation does not explain what actually happens inside the psychic apparatus. It has survived because it approximates the subjective experience of the patient in analysis. The analyst does not make direct use of the theoretical language of psychoanalysis in communicating with his patient, of course. He paraphrases it and translates

it into everyday expressions with similar meanings, with careful attention to the patient's capacity for assimilation. Nevertheless, the theoretical language considered to be most useful by the clinical analyst is
usually that which lends itself to such translation with the least
elaboration and ingenuity.

It has been suggested (Schafer, 1976) that a psychoanalytic vocabulary which closely follows the patient's subjective experience is not only
redundant but obstructive to the analyst's goal of increasing the patient's
sense of personal responsibility for his own feelings and actions. If this
were true, the tenacity of the Freudian language would weigh heavily
against the clinical judgment of psychoanalysts in general.

Schafer has missed an important point. Freud's theory of motivation
has been useful clinically because it recognizes, however indirectly, that
the mechanisms of the archaic ego are automatisms. The decisions of the
archaic ego are motivated—i.e., they are purposeful responses to the
needs and desires of the patient. But they are not *intentional,* as they
would be if they resulted from a conscious problem-solving effort by the
mature adaptive ego. Before the patient can take responsibility for his
archaic ego, he must understand, first, that it exists, and second, that in
denying its existence, he has forfeited the opportunity for his mature
adaptive ego to supervise its activity. Once this understanding has been
achieved (and most of the analyst's work is devoted to this intermediate
goal), the neurotic patient's acceptance of his responsibilities encounters
only minor resistance. It is for this later phase of analysis that Schafer's
language is appropriate.

Throughout the history of psychoanalysis, the complaint has been
heard that Freud's mechanistic theory interferes with the humanistic
goals of analytic treatment. But this is not the case. On the contrary, a
mechanistic theory of motivation is essential if the patient is to give up
the belief that there is something inherently destructive within him
which must be excised. The analyst helps him to understand that he is
an ordinary person with a malfunctioning psychic apparatus. He learns to
view this apparatus with detachment, as a part of himself, yet apart *from*
himself, to be observed with objectivity and understood as a deterministic
system. In this way, his self-esteem can be enhanced while his psychopathology is investigated.

The machine metaphor has other heuristic advantages. The patient
can readily imagine an impersonal apparatus being taken apart, examined
piece by piece until the malfunctioning components or connections are
found, then repaired and reassembled in working order. This analogy
provides a rough first approximation of the analytic process which is

minimally threatening to the patient's narcissism. If the analyst were to take the whole person as the indivisible agent for every thought, feeling, or action, as Schafer suggests, it would be extremely difficult to conceptualize psychoanalysis as a morally neutral step-by-step procedure comprehensible to the anxious and guilt-ridden patient who comes for analytic treatment.

Schafer's "action language" is appropriate to the mature analysand at the conclusion of a successful analysis. It completely fails to capture the quality of the process which leads slowly and painfully to this desired conclusion. For all its deficiencies, traditional Freudian theory offers a much more practical alternative. It stays close to the subjective experience of the patient, but transposes that experience onto an impersonal, deterministic, and morally neutral plane. For this reason, it has been widely accepted by the practitioners of clinical psychoanalysis.

Psychoanalysis as a Science

Of special interest to our discussion here is the fact that the clinical value of the traditional theory is only very roughly dependent on its scientific accuracy. The detailed workings of the mechanisms it postulates are much less important than the general framework of detachment and moral neutrality which it sets up. In this respect it is comparable to the Aristotelian-Ptolemaic cosmology mentioned earlier.

The geocentric theory of the Greek astronomers represented an enormous advance over the fantasies of supernatural power current in the ancient world. It eliminated moralism, capriciousness, and personal whim from the large-scale structure of the phenomenal universe. It integrated the observable regularities in the movements of the planets into a complex overall pattern capable of generating predictions which were sufficiently accurate to solve important practical problems in agriculture and navigation. To banish the astrologers from the psychic universe as well, and to convert its superstitions into practical science, was an achievement of Freud's as great as Aristotle's.*

---

* The parallel between Freud's therapeutic strategy and the development of the natural sciences can be traced back much further than Aristotle. The sixth century Ionian philosopher, Anaximander of Miletus (mentioned by Freud in *Totem and Taboo*, 1913, p. 153) conceived of the cosmos as a gigantic whirlpool of uniform composition. Out of this whirlpool were separated the distinctive elements which

We do not disparage Freud when we acknowledge that his theoretical views were limited by the practical necessities of psychoanalytic treatment with neurotic patients. The geocentric theory was not a failure, but a brilliant success. It made possible the demand for greater accuracy of observation and a more comprehensive point of view which led ultimately to more accurate and comprehensive cosmological theory.

The limitations of traditional psychoanalytic theory become evident to every psychoanalyst who works with patients suffering from a malfunctioning adaptive ego. Unlike the symptomatic neurotic, such patients must have the help of the analyst in activating these deficient ego operations until they have learned to function without his assistance. Traditional psychoanalytic theory offers very little guidance here, and the successful analyst must work out his own rules for judging when and how much his help is required. Psychoanalytic ego psychology is useful to the analyst in this predicament, but the relationship between ego psychology and the traditional theory is less clear in this area than one could hope.

No Copernicus is needed to inform us that the traditional theory works best in the neurosis-centered psychic universe for which it was designed. In that universe, the well-observed subjective experience of the patient provides the data necessary for uncovering the thoughts, feelings, and memories which had been concealed by the operation of his defense mechanisms. But this subjective experience cannot be relied on to tell us any more of the detailed workings of the adaptive ego than the subjective experience of the stationary observer can tell us of the motions of the earth and the planets.

The stationary observer feels that the earth is at rest. The neurotic patient feels that the activity of his archaic ego is without structure, irrational, infantile, violent, immoral, uncivilized, self-motivated, and incapable of being influenced or controlled by his adult personality. These are illusions of the greatest scientific interest, but illusions nonetheless. The illusion of the neurotic patient is dispelled by the success of

---

combined to form a multiplicity of worlds like the earth. De Santillana (1961, p. 39) remarks:

> Anaximander had to devise some kind of coherent mechanism, and he did. Aristophanes was to say bitterly: "They have dethroned Zeus, and Vortex is king." The divine mechanism did not have to be true in detail, but it expressed on this new level what had to be there—the impersonal equivalent of a consciousness, which makes its stipulations alive not only in nature but in men's minds, and superior to all and each.

Freud was trying to do for the microcosm exactly what Anaximander had done for the macrocosm, and met with the same resistance. Freud's "cauldron of seething excitations" is a direct descendant of Anaximander's whirlpool.

psychoanalytic treatment itself, for, as Freud proclaimed in triumph, "where Id was there Ego shall be." The mechanistic subjective language of traditional psychoanalytic theory is ideally suited for describing what the neurotic patient experiences in analysis. However, it does not adequately describe the analytic experience of the patient with a defective adaptive ego, the actual workings of the neurotic patient's adaptive ego during analysis, or the subjective experience of the patient who has successfully completed his analysis.

I would expect the theory of the archaic adaptive ego to provide a useful supplement to the traditional language of psychoanalysis in the clinical situation, but certainly not to replace it. That is not its purpose. Its purpose is to lead us closer to an understanding of the psychological reality which lies beyond the subjective experience of the stationary human observer.

For the psychoanalyst who wishes to be a successful navigator, the traditional theory has been and will continue to be a valuable guide. It offers him a suitable platform from which to make his observations. It tells him, roughly, where he is in an analysis and how much farther he has to go. None of the beliefs or methods that help him do his job will have to be modified.

Once we have separated the defense-determined superstructures from the underlying structures of the adaptive ego, there is ample room for both approaches. We can see, for example, that from about ages four to six, the superstructures take on the tripartite form which characterizes the adult neurotic's subjective view of his own psychic apparatus. The Oedipal child imagines his inner world as a replica of the triangular relationship which dominates his outer world of self and objects. He identifies his archaic ego with his peremptory Oedipal strivings toward the opposite-sexed parent, the loving and protecting object who becomes the model for his mature adaptive ego. Opposed to the wish-programming of his archaic ego he sets an inhibitory ego which is equally powerful and arbitrary, like the same-sexed parent whose rivalry he fears. When his rudimentary mature adaptive ego is unable to come to terms with these warring factions, his defense mechanisms respond by banishing both of them from conscious participation in its deliberations. The stage is set for the familiar drama of later years.

Anthropomorphism is rife in this account, for the inescapable reason that the psychic superstructures are modeled after the representations of actual people (Grossman and Simon, 1969). The various structures of the adaptive ego are subjectively apportioned to the superstructures labeled by Freud as Id, Ego, and Superego, and treated accordingly. In the adult neurotic, these subjective boundaries are rigidly maintained by powerful defense mechanisms. The psychoanalyst does his best to reduce them and restore the patient's adaptive ego to wholeness and flexibility. Where *Id* and *Ego* were, there ego shall be.

The human adaptive ego is the most complicated and interesting entity in the universe as we know it. To see it in terms of the divisions set up within it by the Oedipal child's defense mechanisms is a necessity for the understanding of the neurotic patient's illness. To see it in no other way is to accept an arbitrary limitation which can only bring to an end the great adventure Freud began.

CHAPTER 8

Conclusion

Freud's theory of dreams gave the clinical psychoanalyst what he most needed: an opening to those contents of the human mind which are ordinarily inaccessible to consciousness. The magnitude of this achievement rightly overshadowed the inconsistencies we have been discussing here. Moreover, as Kuhn (1962) has pointed out, the recognition of deficiencies in a scientific theory which has proven its usefulness is extremely difficult in the absence of an alternative with which it can be compared.

As noted in chapter 1, there have been a number of important contributions to the psychoanalytic theory of dreams since the time of Freud's writing, many of them pointing in the direction of the memory-cycle model by emphasizing the relationship between the dream and contemporary events in the life of the dreamer (Greenberg and Pearlman, 1975b).

A new theory does not develop directly from the data of observation. It originates as an attempt to solve the problems left unsolved by an older theory, and it depends on the older theory for a comprehensible statement of the nature of those problems. For this reason, I have tried to retain the traditional Freudian terminology wherever possible, introducing new terms only when new structures were being described.

But the final result of this procedure must be a theory which can stand on its own, a theory which can be related independently to the observational data, and which can be compared point for point with other theories. The opportunity seldom comes in psychoanalysis to settle a theoretical issue by an observational test, but in this case we have had one. The memory-cycle model not only predicted the existence of the correction dream, but told us exactly where to look for it. Only a theory which recognized the interactional nature of mental activity in the archaic ego could have made this prognostication successfully. As we have seen, the new theory differs in fundamental ways from the traditional psychoanalytic theory of dreams.

In the memory-cycle model, the dream compares the representation of an emotionally significant event of the past with the representation of an emotionally significant aspect of the previous day's experience. The impetus for the dream comes not from the representations which are being compared, but *from the information-processing function of the comparison, for which each of the representations is equally important.* This function is the matching of past and present experience in order to determine suitable locations in the permanent memory for the storage of the representation of the new experience.

The memory-cycle model predicts that in most cases the affective charge will be higher in the representation of the past experience than of the day residue, and that the dream which results from the superimposition of the two representations will therefore have a higher affective level than would the day residue by itself. But when the previous day's experience is of unusual intensity, this situation may be reversed, and the reversal will be reflected in the composite image of the dream as a matter of course.

The memory-cycle model permits the dream censorship to intervene at any stage in the construction of the dream, affecting either past memory or day residue or having no affect at all. For example, in the Tuesday-night index dreams of M. A., the censorship removed all cognitive references to Father/analyst from both the day residues and the past memories, as well as the powerful affects associated with both.

The fact that the rooming-house scene of Dream IA was actually derived from a childhood memory is known to us only because of the unusual circumstances of our study. If the patient had not been awakened during Dream IIA, the correction dream, he might never have reported this dream to the analyst on Friday or recovered the memory of the Burgundy Hotel which formed the historical antecedent of both the index dream and the correction dream.

On the basis of the Thursday analytic hour alone, we would have concluded that the rooming-house and its bathrooms belonged entirely to the Tuesday residues, derived directly from a conscious memory on the dream day of a recent visit to Judith's house. In the ordinary course of analytic events, the probability is high that the contemporary antecedent of the manifest dream will be recovered more frequently than the historical antecedent. It is therefore understandable that Freud was drawn into thinking that the cognitive aspect of the manifest dream was derived primarily from the day residue.

According to the memory-cycle model, the affects associated with past experience are necessarily bound to specific memories located in an ordered structure. The appearance of disorder in dreams, on which much of Freud's thinking was based, has three separate causes:

1. The fact that the permanent memory is organized associatively rather than logically; i.e., that the criteria for linking two items in the memory structure are more inclusive than they would have to be during the problem-solving activity of waking consciousness.
2. The manner in which memory representations are displayed during the matching process of the memory cycle; i.e., removed from their normal context in the permanent memory structure and distorted by the process of comparison by superimposition. (Condensation.)
3. The substitutions introduced for defensive purposes by the dream censor. (Displacement.)

While the first two of these causes are present in every dream, the third is not necessarily so. This is in contrast to the neurotic symptom, which derives its disorderliness specifically from displacement and other closely related mechanisms of defense. The usefulness of dreams in explicating neurotic symptoms may rest in part on what they have in common, the distortion caused by mechanisms of defense like displacement.

But the dream is most valuable when it is least encumbered by defensive substitutions, when the distortion is limited to the condensation intrinsic to the matching process. At such times the dream will provide an independent source of information about the early history of the patient; that is, about the stages of his development during which his defensive operations had originally become stereotyped.

The difference between dreams which are burdened by defensive substitutions and dreams distorted primarily by the matching process itself is clearly illustrated by the Tuesday-night dreams of M. A. and their Thursday-night correction dreams. There can be little doubt that the information content of Dream IA was severely diminished by the substitution of the bathroom imagery for the original components deleted from the dream. In effect, the correction dream was able to reverse the substitutions and reconstruct the original matching.

CONCLUSION

The fact that the original components of Dream IA could be retrieved forty-eight hours later and rematched to form Dream IIA implies a mechanism which recognized their importance and maintained them in orderly structures from which they could be recovered when conditions were favorable. If these memory representations had been serving merely as vehicles for the transportation of unregulated impulses and excitations, their preservation and retrieval would have been neither useful nor possible.

Moreover, the impulses supposedly pressing for hallucinatory gratification in M. A.'s unconscious could not have been the same on Tuesday and Thursday nights. During the Thursday hour, there was a dramatic shift in the patient's ability to express his feelings toward his father/analyst, and it was this shift which was recorded so emphatically in the Thursday-night dreams. In spite of this shifting of affects, however, the memory of the identical childhood experience is represented in both the original Tuesday-night dream and the correction dream of Thursday night. (We have seen that nothing remotely related to this memory was mentioned during the Thursday hour except the report of the original dream itself.)

The reappearance of this childhood memory can be explained only by the orderly information-conserving function of the memory cycle. It is this adaptive function of the memory cycle which makes it such a powerful ally of the psychoanalyst. We have seen it at work in this study, bringing neurotically induced deficiencies in the permanent memory structure into consciousness through the Tuesday-night dreams, and applying the problem-solving capabilities of waking consciousness to these deficiencies through the correction dreams of Thursday night.

We have also seen the correction dreams functioning as a medium through which the analyst's interpretations brought about a reversal of the defensive substitutions interposed by the censorship in the construction of Dream IA. This phenomenon surely needs more study, but it raises the possibility that the correction dream may function in the reversal of defensive operations generally.

The memory cycle and the correction dream help to clarify an aspect of the psychoanalytic treatment process which, though it has been taken for granted from the beginning of psychoanalytic work, has been poorly understood. The analyst's interpretive activity does not function in a vacuum. It achieves its therapeutic effect only when it successfully meshes gears with the restorative processes already at work within the psychic apparatus of the patient. These processes must operate through the evaluation, processing, and storage of new information.

Freud's theory of dreams was limited by its reliance on a model of mental functioning largely determined by his conception of a unilateral flow of psychic energy. Some of the evidence for the two-way flow of information in the phenomenology of dreaming was known to Freud; we have seen him try to explain it away with a series of *ad hoc* proposals which on critical analysis reveal themselves to be both inconsistent and ineffective.

Freud believed that the information content of a single dream is incidental to its function as the vehicle for a repressed infantile wish. In order to maintain this conviction, however, it is necessary to minimize the relationship between the information contents of succeeding dreams. The existence of the correction dream, whose full significance is demonstrated in the case at hand, requires that we approach the study of dreams with an emphasis on their continuity and cumulativeness.

Freud's discovery that dreams provide a bountiful source of information about our most deeply hidden feelings and motives had a revolutionary effect on our expectations for human culture. A biological resource, which we had been unable to make use of in the isolation of our individual thoughts, could now become the instrument for a new kind of collaborative human interchange. The achievement of self-knowledge, approached with such painfully slow steps by the process of evolution, had become accessible in a new way to our collective understanding.

A new psychoanalytic theory of dreams does not represent a retreat from the old, but an advance beyond it. The memory-cycle model teaches us not that the dream is less meaningful than Freud knew it to be, but even more so.

Freud revealed to us what our hereditary self-deception had concealed for so many ages. No service could have been more dramatic; the sudden release of pent-up energies is surely an authentic metaphor for the leap in our self-knowledge which resulted.

The memory cycle, of which the correction dream forms an essential part, takes us further. It puts us in touch with the basic biological mechanism of intelligence, the anti-entropic principle which Freud called Eros. For everything of value in life begins with the binding of what is new to the accumulated knowledge of the past, from the DNA molecule to human love.

REFERENCES

Anderson, John R. and Bower, Gordon H. *Human Associative Memory*. Washington D.C.: Winston, 1973.

Applegarth, Adrienne. "The Structure of Psychoanalytic Theory." *Journal of the American Psychoanalytic Association* 21 (1973): 193–237.

Arlow, Jacob. "Ego Psychology and the Study of Mythology." *Journal of the American Psychoanalytic Association* 9 (1961):371–393.

———. "Unconscious Fantasy and Disturbances of Conscious Experience." *Psychoanalytic Quarterly* 38 (1969):1–27.

———. "Fantasy, Memory and Reality Testing." *Psychoanalytic Quarterly* 38 (1969):28–51.

Aserinsky, Eugene, and Kleitman, Nathaniel. "Regularly Occurring Periods of Eye Motility and concomitant Phenomena During Sleep." *Science* 118 (1953): 273–274.

Bowlby, John. *Attachment*. New York: Basic Books, 1969.

Breger, Louis; Hunter, Ian; and Lane, Ron. W. *The Effect of Stress on Dreams*. Psychological Issues Monograph, no. 27, New York: International Universities Press, 1971.

Bruch, Hilde. "Transformation of Oral Impulses in Eating Disorders: A Conceptual Approach." *Psychiatric Quarterly* 35 (1961):458–481.

———. "Falsifications of Body Needs and Body Concept in Schizophrenia." *Archives of General Psychiatry* 6 (1962)18–24.

Colby, Kenneth M. "Experimental Treatment of Neurotic Computer Programs." *Archives of General Psychiatry* 10 (1964):220–227.

———. "Computer Stimulation of Change in Personal Belief Systems." *Behavioral Science* 12 (1967):248–253.

———. "Simulations of Belief Systems." *Computer Models of Thought and Language*. Edited by Roger C. Shank and Kenneth M. Colby, San Francisco: W. H. Freeman, 1973.

Dement, William. "Effect of Dream Deprivation." *Science* 131 (1960): 1705–1707.

Dement, William, and Wolpert, Edward. "Relation of Eye Movement, Body Motility, and External Stimulation to Dream Content." *Journal of Experimental Psychology* 55 (1958):543–553.

de Santillana, Giorgio. *The Origins of Scientific Thought*. Chicago: University of Chicago Press, 1961.

de Santillana, Giorgio, and von Dechend, Hertha. *Hamlet's Mill: An Essay on Myth and the Frame of Time*. Boston: Gambit Press, 1969.

Dewan, Edmond. "The Programming (P) Hypothesis for REM Sleep." *Air Force Cambridge Research Laboratories*, Physical Sciences Research Papers, No. 388 (1967) Also: *International Psychiatry Clinics* 7(2) (1970):295–307.

Edelson, Marshall. "Language and Dreams: The Interpretation of Dreams Revisited." *Psychoanalytic Study of the Child* 27 (1972):203–282.

Eissler, Kurt. "Irreverant Remarks about the Present and the Future of Psychoanalysis." *International Journal of Psychoanalysis* 50 (1969):461–472.

Erikson, Erik. *Childhood and Society*. New York: W. W. Norton and Co., Inc., 1950.

———. "The Dream Specimen of Psychoanalysis." *Psychoanalytic Psychiatry and Psychology*. Edited by R. Knight and C. Friedman, New York: International Universities Press, 1954.

References

Evans, C. and Newman, E. A. "Dreaming: An Analogy from Computers." *New Scientist* 24 (1964):577–579.

Fisher, Charles. "Dreams and Perception: The Role of Preconscious and Primary Modes of Perception in Dream Formation." *Journal of the American Psychoanalytic Association* 2(1954):389–445.

———. "A Study of the Preliminary Stages of the Construction of Dreams and Images." *Journal of the American Psychoanalytic Association* 5 (1957):5–60.

———. "Psychoanalytic Implications of Recent Research on Sleep and Dreaming." *Journal of the American Psychoanalytic Association* 13 (1965):197–303.

Fisher, Charles, and Paul, I. H. "The Effect of Subliminal Visual Stimulation on Images and Dreams: A Validation of Study." *Journal of the American Psychoanalytic Association* 7 (1959):35–83.

Foulkes, David. *A Grammar of Dreams.* New York: Basic Books, 1978.

French, Thomas, and Fromm, Erika. *Dream Interpretation.* New York: Basic Books, 1964.

Freud, Anna. *The Ego and the Mechanisms of Defense.* New York: International University Press, 1948.

Freud, Anna. *Normality and Pathology in Childhood: Assessments of Development.* New York: International Universities Press, 1965.

Freud, Sigmund. *The Interpretation of Dreams.* 1900. Standard Edition of the Complete Psychological works, vols. 4–5, pp. 1–627. London: Hogarth Press, 1953.

———. *On Dreams.* 1901a Standard Edition, vol. 5, pp. 631–686, 1953.

———. *The Psychopathology of Everyday Life.* 1901b. Standard Edition, vol. 6, pp. 1–310.

———. "The Handling of Dream Interpretation in Psychoanalysis." 1911. Standard Edition, vol. 12, pp. 89–97, 1958.

———. *Totem and Taboo.* 1913. Standard Edition, vol. 13, pp. 1–162, 1961.

———. "A Metapsychological Supplement to the Theory of Dreams." 1915. Standard Edition, vol. 14, pp. 217–236, 1957.

———. *Introductory Lectures on Psychoanalysis.* 1916. Standard Edition, vol. 15, pp. 83–233, 1955.

———. *Beyond the Pleasure Principle.* 1920. Standard Edition, vol. 18, pp. 1–66, 1955.

———. *The Ego and the Id.* 1923a. Standard Edition, vol. 19, pp. 12–68. 1951.

———. "Remarks on the Theory and Practice of Dream Interpretation." 1923b. Standard Edition, vol. 19, pp. 109–124, 1951.

———. "Some Additional Notes on Dream Interpretation as a Whole." 1925a. Standard Edition, vol. 19, pp. 125–140, 1951.

———. "A Note upon the Mystic Writing Pad." 1925b. Standard Edition, vol. 19. pp. 227–234, 1951.

———. *Inhibitions, Symptoms and Anxiety.* 1926. Standard Edition, vol. 20, pp. 77–178, 1959.

———. *New Introductory Lectures on Psychoanalysis.* 1933. Standard Edition, vol. 22, pp. 5–184, 1964.

Gill, Merton. *Topography and Systems in Psychoanalytic Theory.* Psychological Issues Monograph, no. 10. New York: International Universities Press, 1963.

———. "The Primary Process." *Motives and Thought: Psychoanalytic Essays in Honor of David Rapaport.* Edited by Robert Holt, Psychological Issues Monograph, nos. 18–19, pp. 259–298. New York: International Universities Press, 1967.

Greenberg, Ramon. "Dreaming and Memory." *International Psychiatric Clinics* 7 (1970): 258–267.

Greenberg, Ramon, and Leiderman, P. H. "Perceptions, the Dream Process and Memory. An Up-to-Date Version of 'Notes on a Mystic Writing Pad'." *Comprehensive Psychiatry* 7 (1966): 517–523.

Greenberg, Ramon, and Pearlman, Chester. "Cutting the REM Nerve." *Perspectives in Biology and Medicine.* 17 (1974): 513–521.

———. "REM Sleep and the Psychoanalytic Process: a Psychophysiological Bridge." *Psychoanalytic Quarterly* 44 (1975a): 388–403.

References

———. "A Psychoanalytic Dream Continuum: The Source and Function of Dreams." *International Review of Psychiatry* 2 (1975b): 441–448.

Greenberg, Ramon; Pearlman, Chester; Fingar, R.; Kantrowitz, J.; and Kawliche, S. "The Effects of Dream Deprivation: Implications for a Theory of the Psychological Function of Dreaming." *British Journal of Medical Psychology* 43, 1 (1970): 1–11.

Grinstein, Alexander. *On Sigmund Freud's Dreams*. Detroit: Wayne State University Press, 1968.

Grossman, William and Simon, Bennett. "Anthropomorphism: Motive, Meaning and Causality in Psychoanalytic Theory." *Psychoanalytic Study of the Child* 24 (1969): 78–114.

Hall, Calvin. "A Cognitive Theory of Dreams." *Journal of General Psychiatry* 49 (1953): 273–282.

———. *The Meaning of Dreams*. New York: McGraw-Hill, 1966.

———. "The Methodology of Content Analysis Applied to Dreams," *Dream Psychology and the New Biology of Dreaming*. Edited by M. Kramer, Springfield, Illinois: Charles C Thomas, 1969.

Harary, Ernest; Norman, Robert; and Cartwright, Darwin. *Structural Models*. New York: Wiley, 1965.

Hartmann, Ernest. *The Biology of Dreaming*. Springfield, Illinois: Charles C Thomas, 1967.

Hartmann, Ernest. *The Function of Sleep*. New Haven: Yale University Press, 1973.

Hartmann, Heinz. *Ego Psychology and the Problem of Adaptation*. New York: International Universities Press, 1939.

———. *Essays on Ego Psychology: Selected Problems in Psychoanalytic Theory*. New York: International Universities Press, 1964.

Hartmann, Heinz; Kris, Ernst; and Lowenstein, Rudolph. *Papers on Psychoanalytic Psychology*. Psychological Issues Monograph, no. 14. New York: International Universities Press, 1964.

Hartmann, William, and Raper, Odell. *The New Mars: The Discoveries of Mariner 9*. Published by the National Aereonautics and Space Administration; Washington D.C., 1974.

Hawkins, David. "A Review of Psychoanalytic Dream Theory in the Light of Recent Psycho-physiological Studies of Sleep and Dreaming." *British Journal of Medical Psychology* 39 (1966): 85–104.

Holt, Robert ."The Development of the Primary Process: A Structural View. *Motives and Thought: Psychoanalytic Essays in Honor of David Rapaport*. Edited by Robert Holt, Psychological Issues Monograph, nos. 18–19, pp. 345–383. New York: International Universities Press, 1967.

Hoyle, Fred. *Astronomy*. New York: Crescent Books, 1962.

Hunt, E. "The Memory We Must Have." *Computer Models of Thought and Language*. Edited by Roger C. Shank and Kenneth M. Colby, San Francisco: W. H. Freeman, 1973.

Jacobson, Edith. *The Self and the Object World*. New York: International Universities Press, 1964.

Jones, Richard. *The New Psychology of Dreaming*. New York: Viking Press, 1970.

Jung, Carl. *Modern Man in Search of His Soul*. New York: Harcourt Brace & Co., 1933.

———. *Dreams*. Princeton, New Jersey: Princeton University Press, 1974.

Kohonen, Teuvo. *Associative Memory: A System Theoretical Approach*. New York: Springer-Verlag, 1977.

Koestler, Arthur. *The Act of Creation: A Study of the Conscious and Unconscious in Science and Art*. New York: Macmillan, 1964.

Kris, Ernst. *Psychoanalytic Explorations in Art*. New York: International Universities Press, 1932.

Kuhn, Thomas. *The Copernican Revolutions*. Cambridge: Harvard University Press, 1957.

Kuhn, Thomas. *The Structure of Scientific Revolutions*. Chicago: University of Chicago Press, 1962.

REFERENCES

Lewin, Bertram. *Dreams and the Uses of Regression*. New York: International Universities Press, 1958.

Lindsay, Peter, and Norman, Donald. *Human Information Processing*. New York: Academic Press, 1972.

Lindsay, Robert K. "In Defense of Ad Hoc Systems." *Computer Models of Thought and Language*. Edited by Roger C. Shank and Kenneth M. Colby, San Francisco: W. H. Freeman, 1973.

Lowy, Samuel. *Foundations of Dream Interpretation*. London: Keegan, Paul, Trench, Trubner, 1942.

Mahler, Margaret. *On Human Symbiosis and the Vicissitudes of Individuation*. New York: International Universities Press, 1968.

Miller, George; Galanter, Eugene; and Pribram, Karl. *Plans and the Structure of Behavior*. New York: Henry Holt, 1960.

Milner, Brenda; Corkin, Suzanne; and Teuber, H. L. "Further Analysis of the Hyppocampal Amnesic Syndrome: 14-Year Follow-Up Study of H. M." *Neuropsychologia* 6 (1968): 215–234.

Newell, Allen; Shaw, J. C.; and Simon, Herbert A. "Empirical Explorations of the Logic Theory Machine." *Proceedings of the 1957 Western Joint Computer Conference*. New York: Institute of Radio Engineers, 1957.

Newell, A., and Simon, Herbert. "Computer Simulation of Human Thinking." *Science* 134: (1961) 2011–2017.

Palombo, Stanley R. "The Associative Memory Tree." *Psychoanalysis and Contemporary Science*. Edited by Benjamin Rubenstein, New York, Macmillan, 1973.

———. "The Dream and the Memory Cycle." *International Review of Psychiatry* 3 (1976): 65–83.

———. "Dreams, Memory and the Origin of Thought." *Thought, Consciousness and Reality: Psychiatry and the Humanities*. New Haven: Yale University Press, 1977, vol. 2, pp. 49–83.

Palombo, Stanley R., and Bruch, Hilde. "Falling Apart: The Verbalization of Ego Failure." *Psychiatry* 27 (1964): 248–258.

Pattee, Howard, ed. *Hierarchy Theory: The Challenge of Complex Systems*. New York: George Braziller, 1973.

Peterfreund, Emanuel. *Information, Systems and Psychoanalysis*. Psychological Issues Monograph, nos. 25–26. New York: International Universities Press, 1971.

Peterfreund, Emanuel, and Franceschini, Edi. "On Information, Motivation and Meaning." *Psychoanalysis and Contemporary Science*. Edited by Benjamin Rubenstein, New York: Macmillan, 1973.

Piaget, Jean. *The Construction of Reality in the Child*. New York: Basic Books, 1954.

———. *Play, Dreams and Imitation in Childhood*. New York: W. W. Norton, 1962.

Pribram, Karl, and Gill, Merton. *Freud's 'Project' Reassessed*. New York: Basic Books, 1976.

Rapaport, David. *The Structure of Psychoanalytic Theory: A Systematizing Attempt*. Psychological Issues Monograph, no. 6. New York: International Universities Press, 1960.

———. *Emotions and Memory*. New York: Science Editions, 1961.

Reivich, M.; Isaacs, G.; Evarts, E.; and Katy, S.; "The Effect of Slow Wave Sleep and REM Sleep on Regional Cerebral Blood Flow in Cats." *Journal of Neurochemistry* 15 (1968): 301–306.

Robert, W. *Der Traum als Naturnotwendigkeit erklart*. Hamburg, 1886.

Rosenblatt, Allan D., and Thickstun, James T. "Energy, Information and Motivation: A Revision of Psychoanalytic Theory." *Journal of the American Psychoanalytic Association* 25 (1977): 537–558.

———. *Modern Psychoanalytic Concepts in a General Psychology*, pts. 1–2. Psychological Issues Monograph, nos. 42–43, New York: International Universities Press, 1978.

Schafer, Roy. *A New Language for Psychoanalysis*. New Haven: Yale University Press, 1976.

Schank, Roger C. "Identification of Conceptualizations Underlying Natural Language."

REFERENCES

Computer Models of Thought and Language. Edited by Roger C. Shank and Kenneth M. Colby, San Francisco: W. H. Freeman, 1973.

Schur, Max. "Day Residues" of "The Specimen Dream of Psychoanalysis." *Psychoanalysis—A General Psychology,* edited by R. Lowenstein, L. Newman, M. Schur, and A. Solnit. New York: International Universities Press, 1966a, pp. 45–85.

———. *The Id and the Regulatory Principles of Mental Functioning.* New York: International Universities Press, 1966b.

Simmons, R. F. "Semantic Networks: Their Computation and Use for Understanding English Sentences." *Computer Models of Thought and Language.* Edited by Roger C. Shank and Kenneth M. Colby, San Francisco: W. H. Freeman, 1973.

Simon, Herbert. *The Sciences of the Artificial.* Cambridge: M.I.T. Press, 1969.

Snyder, Frederick. "The New Biology of Dreaming." *Archives of General Psychiatry* 8 (1963): 381–391.

Spitz, René. *The First Year of Life.* New York: International Universities Press, 1959.

Ullman, Montague. "The Adaptive Significance of the Dream." *Journal of Nerve and Mental Diseases* 129 (1959): 144–149.

White, Robert. *Ego and Reality in Psychoanalytic Theory.* Psychological Issues Monograph, no. 11. New York: International Universities Press, 1963.

Wilks, Yorick. "An Artificial Intelligence Approach to Machine Translation." *Computer Models of Thought and Language.* Edited by Roger C. Shank and Kenneth M. Colby, San Francisco: W. H. Freeman, 1973.

Wolff, Peter. *The Developmental Psychologies of Jean Piaget and Psychoanalysis.* Psychological Issues Monograph, no. 5. New York: International Universities Press, 1960.

———. *The Causes, Controls, and Organization of Behavior in the Neonate.* Psychological Issues Monograph, no. 17. New York: International Universities Press, 1966.

INDEX

Accommodation, 134–136

Acting-out, 99

Action component, in behavior disorders, 170

Action language, 214

Adaptive mechanism: affect in dream cycle and, 51–52; archaic ego and, 188–195; choice of day residues and, 82; condensation and, 62; defensive activities distinguished from, 136–137; definition of Id and, 185–186; displacement of day residues and, 87; disruption of matching process and, 146–147; dream construction and, 24, 91, 133–137; gratification and, 173–174; location of information in memory and, 33; Lowy's conception of, 7; manifest content of dream and, 5–6; matching process and, 51, 132; memory-cycle model on, 13; primary process and, 138; superimposition and, 147–148, 149; theories on dreams and, 6–10; wish-fulfillment and, 178

Affects: adaptive purpose of memory cycle and, 51–52; condensation and, 148–149, 152; in children, 11; gratification and, 173–174; hysteria and, 170; impulse development and, 180, 186; information-carrying function of, 172; insertion of contents of dream into memory tree and, 55–56; interpretation of dreams and, 106; matching process in memory cycle and, 44–46, 51–53; pairing of dreams and, 103; suspension of skeletal-muscle activity and, 173; Thursday-night dreams and, 76; Tuesday-night dreams and, 65; wishes and, 170–171, 183–185

Amnesia, retroactive, 42

Anal imagery in dreams, 118, 119–120, 128

Anal stage of development: associations during interpretation and, 104–105; dream fantasies and, 98

Analysis: analytic hour related to, 107–109; articulation of day residues in memory cycle and, 54; communication and, 12; correction dream analysis and, 19; flight into health in, 103–104; Friday hour associations and, 92; identification of wishes in, 174; memory tree concept and, 36; pairing of dreams during, 102–103; Thursday-night dreams and, 79–80

Analyst: aim of, 4–5; associative process and, 68; correction dreams and, 91; and male object of identification, 115–116; parents and dream production and, 164; psychoanalytic theory and, 216; relationship between analytic hour and analysis and, 107–109

Anaximander of Miletus, 214–215

Ancient world, 3–4

Anderson, John R., 34

Anthropomorphism, 216

Anxiety: castration, 69; correction dream and, 14

Anxiety dream, 17; censorship mechanism and, 120, 165–166; experiential elements in, 112

Applegarth, Adrienne, 181–183

Aristarchus, 205

Aristophanes, 215

Aristotle, 205, 214

Arlow, Jacob, 49–51

Aserinsky, Eugene, 31

Assimilation, 134–136

Associative process: analyst and, 68, 106; complete dream analysis and, 58; correction dream and, 84, 162–163; definition of, 61; denial during analysis and, 108; direction of flow of, 33; in dream IA, 113; in dream IIA, 116–117, 147; in dream IIB, 126, 127; free association and, 89; Friday hour and, 81, 91–100; lack of labeling of memory units in, 33; latent contents and, 101; matching process in memory cycle and, 42; memory tree concept and, 36; monitoring process and, 104–105; permanent memory organization and, 16; primal-scene fantasy and, 102; reversibility of, 195–196; search for information in memory and, 33; Thurs-

INDEX

164; identification of, in analysis, 174; impulse development and, 180–181; matching process and, 172; wish-fulfillment in, 169–178; wish-statement and, 171–173

Wolff, Peter, 11, 132
Working memory, 34; adaptive ego and, 199; features of, 195–196; precursors of, 197; vulnerability of, 196–197
Working through, 8, 36, 68–75, 107–110